MW00561841

PRAISE FOR *FARTHER, FASTER, AND FAR LESS DRAMA*

"*Farther, Faster, and Far Less Drama* is a wonderful book. It provides leaders with tools and techniques to unleash the full creativity of the organization and underscores what leaders must do to clarify their own thoughts and feelings, to better guide themselves and the rest of their team."
—Gene Kim, *Wall Street Journal* Bestselling Author of *The Unicorn Project*, *The Phoenix Project*, and *DevOps Handbook*

"*Farther, Faster, and Far Less Drama* is the book I wish I had fifteen years ago as I started building my first company, or even five years ago as I started building my family. Janice and Jason Fraser have written an exceedingly practical guide to making decisions and pursuing progress with tactics and tools that apply to every dimension of life. They both claim to be ordinary people but they have written an extraordinary book."
—Christina Wallace, Senior Lecturer, Harvard Business School and Author of *The Portfolio Life* and *New to Big*

"Janice and Jason Fraser have managed to write a leadership book that is incredibly useful both for 'elite' leaders of large organizations as well as for 'regular' leaders—those of us who don't have high-powered corporate positions or huge responsibilities, but who nonetheless find ourselves leading others in decision-making, big or small, work-related or not. I may be retired now, but as I read, I found myself mentally applying the 4 Leadership Motions detailed in the book to work I'm currently doing with my community association and decisions my husband and I are considering at home, as well as thinking about how these tools would have made my life easier at my former corporate and government positions. The book is straightforward in both thought and language, with helpful examples and workshops for putting the Motions to use, so it is easy to understand, practice, and implement. It's an entertaining read, with plenty of humor and real-life stories that add life to the Motions. It provides an excellent toolkit for anyone looking for practical approaches to lead people to make durable decisions, large or small."
—Meg McLaughlin, Deputy Director, Presidential Personnel Office, President Barack Obama (Retired)

"*Farther, Faster, and Far Less Drama* is the actionable how-to manual for the modern leader I've been waiting for. The authors give us permission to swap out the outdated, cookie-cutter 'old boys club' methods and swap *in* a more inclusive, collective, intentional way of leading - for the rest of us."
—Femily, Gender/Equity Advisor Executive Director, American Association of Corporate Gender Strategists

"Janice and Jason Fraser have helped me think in new ways about how I can unlock potential to create breakthrough performance and accelerate progress with sales teams and customers. It was fascinating to see their methods trigger new thinking within Naval Special Warfare.

Their work enables leaders to eliminate distractions to help teams execute with speed and precision, in environments of extreme uncertainty, when you have a fraction of the information you'd like to have, but need to make decisions and deliver outcomes fast. *Farther, Faster, and Far Less Drama* grounds these enabling tools with insight, humor, and humility. This book makes it easier to do the hard work and get the boulders moving!"

—Keith Salisbury, Chief Revenue Officer, ASAPP and Former Navy SEAL

"This book is an indispensable distillation of decades of experience helping teams, families, and organizations of all sizes make progress. In these pages Janice and Jason guide us through four simple leadership motions, connect theory to practice through engaging examples, and make them actionable by providing all the tools and frameworks you could hope for to tackle each of them in your own way."

—Martin Eriksson, Product Partner, EQT Ventures and Co-Founder, Mind the Product

"The Frasers have successfully diagnosed what leadership looks like as we come to grips with a generational inflection point in society and business. The Frasers' practical framework is a panacea for anyone grappling with how to be an effective leader as we stagger into this confusing and complex era. I am so pleased to see the techniques that I have long admired in their work distilled so cleanly in this book. The time is surely right for this modern, pragmatic approach to be spread far and wide."

—Edward Hieatt, Senior Vice President, VMware

"*Farther, Faster, and Far Less Drama* engages the potential of people to create new possibilities for organizations. With strategies that are easy to enact and tools that are simple to use, this book is an essential tool for me as both a coach and a leader. Whether you work in the private or public sector, having this by your side will help you thrive in even the most daunting circumstances."

—Tyrome Smith, Director of Strategic Partnership, Common Mission Project & formerly Innovation at National Geospatial-Intelligence Agency

"I met Janice and Jason at the beginning of my product design career. To say they've been instrumental in informing my leadership with startups to big enterprise would be an understatement. They taught me how co-creation trumps selling ideas, that the best ideas emerge when we amplify the quieter voices in the room, and that leading with less ego leads to far greater impact. *Farther, Faster, and Far Less Drama* is for leaders, yes that's you, who want to make an impact with empathy and authenticity."

—Leslie Yang, Senior Design Manager at Lyft

"In a world where things move fast and get complex while you are trying to slow down and focus, the Four Leadership Motions proposed in *Farther, Faster, and Far Less Drama* are the effective easiness you were looking for. They give everyone a 'common horizon to head toward,' filled with empathy that speaks from experience, humbleness, and community. In Latin America, these are key pillars for organizations and people to thrive in their leadership journey."

—Alejandra Dancuart, Senior Product Owner, Colectivo23

FARTHER
FASTER
AND FAR LESS
DRAMA

FARTHER FASTER
AND FAR LESS
DRAMA

How to Reduce Stress
and Make Extraordinary
Progress Wherever You Lead

JANICE FRASER and **JASON FRASER**

Matt Holt Books
An Imprint of BenBella Books, Inc.
Dallas, TX

Farther, Faster, and Far Less Drama copyright © 2023 by Janice Fraser Consulting, LLC

Matt Holt is an imprint of BenBella Books, Inc.
10440 N. Central Expressway
Suite 800
Dallas, TX 75231
benbellabooks.com
Send feedback to feedback@benbellabooks.com

BenBella and *Matt Holt* are federally registered trademarks.

Printed in the United States of America
10 9 8 7 6 5 4 3 2 1

Library of Congress Control Number: 2022040459
ISBN (hardcover) 9781637742891
ISBN (electronic) 9781637742907

Editing by Camille Cline
Copyediting by Michael Fedison
Proofreading by W. Brock Foreman and Isabelle Rubio
Indexing by WordCo Indexing Services, Inc.
Text design and composition by Aaron Edminston
Cover design by Brigid Pearson
Printed by Lake Book Manufacturing

For Evan and Jeana
Say yes to interesting opportunities.
1 x 1.01 every day.

CONTENTS

PART 1: ORIENT HONESTLY

PART 2: VALUE OUTCOMES

PART 3: LEVERAGE THE BRAINS

FOREWORD

By Eric Ries

Over the last decade, Janice Fraser and I have trained entrepreneurs working in the Mission District of San Francisco, in the United States federal government, and at some of the world's largest companies. In all of these contexts, we worked together to help foster innovative thinking in the service of whatever goal or progress was at hand. We acted as guides in the creation of unique systems that helped each individual company or institution make the best possible use of the talents, resources, and time available.

At the heart of each of those processes was a basic framework from which to begin—the Lean Startup™ method, which I pioneered in 2011. Now, I'm honored that Lean Startup makes an appearance in the far-reaching new framework the Frasers have created for making iterative progress. Its four principles serve as a foundation for making incremental, information-based decisions about what to do next in every aspect, not just of business, but of life. They center on honesty, compassion, and thinking long term about where you're heading and where you want to land. Janice and Jason's goal is to help create alignment across all of the areas that make up our daily existences, which together add up to how we move forward in the world: work, home, and the personal passions that provide psychological sustenance to us as humans. Their systems, which draw on their engagement with clients ranging from the military to startups, individuals, and government, combined with interviews with leaders of all kinds, work as well for leading a team as they do for figuring out how to buy a car. As the Frasers say, these are tools for everybody. Understanding your own motivations, strengths, and pitfalls is also part of the process.

Perhaps most importantly, they lead to actionable outcomes, whether you're facing a work issue, an educational choice, or your grocery list. *Farther, Faster, and Far Less Drama* challenges you to start tackling your own life even as you're still reading it. It's packed with exercises and organizational methods, culminating in a clarifying decision-making tool called the 2×2 that the Frasers have used with Navy SEALs and startups and in deciding where to go for dinner in San Francisco. Each tool is tied to considering the needs and abilities of all stakeholders in any given situation, whether they're your kids, your colleagues, or—in the case of one pretty compelling story the Frasers tell in these pages—the rock star whose clear statement of purpose about playing the guitar helped solve a financial crisis at his company once the employee to whom he articulated it considered it from a different perspective. That the Frasers then go on to show how this same method, called cascading intent, worked equally well for them when they needed to buy new kitchen gear, and then again how it can work in a business context, tells you everything you need to know about the wide-ranging applications of their book.

The best frameworks, as I've learned over the years, are flexible. They provide structure without limitations, and they can be used as a basis for change at multiple levels. They serve as engines for transformation. In a world in which everything feels at once chaotic and up for grabs, Janice and Jason Fraser have cleared a path for anyone ready to start sorting it out in order to make the most of the opportunities at hand. We can't predict what's next, but we can get organized to make sure it's more equitable on every level. A collective, collaborative future is the best future for everyone. This book is a great way to get started on the work of building it.

INTRODUCTION

We are not special or extraordinary. We're regular people. We're saying this right now, at the very start of this book, because we want to emphasize that regular people do extraordinary things.

Although we're regular people, we've lived a life beyond our wildest dreams. This may have been a failure of our imagination, but it also points to our essential humanity. Growing up in the Midwest, living decidedly middle-class lives, attending public universities, navigating the challenges of one crazy family of origin, and building our careers in fits and starts as we learned what truly mattered to us, we had what we considered to be fairly "normal" lives.

But over time, we built teams and companies where we led in practical, ambitious, and humane ways. We focused our energies on creating projects that inspired us and taught smart people how to collaborate effectively, all of which propelled us toward a life full of meetings at the White House and client-funded trips to Peru. So today, we eat extraordinary for breakfast.

As such, we've spent a lot of time with founders, think-tank members, corporate executives, and other assorted big shots. Many of them embody the stereotypical Capital-L Leader: the visionary, chest-thumping, self-aggrandizing lone wolf who issues edicts and rejects input. You know the type. They may have been regular people once, but their ascent to power totally rewired their egos. Capital-L Leaders like Steve Jobs and Jack Welch have shaped our world for centuries, making invaluable contributions to

1

business, government, art, culture, and science. But now, we believe their time is up.

The solitary hero stories of these leaders do not provide realistic or useful models for the rest of us. (Especially when the rest of us aren't all cis, heterosexual, white dudes.) Sure, the Old Boys Club has done some great things, but obviously at great cost. In today's world of climate change, transphobia, artificial intelligence, racial reckoning, pandemics, political polarization, and other destabilizing forces, the leaders we need are NOT alpha individualists. The Capital-L Leadership school of changemaking is becoming less relevant by the minute.

Fortunately, there are alternatives that enable absolutely anyone to lead with compassion and humility while making meaningful progress on big ideas. We've developed (or, more accurately, discovered) one of those alternative approaches, and that's what this book is about.

This is a "Take the elevator back down and bring the next leader up" leadership book.

This is a "Well, that just happened" leadership book.

This is a "Nevertheless, she persisted" leadership book.

This is a "Get 'er done" leadership book.

This is an "If you want to go fast, go alone; but if you want to go far, go together" leadership book.

In these pages, you'll find tools that the two of us have used for decades to help all kinds of people—including Navy SEALs and startup CEOs, high school administrators and software engineers—make progress in their professional *and* personal lives by solving hard problems with grace. What you're about to learn will help you do the same, all while amplifying your passion and empathy in ways that can transform your life for the better. You'll get access to tools and build lifelong skills that will help you set bolder goals and achieve them in less time, with less drama, and less hassle. You will find out how to make complex problems more manageable, even in overwhelming circumstances. Even if you're not a cutthroat titan of industry, political wunderkind, or cis/het white dude. (But also if you are.)

In short, you'll be equipped and prepared to lead from wherever you sit in your workplace, community, friend group, and home.

Speaking of home, we want to circle back to our own lives for a moment. In addition to being filled with rewarding and challenging work, our lives are also filled with friends and family, particularly our amazing children. We get paid to teach our tools and techniques to corporate teams and government branches, but we also use those tactics at home. Much of what we share in these pages was conceptualized at work, but refined within our community and family, helping us understand and connect with our son and daughter in deeply valuable ways. In the chapters that follow, we'll talk about how that's played out for us and how it might benefit you and your life. **We do this in part because we believe that leadership isn't just for the boardroom, courtroom, and war room; it's also for the living room.** Good leadership undergirds strong families.

We want to underline that we have permission from our children to share aspects of their stories, and they have read and approved everything we've written about them. We have a family history of talking openly about our experiences in the hope that it will normalize the complexity of "real life" and help others navigate their unique challenges. We won't be giving you the filtered, Instagram-ready version of our backstage life. We'll give it to you straight.

Our hope is that our radical honesty will help you see how these methodologies have worked for us and prove to you that they're effective on tricky, deep-seated problems. This system functions elegantly across work and family and life. Truly, this is holistic, transformative work that will affect everything from your relationships to your speech patterns to your life choices.

We've also come to believe that the tactics outlined in this book are fractal in nature: each subunit has the same shape as the larger whole. Every tiny interaction is a facsimile of a group interaction, which is a facsimile of an organizational interaction, which is a facsimile of a community interaction. In other words, what you do one-on-one has the same shape as what you do in meetings and groups. How you think and behave on a micro level is reflected on a macro level. So if you are intentional and mindful as an individual, that intentionality and mindfulness will reverberate throughout your entire life. When you choose to be honest and collaborative as a leader, honesty and collaboration will infuse everything you do.

Big promises, we know. Luckily, we've used every element of this method in our own lives for more years than we care to count. We worked out the kinks long before we decided to cram it all into a book and share it with you, so we know we're giving you the good stuff.

Now, in terms of the book itself, here's how it works. The core of our method is a simple but transformative set of four principles: Orient Honestly, Value Outcomes, Leverage the Brains, and Make Durable Decisions. They form the structure of the book, and you'll see them pop up many times throughout the text. They are guiding ideas that anyone can practice—at the office, the PTA, the rebel alliance, the DEI council, the board of directors—anywhere you want to go farther, move faster, and (please god) reduce the drama. Each section of the book addresses one of these principles.

The principles are put into practice when you adopt certain behaviors and mindsets, which we describe for you throughout the coming chapters. To make it easy, we'll supply you with various tools to use across situations and settings. And we'll sprinkle in some charts and graphics so this web of ideas is clear.

So why capture this method on paper at all? Why are we codifying and sharing our work *right now*? **Because seeing the collateral damage of ego-driven leadership made us want to equip the emerging generation of humble, practical, everyday leaders.** Human existence is becoming increasingly complex, and the old guard is struggling to keep up. Right now people need mentors, CEOs, managers, teachers, guides, supervisors, directors, and family members who understand nuance and strive for effective, agile collaboration. "My way or the highway" leaders are starting to alienate their own colleagues, stirring up needless drama and fear along the way. In a world that is downright bewildering, everyone from business consultants to stay-at-home parents wish for ease and simplicity. We wrote this book so that everyday leaders could rise up and fill the void that will soon be left by their Capital-L predecessors.

We'd like to acknowledge that we have told a big lie in this book. At the time of writing, best practice calls for diversifying the names of examples, which we have done. At the same time, we want to acknowledge that it is not an accurate representation of the world as we have experienced it, in which women, BIPOC, and LGBTQIA leaders are not promoted, elected, or rewarded in proportion to their numbers or contributions. Despite what you see here, we don't actually exist in a magical bubble that has achieved equity. But we wish to, so we have diversified the names, with the hope that everyone can better see themselves as the hero of this book.

Life is hard, it moves fast, and everything is constantly changing. Much as we'd love to, we can't alter any of that, for you or for ourselves. What we *can* do is equip you to thrive in the face of this hyperdynamism, just as we've done in our own lives. We can share our methods for leading collaboratively and conscientiously, so you can make progress, regardless of what surprises might pop up next. In our experience, nothing keeps overwhelm at bay quite like trusting yourself to handle the unexpected. (And more so when you know that you can trust your family, team, and company to handle the unexpected together, even when you're not looking.)

The world around you might constantly be in flux, but you don't have to be. You also don't have to be an infallible, all-knowing leader to create meaningful change in the world. With the insights you'll gain from reading these pages, you'll be empowered to make efficient progress with less stress—every single day.

Chapter 1

LIFE, NOT WORK/LIFE

Ready for a harsh truth? Your problems aren't unique.

Undoubtedly, they *feel* special and utterly specific to your situation, but what we've learned over several decades of leadership work is that all problems are human problems. The technical challenges or goals-in-process might vary, but the hang-ups and holdups always stem from interpersonal dynamics, snarled communication, and decision-making. We've seen the same frictions crop up in the White House and at nascent tech startups. We've taught the same skills in massive global corporations and in our own home, and they've worked equally well in both contexts. Whether it's the Navy SEALs or the neighborhood watch, we can guarantee they're struggling with the same challenges around clarity, problem-solving, and mutual understanding. Because we're all a lot more similar than we'd like to admit.

This is good news. If the problems you face at work, at home, or inside your own mind aren't so unique after all—if, in fact, they have shared underpinnings—that means you can address them using a single set of methodologies, mindsets, and tools. You can use the contents of this book on everything in your life, and make it all easier to manage. We designed it that way on purpose. We knew we needed to find a method that could be used with any group of any size in any context, and still be transformative. We wanted it to work everywhere, all the time.

And it does.

To be clear, though, we're not saying that people are problematic, or bad, or obstacles that need to be overcome. In fact, that's a problem we've got with Capital-L Leaders: they often treat people like assets instead of living, breathing beings with important perspectives. Humble leaders know that we succeed together through aligned action, and grounded leaders are collaborative to their very core. But even humble, grounded, collaborative leaders get dragged to meetings that could've been emails, and struggle to articulate their desired outcomes. Even everyday leaders with amazing teams or families can be challenged by creating clarity, solving thorny problems, or fostering mutual understanding.

Enter 4LM—the Four Leadership Motions, a deceptively simple set of leadership behaviors and mindsets that enable progress. It's the life-navigation method you never knew you needed. But *we* knew you needed it because, frankly, **every adult human needs better ways to deal with the unknown and unpleasant**. We've seen how challenging it is to move ourselves forward as individuals. And once you get a bunch of people together and they *all* have to make progress collectively? It gets complicated. Fast. No matter where you lead from or what kind of group you're leading, you need a way to manage those complications and make everything you do easier, simpler, and more effective. The Four Leadership Motions can help.

THE FOUR LEADERSHIP MOTIONS IN A NUTSHELL

The core of 4LM is a set of principle-driven behaviors that help you navigate a wide variety of complex circumstances. It creates clarity around both individual and shared goals, helps people to articulate and agree to parameters, and gives everyone a common horizon to head toward. We have honed it over many years and through many experiences, and it's become part of how we approach every challenge and problem.

The Four Leadership Motions are to the right:

The order in which we present them in the book enables us to show how the motions build on one another. But they work in any combination, alone, and as a stepwise process. Each can be transformed into a question that you can ask yourself whenever you feel frustrated or lost, when you need to make decisions or lead a discussion. (Are we Oriented Honestly around our current situation? Is this the best way for us to Leverage the Brains available to us?) Each motion forms one part of the book with multiple chapters and tools to help you use them, so here they are in brief:

1. **Orient Honestly.** Get real with where you are now and where you are going, including the ugly bits that make this moment challenging.
2. **Value Outcomes.** Place more value on what you want to achieve than on the activities you have planned. Instead of creating outputs, measure your progress toward shared outcomes, and continuously strive to improve how you work as a team.
3. **Leverage the Brains.** Involve the right people and ensure they can all participate fully and equally.
4. **Make Durable Decisions.** Focus most on making a decision that all can live with, rather than going it alone, aiming for perfection, or striving for consensus.

We've organized this book around these four motions so you can see how they relate and interconnect. In our own lives, these principle-driven motions offer grounding when we feel stress and guidance when we feel stuck. They've helped us through loss, transitions, disagreements, and apathy, as well as guiding us through joyful life events and decisions. These principles are like the duct tape of human existence: versatile, reliable, and surprisingly strong in the face of resistance.

GREASING THE RAILS, NOT CUTTING CORNERS

We understand the temptation to take shortcuts and compress timelines, and we're eager to promise that the Four Leadership Motions will help you move faster. But we want to be very clear before diving into the details: This system is about reducing unproductive complexity and friction, so that you can set bolder goals. **This system won't make people's jobs easier; it will make** *progress* **easier, so you can accomplish even the hardest things.**

The Four Leadership Motions are not less work. By excising the waste, this method helps motivated people accomplish more because you've greased the rails. In this way, it can feel more demanding rather than less. The amount of waste caused by people doing a lot of activity for zero benefit is shocking. This method shifts attention to different parts of the work in order to reduce wasted time (and social capital, patience, money, energy, and activity). This can be exhilarating but also exhausting, so we encourage rest. **Successful leaders nap,** then get up and run some more. Let's say that again: successful leaders nap!

We want to introduce 4LM right now because the pace of change is slower today than it will ever be for the rest of our lives. Sit with that for a few moments. Our world is simpler now than it will likely be again for generations. COVID, racial and economic inequality, splintered families, government upheaval, educational gaps, sexism, and climate change are just a few of the disrupters of our day-to-day lives, and others are already cresting on the horizon. We're in for one hell of a century, and we need your leadership.

These forces are at work on us right now, and they're pushing us to be more flexible and adaptable. We need to be able to respond to unexpected macro and micro changes effectively, mindfully, and calmly, yet most of us have never thought about how to do that. Perhaps you've been doing fine with it all so far, but you don't have a system and you don't really know how you've done it; you just feel lucky (and maybe tired). Probably you've used some of the tools we have included, and the benefit of this book will be to lay it out as a system for easy recall when you need it. The leadership and life-living models that have historically been available to us simply will not work for the fast-changing, more inclusive future.

THE MYTH OF WORK/LIFE BALANCE

This is ostensibly a business book, aimed at business leaders who do business things. But the traditional approach to business writing omits so much. Not everyone has a "jobby job," as our friend Kim calls it. She's the person you hire when you need to set up design practices in your consulting company. Like so many of us now, Kim alternates between high-powered leadership roles and independent consulting. This is what is starting to be called a "portfolio career," in which multiple elements are brought together to craft a legitimate, high-performance, high-impact work life. And beyond "business," people who lead work in all sorts of contexts: public sector, nonprofit sector, hybrids, music, and the arts. Our friend Jill is a leader in her faith, as a stay-home mom, and really anywhere she goes. For a decade, though, she was a professional touring musician. The idea that we will have a "business" job for decades, where we will work our way "up" until we reach our ideal "level," simply doesn't apply for most people.

So we no longer believe in work/life balance: It's all just life. And we need to know it's a life that we want to live, filled with security, confidence, love, and meaning.

The idea that we turn "off" life when we turn "on" work is outmoded. What happens to us at work, the choices we make at work, how we lead at work—all of this impacts our macro and micro quality of life, and the nature of the world we live in. We need to see what has worked for leaders like our mentor and friend Wanda Brown. She's a very successful salesperson, coach, and leader. She can't help but lead wherever she goes, and she makes it look easy, even in unlikely circumstances. We have spent more than a decade studying what makes it possible for humble leaders like Wanda to get so much more done with so much less drama. In her story (see page 12), we can find so many of the lessons that we present in the book.

The tidal wave of urgency in our shared world is a problem that decision-makers must face. And as it turns out, we're all decision-makers: from choosing whether to freeze our eggs to choosing a vendor for a marketing campaign. Our ability to make informed, levelheaded, leaderly decisions is becoming increasingly vital. Despite everything we've just said about choice complexity, we don't see easier decision-making as the true goal.

Progress is the goal. But in order to make progress, we need to get better at making decisions more easily and quickly, because decision-making is hard, and it's not your fault.

WANDA BROWN: MAKING PROGRESS HAPPEN

Wanda Brown spent her career in high-stakes business-to-business sales. She taught us to approach business relationships "on a completely level playing field, psychologically, emotionally, intellectually, and to let everything flow from that position, which is one of integrity." She taught us that it is possible to make a good living without compromising our principles. She also taught us a great deal about love, marriage, and lifelong commitment. We are deeply grateful to Wanda for sharing a chapter of her leadership story with us.

A large part of leadership has to do with showing up. You just show up. In 1974 I met my dear wife, Phyllis. She died in 2020, after forty-six amazing years together. We felt from the beginning that we would be out in every circumstance in which we felt it was relatively safe to do so, which means I've been an out lesbian for almost fifty years. (We were so crazy, madly in love with each other, there was no way we could hide it anyway.) This decision meant that we showed up for things. We spoke up. We marched in Washington, D.C.; in San Francisco; and Portland, Oregon; and Minneapolis and St. Paul and everywhere. We wrote letters to the editor (back when people did that). We were interviewed, and on television, and in the press.

We said yes. Leaders have to be prepared to say yes. You do so in such a way that you can still have a somewhat relaxed life without getting burned out, which is a high risk, as you know.

Eventually we settled in our little town of River Falls, Wisconsin. We were still new to that town when the wars in Iraq and Afghanistan started. Phyllis wrote a letter to the local newspaper editor condemning the wars, which prompted an economics professor at the University of Wisconsin to contact her and ask, "What should we do?" And Phyllis said, "Well, we should have a Peace March." So we started one. We showed up.

The March started out with maybe half a dozen people, and gradually we collected more and more. Every single week we marched. And then the counter protesters showed up on Main Street hollering and waving American flags. So we thought we should carry American flags, and we did, and the March grew bigger.

That winter was bitter cold. It was below zero sometimes and snowing and blowing, but we just kept on showing up. We met amazing people while we were all bundled up and marching together and talking, and eventually somebody started saying, "You know, we're all Democrats. Isn't there a Democratic Party around here? How come we never hear about it?"

There *was* a Democratic Party, and bless their hearts, they were folks older than I am now meeting in the basement of the town building under very bad fluorescent lighting. They didn't even have coffee or cookies! They were just this group of folks who had been gathering to talk with each other since God was a baby. So we started going to their meetings, and they were so happy to have us; no one under the age of fifty had been at their meetings in forever.

After a while, I spoke to an older guy who'd been the chair of the Pierce County Wisconsin Democratic Party forever. And I said to him, "Would you like me to take over as chair?" "Yes," he said. "But it's a big job. A bigger job than people realize." I said, "That's okay. I'll toss my hat in the ring." And I did.

We had a great big holiday potluck in December at someone's big, beautiful, full house. And I gave a speech. And the heart of the speech was, "Now is the time! Now is the time! If you've never stepped up before, now is the time!" That's how my chairmanship of the Democratic Party in our little town in Wisconsin began.

So my point is, if you want to lead, you have to be prepared to say yes when the time is right. Just say yes.

MAKING DECISIONS: THE STRUGGLE IS REAL

Do you remember that hazy period in the middle of COVID lockdown, after the toilet paper shortages, after we learned to sing "Happy Birthday" twice while washing our hands? There came a period when time stopped and every day blended into the next. Do you remember how feeling utterly unmoored made simple tasks feel impossible? That wasn't just fear or fatigue messing with you; it was your brain short-circuiting. In her 2020 article for CNN, neuroscientist Daphna Shohamy wrote, "In a world reeling from the coronavirus pandemic, mundane decisions can feel as difficult as existential ones. The real issue isn't about something as minor as a meal choice, but about understanding how, as so many decisions are taken away from us, we can feel paralyzed in the face of those we still need to make. Your brain does not distinguish between consequential and trivial decisions now. The line between them is blurred by uncertainty."[1]

Most of us were lucky enough to move past that untethered confusion, but its aftereffects lingered. Even a year or two later, choices felt more onerous and confusing than they used to, because our templates were shattered. In the COVID "before times," our lived experiences were useful templates for effective decision-making. But in a post-pandemic world, some facts we knew for certain are completely out of date today. We are constantly trying to process new inputs instead of relying on our knowledge of how things used to work, and this is exhausting. *So* exhausting. We were starting from zero on so many fronts, even as we wrestled COVID under control, and that's why our thinking went from fast to slow even around the simplest decisions.

Some things have settled down since then; others remain complicating factors in our lives. Some have resolved; others lurk in our minds and continue to make every choice feel strange and burdensome. Decisions were always tough, but living through a global pandemic has made them that much tougher.

Even if you haven't examined this issue head-on, you've likely felt its impact. And, of course, you already knew that human life is hard and complex in general, or you wouldn't have bought this book in the first place. But you might not be aware of all the ways in which it's hard and complex, the unavoidable constraints that make it feel even harder and more complex than it should be. While we don't want to load you down with discouraging information about the nature of decisions, we do want you to feel validated in your struggles to make good decisions.

And since understanding a problem helps us move toward meaningful action, we're going to talk about why collaborating, making choices, and forging ahead can feel so challenging, even when we're not suffering from COVID Brain.

WHY IS CHOOSING SO HARD?

As humans, we love having the freedom to choose, and yet actually making choices has become increasingly difficult. We have more options than ever to select from, and "choice fatigue" is a very real phenomenon. Voices around and within us shout about priorities, urgency, and speed, causing us to freeze up instead of move forward. Our time is limited, so even if we'd like to take a couple of weeks to mull over a decision, we rarely have that luxury. Our resources are also limited, forcing us to make choices we might not otherwise make. Most of us juggle a variety of roles and responsibilities, splitting our focus and splintering our attention.

What's the most important and severely restricted resource impacting this process? Our brains.

The prefrontal cortex is the part of the human brain involved in planning, executive function, decision-making, and reasoning. What most people don't realize is that this crucial piece of our minds is really quite small. When we see diagrams of the brain, the prefrontal cortex appears to encompass the front fifth of the entire brain, but it's only a few millimeters thick. It's just a wrapper around other sections of the cerebrum. Neuroscience author David Rock says that if we define the capacity of the prefrontal cortex as equivalent to a single cubic foot, the rest of the brain's capacity would be equivalent to the entire Milky Way galaxy. And our brains task that single cubic foot with making *all* our choices and decisions. No wonder we struggle, and our brain has developed some effective hacks.

In order to ease decision-making, we (humans) instinctively try to get ideas out of our heads. We write them down, we record them into our phones, we discuss them with friends or team members. We do our best to hold as little as possible in our overtaxed and scarce prefrontal cortices, and yet that tiny sliver of brain matter is where all choice-related thought happens. Physiologically speaking, we have very little capacity in our neurological centers of choice and reason. Our capability for holding even a handful of ideas or options there gets exhausted really, really easily.

Add other people to the decision-making mix, and our brains start to malfunction in other ways. Entering into conflict with other people—as we often do when making collective decisions—lights up the same areas of our brains that register physical pain. In the brain, belonging (and threats to belonging) are actually understood and aligned with physical safety. Because of this discovery, UCLA professor and social neuroscience researcher Matthew Lieberman says that Maslow had it wrong, and that feelings of belonging are more essential to our survival than even food and shelter.[2] Our desire to feel like we belong is ferociously strong, and the drama associated with being forced to argue, cajole, and debate with other people in order to reach consensus is (literally) neurologically painful.

Some of these factors crop up even when we're making decisions solo. However, when choices require consensus from a large group of stakeholders, the process becomes considerably more difficult and exhausting.

TOO MANY HANDSHAKES

To understand why this is, let's walk through an exercise that we use in our leadership trainings.

Imagine that one of us—let's say Jason—is standing on a stage with four volunteers. Three of them stand together, while one stands off to the side. Jason says to the three, "I want you all to shake hands with each other as though you're meeting for the first time. And as you do, count the handshakes." Between Person 1, Person 2, and Person 3, we arrive at a total of three handshakes.

3 people = 3 hand shakes

Then, Jason brings in that fourth person, and asks the group to do it all again, counting handshakes as they go. When the handshakes are counted, we've gone from three to six. We've only added one person, but we've doubled the number of handshakes.

4 people = 6 handshakes

We use this exercise to illustrate the complexity of communication overhead, and it comes with a handy formula: Handshakes = $n(n-1)/2$, where n is the number of participants in the group. As you add people, the number of individual relationships increases:

3 people = 3 relationships
4 people = 6 relationships
5 people = 10 relationships
10 people = 45 relationships

This matters because:

1. People only make decisions when, among other things, they agree to stop talking.
2. People stop talking when they feel understood. Not when you actually understand them, but *when they perceive that they have been understood.*
3. Understanding happens between individuals in a group, not just between one individual and the rest of the group.
4. The more individuals involved in making a decision, the more understanding needs to be driven out, and the harder it is to come to a durable decision.

This comes up at meetings in workplaces around the world on a daily basis, but it also applies outside the office. Say you're at a conference with a large group of people and everyone wants to head out together for dinner. Getting that group to make a choice about where to go can feel absolutely impossible! Coming to agreement on where to go and how long to stay and what route to take among eight or ten people with individual ideas, opinions, and needs is an absolute nightmare. That's n(n-1)/2 wreaking its interpersonal havoc. That's the overhead around decision-making. This overhead slows you down and limits what you can accomplish.

This is not a problem to be solved, but an interpersonal dynamic to be navigated. And we'll give you plenty of tactics for navigating it effectively and with minimal drama in the chapters to come. For now, though, since we're just exploring the reasons why decision-making feels hard, remember this: it's not your fault. This is a naturally occurring complexity that arises in all groups, no matter how skilled they are or how well they work together. Making large group decisions is just plain hard, especially in the high-pressure environment of a workplace.

On top of all this, the culture we've cultivated around meetings is often both toxic and counterproductive. So, when we gather to make a group decision, that's when things *really* get hairy.

MEETINGS ARE A WASTE OF TIME, PATIENCE, AND SOCIAL CAPITAL

Back in 2010 we founded LUXr, a Lean Startup coaching and training firm for early-stage companies. Over its four years of existence, the LUXr accelerator program served more than fifty startups in San Francisco and New York, and our team taught thousands of entrepreneurs in workshops around the world in places as diverse as Bangkok, London, and west Tennessee.

One of the teams we coached through LUXr was a group of four men who created an app that allowed people to find their families during and after natural disasters. Sort of a "find my phone," but for people and families. The app was inspired by the aftermath of Hurricane Katrina, and the company had already won a major prize from Google for innovation when they came to us to help them develop it into a successful business. The founders were all roommates, all the same age, and they argued constantly. Bickering and jockeying for the mic, talking over each other, not listening. They weren't making efforts to understand each other; they were only making efforts to sell their own individual visions. They all behaved as if they had the right to continue talking until they personally were satisfied.

After several weeks of stalled progress, we sat them down and said, "We love you guys and love what you're trying to accomplish, but if you don't stop bickering and move forward, you're not going to get what you want out of this company." By that time, they'd lost weeks of time in useless meetings and damaged some of their relationships with each other. They'd mistaken arguments for communication and conflated having meetings with making progress. In the weeks that followed, the team gave our collaboration tools and advice an earnest try and began to accelerate their progress. The happy ending to that story is that the team course-corrected and eventually went on to a successful IPO.

Larger organizations have different symptoms. In big companies, the most telling evidence that meetings are essentially bankrupt is the prevalence of "pre-meetings." This is the phenomenon where key participants have smaller meetings in advance of a larger, planned meeting to build support for whatever they'll be presenting, sometimes orchestrating multiple conversations with each person before bringing them all together. Their goal: to make sure nothing surprising happens at the meeting.

When people create multiple levels of meetings before actually coming together face-to-face to say, "Yes, we agree to this thing," it's equivalent to staging the outcome. When we pre-sell our position in advance of a meeting, we can't benefit from the range of thoughts and insights that other humans might bring, literally, to the table. (Spoiler: That's Leveraging the Brains.) Instead of harvesting the best thinking, pre-meetings stymie important conversation and trap wisdom in silos. They don't allow for the necessary discussion, what Harvard researcher Linda Hill calls "creative abrasion," to unfold when we meet as a group. And why? Because we fear what might happen if we fail to control the outcome. And rightly so. It's often a sh*t show. The problem we're trying to solve with this behavior is real, but the pre-meeting solution has its own costs.

Of course, encouraging creative abrasion is contrary to human nature. We just pointed out that our brains desperately avoid anything that threatens relationships, makes us feel unsafe, or endangers our feelings of belonging. So how can we create an environment where conflict feels positive and productive? How can we make teams (or families) feel so safe that productively challenging each other's ideas just naturally happens?

We experimented with this question continuously at LUXr. Each week, we tried to stage the environment to predispose positive social dynamics, so that people could challenge each other in nonthreatening, maximally productive ways. When we did that, the right conversations happened simply because of how we'd set up the environment and the conditions. We found that managing the details of how participants would interact—everything from the color of the sticky notes to the size of the pens participants use—could improve the quality of conversation. By controlling the context, we can let go of trying to control the outcomes and make more progress with less pain. We can create space for the challenging but very necessary phenomenon of creative abrasion. Some meetings will always suck, but the ones you lead can suck a lot less. (We'll tell you more about that in chapter nine.)

The moral of *this* chapter isn't just that making decisions is hard. It's that making decisions is hard, **and that's not your fault**. It's also not the fault of your obstreperous teen, your naive new hire, or your opinionated PTA cochair. As a leader, you must cultivate compassion around the decision-making process for yourself and for everyone else. Every morning, people everywhere wake up and try to make choices that move us forward in our lives. At work and at home, we struggle to do that because of neuroscience, social dynamics, and relationship complexity. Now that you know what's gumming up the works, you can start to adopt new mindsets and behaviors that will help make tough decisions feel easier. For you and for the people you lead.

Because as a leader, you can't just apply these ideas to your own decisions; you need to guide others toward more effective processes and mindsets. It's not your fault that making decisions is hard, but it is your responsibility to do what you can to make the process less painful. It is your job as a leader, in whatever context, to help those around you navigate the interpersonal dynamics of choice.

The world is changing stupidly fast, decisions are hard, people are abundant, and work/life balance is a myth. If we're going to be effective, we need simple strategies that we can use anywhere, anytime. Each of the four parts of the book from here will introduce you to a principle and provide you with tools. The Four Leadership Motions are stated as one-line instructions for what to do right now: Orient Honestly. Value Outcomes. Leverage the Brains. Make Durable Decisions. Any one of them can be useful in virtually any situation. But let's start with knowing where you are right now, and what makes this moment complicated. We call that Orienting Honestly.

Workshop with Janice:
CHOOSE ONE CHALLENGE

1. Make a random list of ten things that are bothersome in your life. Any ten things; they could be family, they could be work, they could be anything. Don't worry about the order. Don't worry if they're "right." Just make the list and don't judge or overthink what you write. If you're a fan of sticky notes, use them. Write one thing per sticky note. (This is how we do it. Sticky note + Sharpie Fine Point = Brains on fire.)

2. Now read through your list and pause at each one. As you pause, ask yourself, "How important is it to fix this?" If you're like me, they'll all seem monumental and looking at the list may give you a bit of a panic attack, so create focus. As you go through the list, draw a line through five of them. (Or crumple up five stickies.) You should have five items remaining that are pretty darn important. I like stickies for this because you can sort them into piles and rearrange the piles. If you need help choosing which five to eliminate, try thinking, "Just for today, I'll pause to think about solving five of these." The just-for-today part is what makes it manageable. Tomorrow you can think about everything else, but today, let yourself focus.

3. Number the remaining items one through five in terms of urgency. (One is the most urgent, five is the least urgent.)

4. Now circle the item you marked as number one. If you're using stickies, set all the rest aside and look at just this one. Rewrite that item on a fresh sheet of paper and make it a sentence that declares an intention. I chose the sticky marked "talk track," which is my term for what communications professionals might call a messaging platform. Strategic communications is three parts strategy, one part people leadership, and one part showmanship, so it's a daunting task for me. I tend to put it off and then wing it (I'm good at improvising), but it's an approach fraught with drama. So, I write, "I will create my talk track for the next six months."

If you were to make progress on this single problem as you read this book, would that feel like a valuable use of your time? If not, choose the next item/ sticky and ask the same question. What's one thing you can do to move that forward today?

Part 1

ORIENT
HONESTLY

Chapter 2

THE FUNDAMENTALS: POINT A & POINT B

J anice has a saying: "Figure out what's true and make that a good thing." It's connected to the tool behavioral psychologists call "Radical Acceptance." It means that no matter how unpleasant an underlying truth might be, you're better off if you do the work to uncover it, look it squarely in the face, wrestle yourself into accepting it, and then find a way to thrive nonetheless.

In August 2020, startup founder Devin began working the bid for a large military contract for the U.S. government. By the time February of 2021 rolled around, she was getting antsy. She knew that government work is slow and process-intensive, and that her proposal would need to be reviewed by multiple parties—these things take time. On top of all that, Devin knew that the department she hoped to work with was waiting for Congress to approve the annual budget. Yet she was still feeling anxious. She understood all these pieces of information intellectually but was still acting as if she could make it go faster. She was twisting herself in knots, convinced that if she just did or said the right thing to the right person, her bid would get approved. Devin thought that if she searched hard enough, was good enough, she'd find a tactic to speed up this glacial process. She wanted to have more power in the situation than she actually did, she believed she could manipulate the out-come through her actions, and in this way she was not being honest with herself. In retrospect, it's easy to see, but in the moment, there was an illusion of control, and it created a huge load of stress and self-doubt.

Working alone, Devin had lost sight of which thoughts were plain facts, and which thoughts were her own assumptions, wishes, and beliefs. It helped to talk with an advisor and separate unchangeable facts (congressional bud-get approval) from the wishes that something could be different (finding a way to speed up Congress). Once she saw her thoughts laid out this way, Devin became unstuck. Orienting Honestly meant accepting the uncom-fortable truth that this approval was out of her control. It meant recogniz-ing where she was in the present moment, with full and complete honesty, instead of subtly retouching her situation to make it more palatable.

Once she did that, her action plan for getting the federal government money became very simple. She needed to keep in touch with her top five contacts, talk to them every week or two to stay on their radar, and wait until the budget was approved and the wheels of the federal government began to turn a bit more swiftly.

Before she Oriented Honestly, Devin's action plan was, in essence, "Try to squeeze juice from a tennis ball." After she Oriented Honestly, her action plan was, "Build my relationships with key contacts while focusing on other projects." There was no persuasion work to be done, and no way to accelerate the process. It was still a tense time, but it flowed much more easily. She won the contract (and then some).

One of the ways we may inadvertently sabotage ourselves as leaders is to obscure the truth about our own circumstances. We may do this to make ourselves feel more productive or comfortable or in control. We may do it because we don't want to make waves. We often lie to ourselves about our current circumstances without even realizing we're doing it. If we move for-ward under the premise of that lie, we are far more likely to be moving in the wrong direction.

And that's why Orienting Honestly is so crucial.

It can be painful to recognize that we haven't made as much progress on a personal goal as we'd believed. It can be equally disheartening to admit that the team we lead is happy and chummy, but they're not actually aligned on anything important. But what's the most painful and disheartening of all is realizing how badly we've misjudged our starting point when we've already charged seventy-five steps ahead. Admitting a miscalculation, retracing steps, and redoing work is far more demoralizing than taking the time to Orient Honestly early. (And reorienting often so that you can make adjustments along the way.)

Defining our current situation fully and honestly brings clarity; and *lack of clarity* is a pernicious roadblock to progress. When people struggle to understand their current circumstances or fail to articulate a shared goal, activity grinds to a halt. When we refuse to Orient Honestly, we do things without understanding why we're doing them. We mistake activity for progress. Mistake arguing for collaborating. We spin our wheels instead of moving forward.

Over the years, we've discovered that honestly and clearly defining where we are right now *and where we would like to go* makes progress exponentially easier. This method for Orienting Honestly can be put into practice across the gamut of situations using a simple technique that we call Point A and Point B. In this chapter we'll teach you how to identify and articulate them both. We'll show you how to notice your current state (including complications), then directly, boldly, and without over-specifying, describe a desired future state. And we'll explain how learning to define and articulate Point A and Point B will change your life for the better.

UNDERSTANDING POINT A AND POINT B

The Point A and Point B concept is exactly what it sounds like: "We're here now, and we want to be over there, so we will need to take these steps to get there." It's a simple metaphor, and when you examine it, it can reveal so much about how we mess up.

Imagine you are an airline pilot who is based in Denver. You need to get a plane full of antsy passengers to Albuquerque, so you request a flight plan. If the plan you're given shows you how to get from Miami to Albuquerque, you can't possibly retrofit it to work: Miami is on the opposite side of the country and farther south than Denver, so you'd have to go ridiculously far out of your way to even begin using this set of directions. A flight plan with the same destination city but the wrong departure city cannot be put into action. This is why you need to have a sense of *where you are right now* before you start setting goals and taking action.

Now, if you're given a plan that shows you how to get from Denver to Cincinnati, you're equally screwed. Cincinnati is nowhere near Albuquerque, and even if you flew there, you'd need to get an entirely new flight plan to get from Cincinnati to your intended destination. This is why you need to have a sense of *where you would like to go* before you start setting goals and taking action.

You need both. We cannot emphasize this strongly enough, good people. You need a Point A and a Point B to Orient Honestly and identify the outcomes you want to enable as a leader. It may sound simplistic, but we're willing to bet that you've made most of your life's most important decisions without identifying those two guardrails. If you begin defining Point A and Point B before you take action, the decisions you make and actions you take will immediately become more informed, comprehensive, and cohesive.

What Makes a Good Point A?

When you sketch out Point A, your point of departure, you need to be brutally honest about it. Point A describes the farthest edge you've reached and includes any associated disorder or messiness, because those issues are critical data points that reveal the complexity of your situation. This is the hardest piece to get right and the part that's easiest to gloss over, but we believe it's where your best insights can come in.

Point A describes your current situation honestly but succinctly. Do your best to write that out word for word in a few sentences. (It'll be too long, but that's okay; allow yourself to do a brain dump now so you can sharpen your focus later.) As you write this first draft, be sure to capture two things:

- Your hardest won, most durable markers of progress (Situation).
- Your points of tension, messiness, and uncertainty (Complication, see sidebar on pages 33-35 for more on this).

Here's an example: "Since COVID, our company has been tasked with releasing Software Product X in eighteen months, but the current plan is three years. We don't know how to change our plan, and some people think it's impossible." It's short but descriptive and includes both salient details and overarching concerns. Can you spot the complication in this Point A statement? (Hint: It has to do with the timeline.)

Here are a few more true-life examples:

- **Business Development:** "We need to decide whether to enter into a deal with Microsoft, and our strategy team has presented great arguments both for and against."
- **Compensation Cycles:** "We have a fixed amount of money to award in pay increases this year, and it's not enough to give everyone what they deserve."
- **Vacation Planning:** "We haven't taken a proper vacation in years, and we don't know how to carve out the time and money, or whether there's a destination that will satisfy everyone."

If your initial draft is longer than two or three sentences, wordsmith it until it's fairly brief, true, and *not* wishy-washy. You want it to both represent the essence of the current circumstances and capture the tension that those circumstances are causing. This tension point suggests and represents the work to be done.

With Point A nailed down, you can move on to identifying the desired outcome. What is Point B? Where do you want to be, how do you want the team to behave, what would be an ideal end-state for the entire company? With Point B, you're not necessarily devising a solution, you're setting a singular outcome for a finite period of time that is achievable yet ambitious.

What Makes a Good Point B?

This is the very simple statement of what you want to achieve, feel, or experience after making mindful changes or taking strategic action. Since you can create a Point A/Point B set for a single hour-long work session or an entire year's worth of life, Point B may be narrow or broad. But just like Point A, it should be honest and succinct. Do your best to write it out word for word in a few sentences (as you did with Point A). If you're establishing a Point B for a single working session, we have found that it *always* helps to start with the words: "At the end of our time today, we will have accomplished_____."

Here's an example Point B to accompany our Point A from above: "At the end of our two hours today, we will have at least FIVE BIG IDEAS that could enable us to release Software Product X in eighteen months vs. thirty-six months. These concepts should enable us to remake the overall release plan."

Here are a few more true-life examples:

- **Business Development:** "At the end of this week, we will have made a decision about whether to accept the Microsoft offer."
- **Compensation Cycles:** "By the end of this working session, we will have three lists: people who must get a pay increase (due to pay equity issues), people who are not getting one, and the 'maybes,' who we will discuss next week."
- **Vacation Planning:** "By the end of the family call on Sunday, we will know how much time and money each person wants to spend on a vacation together."

Your Point B should be specific enough to guide your actions, but not *so* specific that it points you toward a single possible outcome. A well-formulated Point B is flexible, more like a destination city than a destination address. It guides you in the right direction without putting too many parameters around where you'll end up.

Not sure your Point B is spot-on? Try asking yourself, "If I were to accomplish this, would it have been a good use of my time?"

Let's walk through an example scenario that shows someone refining their Points A and B to be as effective as possible. Say Amir is considering quitting his job. He's highly valued as an employee, paid well, and doing work that he thinks is valuable, but the management structure has become dysfunctional and oppressive. Defining Point A as "I don't know if I should quit my job or not" would be a mistake. It's a true statement and a good starting point but isn't specific enough. A good Point A is a short, accurate statement that reveals the tension behind the current stuck point. Point A should succinctly capture the messiness and clarify the complications. Something like, "There are many things I love about my work, and I feel like I'm doing valuable work, but the management situation is making me unhappy, and I don't see it resolving anytime soon." That is Amir's Point A. It explains why he's conflicted about leaving. Perhaps there's a simpler way to say it ("I'm not happy with how I'm being managed . . ."). But most times, our thoughts aren't clear from the start. So let's keep it messy and find clarity as we move forward together.

Point B is a statement of what will be true once Amir has resolved the complication in Point A. If we think of Point A as a problem, defining Point B means asking, "When this problem is solved, what will it be like?" It's envisioning a future state and describing it. Something like, "I'll be happy at work" is a good start, but it's not specific enough. It needs a little more definition and an achievable time frame. "In three months, I will be happy to go to work in the morning," is a solid Point B for Amir to use. And it gives him enough flexibility to consider staying at his job and making changes or finding a better position elsewhere.

SITUATIONS AND COMPLICATIONS

Legendary business consultant Barbara Minto worked at McKinsey & Co. for just ten years, but during that time she completely transformed how the consultancy operated.[1] While there, she created the Minto Pyramid Principle for communications. Her method is a series of steps that helped everyone at McKinsey to think more clearly, solve problems quickly and successfully, and as she intended, they also came to write better.

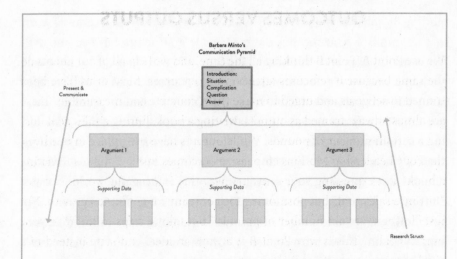

The pyramid has three tiers: introduction, argument, and supporting data. We're most interested in that top tier. In Minto's method, the introduction captures the entirety of whatever challenge lies before you. If you understand that, you're most of the way to solving your challenge. Her "introduction" is structured in four parts:

Situation > Complication > Question > Answer (SCQA)

The situation is a statement of where we are now, so that's half of Point A. Minto then asks us to articulate a complication, which is something inside the situation that is creating tension, which completes our Point A. Only after we've identified the situation and complication can we progress to the question (how will we resolve the complication?) and the answer (here's what we'll do to address it).

The genius of SCQA is the C; the complication. Minto's tool forces us to Orient Honestly, and include the ugly and problematic elements of our situation. She makes us say, "What am I not allowing myself to see or acknowledge?"

"The pyramid is a tool to help you find out what you think," Minto says. "The great value of the technique is that it forces you to pull out of your head information that you weren't aware was there, and then helps you to develop and shape it until the thinking is crystal clear. Until you do that, you can't make good decisions."[2]

OUTCOMES VERSUS OUTPUTS

We use Point A/Point B thinking all the time, and we help all of our clients do the same because it refocuses attention on outcomes. Most of us have been trained to set goals and urged to make them concrete and measurable. These are almost always framed as outputs: writing a book, hitting a sales goal, losing a certain number of pounds. While outputs have their place in our lives, the Four Leadership Motions emphasize outcomes instead: not just "writing a book," but expressing your ideas in a way that impacts the world. Not just "hitting a sales goal," but positioning the company for continued growth. Not just "losing a certain number of pounds," but taking steps to improve your overall health. This is why Point B is always an ideal end-state instead of a single achievement: Point B is an outcome.

When we orient around outcomes, we define what we want to have, change, or be, and put loose parameters around that; we decide on an ideal end-state that could come to pass in a variety of ways. When we decide that only one output (loss of weight) will satisfy the outcome we want (better health), we strap on a pair of blinders and refuse to see the vast universe of other possibilities that could also contribute to getting us what we want to have, change, or be.

Let's see how this plays out in the example of Amir and his misery at work.

Remember that Amir is highly valued as an employee, paid well, and doing work that he thinks is valuable, but the management at his workplace has become dysfunctional and oppressive. Initially, he was just wondering if he should quit his job: quitting would be an activity. Just because he quits this job doesn't mean he'll find a better one, or get hired right away, or be happier in his working life overall. What Amir actually wants is to manage, mitigate, change, or get away from the dysfunction he's facing in his role. What he wants is less stress, less drama, less conflict. Which is why we recommended his Point B be defined as "In three months, I will be happy to go to work in the morning." That outcome still has specificity and can direct his actions but encompasses many possibilities. Amir still might quit, since he could end up happier going to work at a different company. But now he has alternatives—he could change roles, have productive conversations with his supervisors, create a new project for himself, or build more social support among his colleagues. With a Point B/outcome that describes the ideal future state, Amir has the opportunity to explore how he will reach that state. He can be creative in how he problem-solves and decide what he wants to have, change, or be, instead of just choosing a single output and embracing it without looking back.

Outcome (Choose One as Point B)	Activities	Outputs
Be happy going to work in the morning Have less stress, drama, conflict Manage or mitigate the dysfunctional situation	Quit job/company Find a new situation Talk with supervisors Build relationships with coworkers	New job & company New role at same company New project with different team Support within current role

What about at home, where frictions often feel simpler and more concrete? Yep, even there we need to consider the differences between outcomes and outputs and do our best to focus on the former. Let's walk through another example. In this case the "team" is a family of five: two parents, an adult daughter and her spouse, and a teenage son. They have just completed their annual summer vacation, and it is time to begin planning the next one. They were a little bit bored this summer and have decided to go someplace new. As they work on discussing and planning together, there are many factors to consider. We'll start with these:

- Everyone having fun together
- Research destinations
- Top 10 list of destinations
- Be ready to fly on travel day
- Pack suitcases
- Plane tickets and Airbnb reservations
- Something for everyone
- Set up Google Doc to capture things each person likes to do

THE FUNDAMENTALS: POINT A & POINT B

- Destination guide
- Not spending too much money
- Family Zoom call to discuss costs
- Travel budget

Some of these items are activities that *link* outcomes to outputs, or vice versa. Since we know that outcomes are ideal end-states and outputs are concrete goals, here's how we'd categorize everything on the list:

Outcome	Activity	Output
Everyone having fun together	Research destinations	Top 10 list of destinations
Be ready to fly on travel day	Pack suitcases	Plane tickets and Airbnb reservations
Something for everyone	Set up Google doc to capture things each person likes to do	Destination guide
Not spending too much money	Family Zoom call to discuss costs	Travel budget

We have an entire section later in the book on Valuing Outcomes since it's one of our Four Leadership Motions, but we wanted to introduce the concept here since it is so intertwined with the creation of a helpful, productive Point B. It's easy to conceptualize Point B as a goal, accomplishment, or output because that's what we've been taught to do our entire lives. At school, at work, in our hobbies, everywhere. Goal-setting is very sexy, but it's also problematic because *you can set a goal without being honest with yourself.* You can set a goal without taking stock of your resources or understanding anything about where you are, right now, in this moment. You can quit jobs over and over again without doing any sort of self-reflection and be totally dumbfounded when you aren't any happier at your new jobs! Point B must be framed as an outcome because when it's an output, there's a very real chance that you will arrive there having failed to address what was wrong in the first place.

A good Point B can't be formulated by focusing solely on the future. It requires reflection, introspection, and Honest Orientation around present circumstances. And that kind of inward-looking evaluation is something that most leaders must learn to do as individuals before they can do it in group settings.

Most leaders need to practice on themselves first.

START WITH YOURSELF

Remember earlier in the chapter when we said that learning to identify Point A and define Point B is guaranteed to change your life? Here's the part where we explain why that is.

Understanding where you are and articulating where you want to go will give you clarity and agility that most people crave but lack. And, as you've just learned, these two linked practices can be applied to everything from business decisions to personal goal-setting, colossal questions to mundane issues. When you learn to think in terms of Point A and Point B across circumstances, you'll be a positive force wherever you lead.

That said, if you want to transform anything—a situation, team, or family—you need to start with yourself. Not because you're broken and need an emergency makeover, but because practicing transformational tactics as an individual will make you more trustworthy and insightful when you apply them with others. Even more important, though, is the reality that incorporating the 4LM principles and practices into your relationships and personal experiences will make your life easier. And we mean exponentially easier.

By embracing this system, you'll be able to understand your present circumstances with crystal clarity and orient yourself toward improving them. You'll know when to ask for help and who would be in the best position to support you. You'll be able to make tough decisions more easily and trust that you've chosen wisely. You'll worry less about the things that don't matter and focus confidently on the outcomes that do. We promise that mastering

Point A and Point B can make every relationship, choice, conversation, and progress-blocking situation simpler and less stressful.

Especially when you have the courage to apply it to yourself. Especially when you acknowledge that being a great leader starts with learning to lead yourself effectively.

Because, after all, you are the center of the universe. No, really. We are each the axis around which our personal worlds and identities revolve. We bring ourselves to work, to school, and into our own homes. We insert ourselves into an immense variety of situations every day and navigate them all using our experiences and skills. We may adjust our behaviors, speech, and attire to suit the audience or context, but we're still fundamentally ourselves. How we show up in various aspects of our lives is an expression of who we are as individuals, and that affects every relationship we cultivate. So if we want to be more effective at work, in our careers, in our personal lives—really, anywhere across the board—it makes sense to work on ourselves first, because that's our point of greatest leverage.

When we think about situations outside of ourselves, it's a lot easier to make objective observations, identify the facts, and describe the complications dispassionately: "Sales were down in Q2 and our earnings call is two weeks away," or "My dog has a strange cough and started vomiting—maybe it's because the air quality is poor and we just changed his food." (That one's a true story for us right now.) But when it comes to our internal lives, figuring out Point A gets much trickier, because our minds are masterful at keeping secrets: Why does that person at work irritate me? Why can't I finish the memoir? Why do I wake up with the same worry spinning through my head in the middle of the night? Why am I afraid of public speaking? Why do I still bite my fingernails? For most of us, it takes a few visits with a therapist to get answers to questions like these.

Even worse than keeping secrets, our minds *lie to us* all the time. ("I'm a terrible housekeeper." "I'm not qualified for this job." "If I were a better person, I'd have a better relationship with my mother.") Often these lies originated from messages we received early in life—from toxic parents, well-meaning but misguided adults, playground bullies. It's not necessary to understand their origin. Somewhere in our minds, though, we know that this self-talk is neither kind nor factual, and probably we have a lot more answers than we think we do.

So the first step in leveraging the Four Leadership Motions for your own benefit is to find better ways to Orient Honestly. The first step is to start with yourself.

THE BENEFITS OF USING POINT A AND POINT B

Honestly? The benefits are both innumerable and totally specific to each person who uses the Point A to Point B structure. This system is so flexible it can be used at home and at work, with your colleagues and with your family. It can be applied in complex situations and simple ones and can help make seemingly complex situations feel simpler. When you use it to conceptualize personal struggles, it can shed light on thorny issues and bring both clarity and relief. When you use it in groups, you'll reach understanding and alignment faster and be able to tackle projects with a shared sense of purpose.

And now that you recognize A and B as an underlying structure that exists in human life, you'll begin to see it everywhere. Hopefully, you'll also begin to see where it is missing and would be helpful.

For example:

Topic	Point A	Point B
Medical	"I haven't been sleeping well for the past few years. My doctor and I have tried a number of treatments, and they haven't made a big difference."	"By the end of the next month, I will find at least three nontraditional options that I can try next. If they don't work, I'll go in for a sleep study."
Money	"We have built up $30,000 in credit card debt in the past year, and it's starting to feel scary. We don't know how to turn it around."	"At the end of this weekend, we will understand what we spent all of the money on."

Mental Health	"It seems like I'm angry all the time and I pick fights with my partner. I love my partner and want to make it work."	"In six months, I will have figured out how to settle my temper and let go of some of the anger."
Groceries	"We have noticed that if we don't do grocery shopping on Saturday, we end up eating a lot of take-out food during the week. We want to enjoy Saturdays, which makes it hard to find time for grocery shopping."	"By Friday night, we will have an experiment to run this weekend that will allow us to get the grocery shopping done and still enjoy our Saturday."

Start by attuning yourself to discord and friction in your daily life. At any point in a given day, when you find yourself worrying, stuck, angry, or unsure, pause and frame up your situation in terms of Points A and B. What is a clear and honest way of describing your current state, including any complicating factors? When the complicating factors are resolved, what would the future look like instead? Even if there's no one else around and the conflict is entirely internal, simply articulating what's happening now and envisioning what you'd like to happen next will bring greater clarity and ease.

This practice is beneficial at the neurological level, too. Doubt and confusion are dealt with in the prefrontal cortex, which, as we've learned, is a remarkably small part of the brain that is responsible for a remarkably long list of mental processes. When you know something is wrong but cannot articulate or identify it, you're sucking up precious bandwidth in your overtaxed prefrontal cortex.[3] By pursuing and creating clarity for yourself, you free up room in your mind for other matters. In essence, learning to describe Point A is good for your health.

On top of that, learning to utilize the Point A and B framework positions you to achieve outcomes that are desirable and deliberate. You arrive there faster than you would using a less transparent and clearly defined system for decision-making. And perhaps most importantly, you make progress with *far* less drama! We are all drowning in drama spurred by anger, fear, loyalty, and other interpersonal dynamics, all of which are aggravated by our hyper-dynamic world. If we can turn down the volume on the drama, we will all be happier, and our lives will be easier.

Workshop with Janice:
POINT A AND POINT B

1. Pull out the challenge you defined in our chapter one workshop. At this point, it will probably be helpful to choose a notebook (or, if you're using sticky notes, a section of the wall) that will serve as your project work area. Because this is now a project. I want you to make progress, and I want it to be easier than it has been in the past to do so.

2. Write out your Point A as a complete sentence or paragraph. Describe your hardest won, most durable markers of progress. Also list or describe your points of tension and messiness (situation and complication). As you write, ask yourself, "Am I telling the whole truth here? What am I not letting myself see clearly?"

   You'll recall that I'm working on my own challenge right alongside you. I need to figure out my talk track for the next six months. So here's my Point A:

   My business has a range of external stakeholders, and each one seems to need a different kind of information and insight from me. New customers, existing clients, and startup founders are all affected by recent changes in my business focus. I like improvisation and tend to trust my judgment in the moment to know what to say, so I often put off planning strategic communications. But I can see that they are becoming confused, and I fear that this may affect the size and frequency of future contracts.

   It's more detailed and tells the messy story that is truer than the short one-liner I shared before. All these pieces of the puzzle are relevant, though, so it's good to see it laid out in front of me.

3. Now write out your Point B. Often this is the simpler, easier part to write. Aim for an outcome that's achievable in one to three months. (Bigger than a breadbox, smaller than a pickup truck.) Here's mine:

Point B: In thirty days, I'll have a prioritized understanding of my most important stakeholders and the kinds of things they need to know in order to feel confident.

4. Read the whole thing—everything you've written about Point A and Point B—and understand the problem, with all its complications. Have some compassion with yourself. If it were a simple fix, you'd have done it already.

Chapter 3

YOUR PANTS ARE ON FIRE

When we think about honesty, there are a lot of "shoulds." Honesty *should* be table stakes. Leaders *should* be candid and *should* encourage everyone they lead to do the same. By the same token, we *should* all be able to give and accept constructive criticism. We *should* be able to express our views knowing that they will be acknowledged respectfully even in disagreement. And we *should* be able to trust that the people we love will never lie to us.

But we all know it's not so simple, right?

Virtually every form of human society places high moral value on truth, honesty, and candor, and yet an all-truth, all-the-time policy can make actual human life indescribably miserable. Sometimes obscuring aspects of the truth can prevent unnecessary pain. Plenty of people prevaricate when being fully honest would be socially awkward. (Responding to an invitation to go axe-throwing with your in-laws by saying, "I've got plans that afternoon," versus saying, "I never want to try axe-throwing with anyone, especially not my in-laws.") And all of us lie to ourselves without realizing we're doing it. (For the record, Janice would throw axes with her in-laws, but Jason would not.)

So we enter this chapter acknowledging that "honesty" is a nuanced and complex set of ideas, but also insisting that it's one worth embracing in all of its gorgeous messiness. Especially in the context of making meaningful progress, as an individual or with a group. Honesty, as difficult as it may feel to manage, is essential to effective everyday leadership.

We've already talked about Orienting Honestly as a vital practice and explored an example through Devin's government contract story. Hopefully by now you agree that clearly and honestly defining **where we are right now AND where we would like to go** are practices that make it easier to lead. It would be absurd of us to tell you, "Be more honest with yourself!" without explaining what that means or how to go about it. So we *should* probably take a look into the mechanisms of honesty, the ways to dig deeper and uncover obscured truths.

Let's do that now.

HOW AND WHY WE LIE TO OURSELVES

Yes, lie. It's a strong word, but we feel a need for some radical candor here. Your brain and your mind lie to you, all the time. It can be a defense mechanism or a response to anxiety or a completely unconscious reaction. The reasons we lie to ourselves aren't nearly as important as understanding when it's going to impede our progress and how to Orient Honestly instead.

First and most importantly, quoting Robert Fulghum and about a million therapists, "Don't believe everything you think!" A very common way we lie to ourselves is to **believe that we already know everything we need to know**. You see this acted out in so many ways: jumping to conclusions is a form of this, and so is "splaining," a word that has recently been embraced by the lexicographers. We were working with the president of a new business unit at a very large company a few years ago. He was a charismatic leader and was well known for his ability to critique new business pitches. We watched several of these sessions and were struck by how often he made declarative statements, telling these innovative employees which direction to go with their ideas. It's as if he believed his job was to "know" rather than to "learn." (Hello, Capital-L Leadership!) Having all the answers has been rewarded so often and so completely that we've learned to overlook important questions and plow ahead with pseudo-confidence. Questions like *What do we know? How do we know it?* and *What are we missing?* are the leader's best friend. Failure to ask them can leave us with incorrect information about our Point A starting place, with disastrous consequences as we charge off in the wrong direction.

Closely related, a second way we lie to ourselves is in **believing that our truth is universal truth**. Say Janice shows up to a marketing strategy meeting believing, based on her past experience, that Influencer Marketing is the most powerful tool. But Jason believes that Influencer Marketing is a complete waste of time and money, based on his experience. Both have lived experience to back up their claims, and both enter the room assuming that their viewpoint is a self-evident fact. Who would want to sit through that disastrous meeting? Projecting our experience and beliefs onto others causes endless strife. We set ourselves up for conflict when we fail to consider that other people may legitimately believe different things than we believe. Projecting our beliefs onto others is an unconscious habit that feels disrespectful when you're on the receiving end and prevents us from developing a wider, more accurate understanding.

A third way we lie to ourselves falls under the umbrella of *cognitive bias*. For instance, *confirmation bias* makes us pay more attention to information that reinforces our previously held beliefs while we ignore or disregard conflicting information. So, if Janice sat on a search committee and she believed that women are more resilient, she might unwittingly focus on any resumes that highlight the resilience of women applicants. Or if Jason grappled with *choice-supportive bias*—meaning once a decision is made, we only see its benefits and minimize its flaws—he might choose an ill-suited vendor for a particular job just because they'd done well at other tasks in the past.

These subtle lies are roadblocks to progress.

It's worth noting that these are generally unintentional self-deceptions. They're based on biases and unvalidated assumptions, which we all have. We may also lie to ourselves more deliberately if doing so serves a social purpose. It might be politically expedient or more comfortable to disregard facts than it would be to face them and cope with their unpleasant consequences.

Here's an example.

Many years ago, the two of us built a business that was based around video training. We had decided that prerecorded sessions were the most efficient and effective way to disseminate information to startup businesses around the world, so we went all in. At one point, a trusted employee sat us down and said, "Look, I've been out there in the field doing research, and I've got to tell you, entrepreneurs don't want video." This was before the work-from-home revolution swept the planet, and customers at that time wanted a real live person to look them in the eye and empathize with their problems.

But video distribution was core to our business model. We had invested everything in a system that created stellar video content, so we resisted. "I hear you, and that might be true," Janice replied. "But if it's true, then our business is dead, so I'm going to keep believing video can work." She recalls saying those words out loud, and she wasn't alone.

Jason remembers meeting with the founder of a Ukrainian accelerator program outside her hotel on Sutter Street in downtown San Francisco to deliver the product to her. As he was handing her the boxes she'd need to take back to Kiev with her, she said, "Great, so when are you going to come out and walk us through it?"

He said, "All of the coaching content is delivered through the online videos. You won't need me for anything!"

And the founder said, "Yeah, cool. When are you going to come out and walk us through it?"

Even though the demand was literally standing on the sidewalk in front of Jason, telling him the client wanted a human being to come to Kiev, he brushed it aside, because it would have been so disruptive. (This is another self-deception that's so common it has a name: the Sunk Cost Fallacy.)

Of course, the employee was right, and online videos never took off for us. If we'd listened and pivoted, we might have found a way to keep the business growing long enough for video to catch on. (We were about eight years too early.) But because we hid from the truth, we lost out.

HOW ALL THIS SELF-DECEPTION PLAYS OUT

When Janice's client Mafalda was assigned a new boss after a company reorganization, she and Janice spent a month strategizing. Mafalda had seen this new boss hiring a fleet of people and starting some exciting new projects, so based on her current position and recent experience, she assumed she'd soon be appointed head of a new division. In advance of a leadership meeting, she and Janice polished up Mafalda's proposal, only to find out that the new boss didn't think she'd wanted the division head job and had already made different plans for her.

The result was two months of negotiations, backpedaling, fear, agita, relationship erosion, and a situation that was borderline unrecoverable. At the end of all that drama, Mafalda got the position she wanted, but since her boss had spent all that time creating infrastructure without her input, she was saddled with an organizational structure and staff that she would not have chosen herself.

Both Mafalda and her boss thought that they had been acting with accurate insight, but both failed to ask basic questions. They didn't Orient Honestly, together or individually. They were dishonest with themselves. They each chose to think, "I know what's happening. I don't need to risk the social discomfort of a probing conversation with anyone else. I'll just assume my understanding of this situation is right and behave as if it is." If they had taken a week up front to align, they could have avoided months of delay and difficulty later in the year.

The act of Orienting Honestly is often one of taking a little time to ask questions. It may even start with questions about questions, such as, "What questions should I be asking right now?" That spills over into, "What do I think I know, and how can I confirm if my assumptions are true or false?" This is deeply uncomfortable territory for many of us, especially if our situation involves other people. In many cases, we *know* we need to do some investigating and questioning, but it feels inconvenient or scary or politically touchy to do so. We must find the bravery to ask, though, or risk disaster. Both of us have watched senior executives who are twenty years into their careers and pulling half-million-dollar salaries shy away from asking questions. Because asking questions can feel threatening or demeaning. It can imply you don't have all the answers, which can feel untenable to some leaders, regardless of experience or standing. But we coach them toward courage and push for them to cover these two fundamental questions at the very, very least:

1. What do I know?
2. How do I know it?

Skipping those questions is equivalent to pulling the wool over our own eyes. This is not a character flaw or point of shame; it's a part of being human. Self-deception is a fact of life. But when we act on inaccurate information, especially a false picture of the current state, we set ourselves up for one of these deeply undesirable outcomes:

We treat a symptom rather than a cause: If we don't Orient Honestly before we begin addressing a problem, we can squander our time, energy, and money on a "solution" that doesn't actually resolve the problem. Let's say you have a public relations team that isn't performing well. They aren't getting stories out there, and you just don't know how they're spending time. You set them up with specific and measurable goals, and things improve—but not for long. Because it turns out that the real problem is that they hate each other and will do anything to avoid talking.

We waste resources: If we don't understand the true present circumstances, we can pour resources into the wrong efforts. We've seen scores of companies build products based on their own ideas only to discover that nobody wants to buy them. A waste of resources, imagination, and effort that could have been avoided by asking questions of the customer up front to validate their ideas.

We erode trust: Acting on unconfirmed assumptions can have devastating effects on our relationships, especially when those assumptions are ungenerous to others. When we mistake assumptions for facts, we close ourselves off to other perspectives and can alienate our stakeholders—friends, coworkers, family members—and set the table for friction and disagreement.

We lose perspective: Jason met an old friend last weekend for coffee. Phil was struggling at work, and it quickly became clear that this was because his boss was really being nasty. The boss convinced Phil that his struggles were his own fault and he just had to try harder, but in reality he needed to find another job—fast! When we make an effort to articulate our situation and complication (remember Minto!, page 34), we carve a little porthole to light up the dark places. We can see outside the situation, regain perspective, and begin to make progress again.

Worst of all, we stop learning: You don't have to be an ego-driven Capital-L Leader to become closed to new information. It takes awareness and deliberate attention to practice open-mindedness. When we start believing we already have the full picture, we stop exploring beyond what we already know. We think, "I got this. No need to investigate any further." This is the equivalent of using Stop Hands.

This gesture, and the mental process that accompanies it, signals resistance, closure, and an unwillingness to listen or accept further information. We are committing to the path we've chosen, and to ignoring any signals that other, better paths might exist.

By contrast, when we move to a mindset of inquiry, we switch to Open Hands.

This is not only a physical metaphor for receptiveness; the act of turning your hands over and putting them on your lap also creates a neurological change toward receptiveness. We open ourselves to new possibilities. *This* is how we need to be in order to Orient Honestly.

HOW TO RECOGNIZE WHEN WE'RE NOT BEING HONEST WITH OURSELVES

A big part of Orienting Honestly is learning to recognize when we need to check the facts. Learning to sense the clues and cues that suggest maybe there's something more under the surface, or that the truth is more complicated than we might wish.

For many years, we've had a saying, "Acknowledge what's true and make that a good thing." It's not always possible, we understand that. But this ethos has helped us move through the world with more integrity and far fewer dramatic surprises. We find that having an explicit strategy, even for grappling with unpleasant truths, is far smoother than the alternative. So here are some indicators to help you notice when you need to pause, check in with yourself, and see if there's an uncomfortable truth that you need to accept.

Behaviors & Social Signals

- **The fidgets:** Your body will react when your mind is up to no good. If you're fidgety, twitchy, or incapable of settling into a comfortable position, that could indicate that whatever you're thinking or saying doesn't feel right.
- **Back-channel conversations:** If you're only discussing something through sneaky back channels, ask yourself why. What's the reason this topic can't be brought out into the open? Maybe it's because you're avoiding some unpleasant truth.
- **Avoidance:** Avoiding a root canal is understandable. But if you're steering clear of a topic or feeling reluctant to surface an idea at work, examine that behavior. When we're lying to ourselves, we tend to keep the subject at arm's length.

Words

- **"Let's move forward":** This phrase is inevitably spoken when some niggling issue remains unresolved. If that issue is yours, the phrase might come from your own lips. And when that happens, take a step back and try to identify what's bothering you.

- **"I'm not X, I'm just Y"**: That little word—*just*—is a verbal cue that you may be engaging in self-deception. "I didn't mean to hurt him, I just wanted to teach him a lesson," or "I'm not unhappy, I'm just overwhelmed." What difficult truth is the word *just* covering up?
- **Emotions and words clash:** If you find yourself saying things aloud that don't align with your feelings, take a private moment to consciously ask yourself, "What's true for me right now?"

For the record, very few people know themselves so well and live their lives so in tune with their intuition that they avoid self-deception. In fact, we lie to ourselves about fundamental elements of our identities, like how biased we truly are.

Dr. Akiko Maeker is one of the founders of Interculturalist LLC, a company that helps organizations foster inclusion. One of the tools she uses is the Intercultural Development Inventory (IDI), an assessment that measures a person's ability to engage effectively across cultures. The test results show test-takers three key metrics: where they *expect* to fall on the so-called Intercultural Competence Continuum, where they *really* fall, and the difference between the two scores. That last score captures the distance between their self-image and actual competence; between how they aspire to behave and the reality of their current behaviors. Dr. Maeker calls this difference The Gap.

Everyone has The Gap. Nearly every single test-taker believes they are more interculturally evolved than they actually are. Which means they have all unknowingly lied to themselves about how biased and empathetic they act in their lives.

It's worth repeating—this is not a character flaw or point of shame; it's a normal part of being human. Self-deception is a fact of life. In conversation with us, Dr. Maeker pointed out that no one can actually *close* their Gap, but everyone can chase it.

"The Gap should always exist. Its existence drives us forward. We should envision ourselves chasing it, instead of catching up to it," she explains. "The process of building an intercultural knowledge base and thinking reflectively helps us build capacity and become more capable of developing even more. When we push our aspirations outward, reaching for deeper learning, we become more capable of relating to the experiences of other people.

Aspiration drives development. When we simply close our gap and stop, we don't develop very much or very well. After all, if we reside exactly where we think we reside, what's our impetus to improve?"

SASSIE DUGGLEBY: STAYING HONEST AT HYPERSONIC SPEED

One of the hardest challenges an entrepreneur can face is the disruption that comes with growth and success. As you go from zero employees to ten, to twenty-five, to fifty, and from zero funding to $1 million to $20 million to $40 million—every week the requirements change, and the context feels different. As CEO of Venus Aerospace, Sassie Duggleby is one of the most ambitious, humble, and driven entrepreneurs we've had the honor of working with. We sat down to get her best tips for how she stays honest with herself, and the truths she's accepting about her business.

Nurture Health: Our motto is "Home for dinner." We want to be able to fly you to one side of the world and have you home for dinner. And if you work for us, we want you home for dinner. We're solving thousands of problems, and every problem we solve will open up a hundred more problems. In order to solve those problems, we need to have you at your best as an employee. At your best, you're rested, you're eating healthy, you're fueling your body. If you're working hundred-hour weeks, we don't believe you'll have the mental capacity to solve problems creatively.

Normalize Your Adventure: At the end of the day, I'm still just Sassie Duggleby. I'm just a standard person who's got this crazy idea and I happen to be executing on it. I still pinch myself. I ask Andrew (my husband and cofounder) every day, "What are we doing again?" He says, "Oh, we're just building a space plane." I say, "Oh, okay, no big deal." We make it a joke. We try to normalize the grand vision, because whether we're building a space plane or making a new shampoo, there are some processes we just have to go through that are true, no matter what we're building. At the end of the day, I'm still a mom—I make dinner for my kids and get to soccer practice just like everyone else.

Stay Grounded: I want to jump up and go, go, go, but every morning, I try to force myself to get up and start the day with some quiet time and reflection. It's not easy to stay grounded. Being active helps, being with my family helps, making time for my friends helps. I lean on my faith a lot. I know that we were called to this work.

More Brains: It's easier to be clear about what's happening, because I'm surrounding myself with great people who have seen and done things like this before. So when I say, "Hey, this is what's going on," they can say, "Of course that's happening—here's what you might expect next." Having people who are ahead of me in their growth, who can share, "Here's something that's going to bite you because it bites everybody," is so helpful. I really tap into those resources, because I certainly don't know all the answers. I'm happy to reach out to experts and get their help, I like to remind myself it never hurts to ask.

Embrace Life's Messiness: As a leader, I want to know that my employee was up with a crying baby all night long. Then I understand, "Oh, that's why they're grumpy. Let's give them a little extra grace and some extra coffee." There's never *not* something going on outside of work. You've got all the stresses and things at work, but we all have things happening outside of work that require context for what's happening within. Ignoring context can set you up with false expectations.

Plan for the Long Haul: I tell people all the time, at the end of this journey, our kids are going to be out of the house. And if we miss their childhood, we can't get that back. Andrew and I have seen people burn out at some of the world's most renowned space companies. They recognize that they just can't put in another a hundred-hour workweek, so they're looking for something different. The very best people are coming to us, and they're staying. It takes, what, six months to a year to bring someone in, train them up, and get them working at the same level? Think of the mind loss when great people leave.

Lift Out of the Moment: As leaders, we get inundated with all the problems. For example, we just got back from vacation. I was swamped with everything that arose while we were gone. I came home from work that day and I felt rough. As if everything was terrible. I had to stop, step out of that moment, and remind myself that, actually, everything is great. We've got a team. We just received more investment money, and others are banging down our door to invest. I spent this morning with a videographer, and he said it was the coolest thing he'd ever filmed! We're doing cool, cool things. We're the hottest company in town, and everyone is talking about us. Sometimes it helps to stop, orient yourself with honesty, and remind yourself that the way you feel in a certain moment isn't always the whole story, nor is it the larger picture.

A TOOL FOR FINDING THE TRUTH: FIVE WHYS

If you're going to Orient Honestly, you sometimes need to dig up details to figure out what's really going on. Maybe you have a surface understanding but suspect there's something more. Here's a tool for finding the truth below the facts: Five Whys.

Sakichi Toyoda—Japanese industrialist, inventor, and founder of Toyota Industries—created this technique in the 1930s, and Toyota still uses it to find the root of problems and thorny issues today.[1] Toyota has long adhered to the "go and see" philosophy, meaning that decisions about production should be based on an in-depth understanding of what's actually happening on the factory floor, and *not* on what someone in a boardroom posits might be happening.[2]

The Five Whys tool follows this tradition. The method is straightforward to describe but can feel nuanced in practice. When a problem arises and you want to understand "What's really going on here," the Five Whys has you drill down to the root cause by asking "Why?" five times in a row.

Here's a true-crime example:

"Who drank the last cup of coffee? You interns always take the last cup and never make more! Why am I the only one who makes coffee?" This person has told herself a story, but is it an accurate story? How can we approach problem-solving? Perhaps putting up a sign in the breakroom that says, "Refill the coffee if you take the last cup!" Maybe making an announcement at the next team meeting. But if, instead, the people involved get together for Five Whys, we might get this picture.

WHY NUMBER	QUESTION	ANSWER
1	WHY is there no coffee in the coffeepot?	Because we're out of coffee filters. (*So much for blaming the interns.*)
2	WHY are there no coffee filters?	Because nobody bought them at the store.
3	WHY didn't someone buy them on the last shopping trip?	Because they weren't on the shopping list.
4	WHY weren't they on the shopping list?	Because there were still some left when we wrote the list.
5	WHY were there still a few left when we wrote the list?	Um. I don't know?

When you get to the "I don't know" stage, that's when you've probably reached a "root cause," and you can begin to problem-solve. There wasn't any coffee made on the day when our story's hero blamed the intern because the company still had a few coffee filters left in the box when the last shopping list was compiled. Once you have the root cause, you can find an operational solution: when you take out a filter, if there are only a few left, put "buy coffee filters" onto your shopping list.

Another example might be around poor quarterly sales performance. We're going to make this a little messier, to show how you may need to reframe the next "Why" question to get to the heart of what you can control and get past our tendency toward knee-jerk reactions and cognitive biases.

WHY NUMBER	QUESTION	ANSWER
1	WHY was sales performance low last quarter?	Because the economy was down. (*Blaming externalities for failure is called "Self-Serving Bias."*)
2	WHY were we not prepared for a down economy?	Because our strategy was developed six months ago, and nobody knew it would happen.
3	WHY didn't we know it would happen?	Well, some of us did, but we didn't take them seriously.
4	WHY didn't we take them seriously?	Because we would have had to replan and we didn't have time. (*Rejecting things we don't already believe is called Confirmation Bias.*)
5	WHY didn't we make time to replan?	Um. I don't know?

As you can see, when you do this on more complex issues, you sometimes find that every "why" is harder than the last. You may need to dig and rewrite each question or answer a few times to get to something that feels like a root cause that's actionable. It's no good to throw up your hands and say, "Welp, the economy was down, so we're off the hook!" It's important to reframe around what is actionable that you have agency over. This team can now identify that it might be a good idea to create a contingency plan when someone on the team sees an external threat.

For a final example, let's consider how you might use Five Whys to understand why a team that we have coached is struggling.

WHY NUMBER	QUESTION	ANSWER
1	WHY is the team struggling?	Because they are having difficulty getting along with the new team member.
2	WHY are they having trouble getting along with the new person?	Because that new team member tends to be directive and thinks of themself as the leader of the team.
3	WHY do they think they are the leader of the team?	Because in previous roles with the same title at other companies, that role was expected to be a directive leader and sole decision-maker.
4	WHY have they not adapted to their new context? (At this point, we need to keep digging, and that means adapting this next why question.)	Because they were trained and scarred by previous work environments where they were punished for not being directive. Habits, defenses, and expectations were built up over ten years in environments that expected something different. **They don't yet trust that this place is different.** (Note that sometimes it takes a few sentences to get to the heart of the matter.)
5	WHY haven't they begun to trust yet?	Um. I don't know?

Drilling down is challenging. It can be ambiguous, and there may be some false starts. Sometimes you won't even need all five to get to a good place to start resolving. Other times, you might need six. That's all fine. Practice Five Whys several times and you'll get the hang of it. The goal is to reduce problems over time by discovering and resolving root causes, rather than treating symptoms. In this example, the salient point is that the new team member doesn't yet trust, so the whole team, including the leadership, will need to reinforce trustworthiness over time. Having compassion for a challenging team member can help to unlock their greatness.

A TOOL FOR CHECKING IN ON YOURSELF: THE LIFE PIE

"How are you doing? You seem a little stressed."

"No, I'm fine."

"Really?"

"Yup."

"Really, really?"

It's one thing to keep your feelings to yourself. It's quite another to hide your feelings *from* yourself. We make it a habit to check on each other—really check—pretty often. We've learned that we move so quickly through life, and life moves so quickly through time, that it's easy to lose sight of our inner state. And before you know it, we're grouchy, or high strung, or can't sleep.

The Life Pie is a miraculous framework for checking in on yourself. It brings clarity when things feel confusing, overwhelming, or when you can't see how to get out of a funk. Long ago, when Janice was going through a divorce and setting up life as a newly single person (her quarter-life crisis), the Life Pie tool became a daily companion, coach, and cheerleader. Today it's an occasional check-in, especially when work stress or life worry creeps up. It's easiest to understand if you just jump right in and do it, so let's do that now.

To make a Life Pie, you start by drawing a circle, then dividing it into eight pie slices and labeling them like so:

The purpose of this exercise is to create a visual representation of how "full" or satisfied you feel in these eight key areas of life. How content are you with your current state of physical well-being? How connected do you

feel with your community right now? How full is each slice, assuming that "totally full" is perfect and "totally empty" is the worst?

Starting from the center and working outward using a light-colored marker or highlighter, color in each wedge of pie to show how satisfied you are with each part of your life. If you feel 80 percent satisfied with your own understanding of your emotional well-being, fill in 80 percent of that wedge, and so on. When you're done, you'll have a snapshot of your current life situation.

Take a good look. Which wedges of pie are full and which are empty? Is there one wedge that feels overfull? Looking over the whole picture, you're likely to notice some spots that need attention to *bring your life into a more satisfying balance* (that's our Point B). Then use what you're seeing to create a statement that describes your present situation, including any complications. Now you have your Point A. Use these insights to formulate a plan that will make your life more satisfying, calmer, and more balanced. Here's an example:

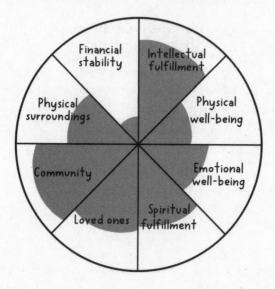

- **Point A:** "I've been focusing a lot of energy into finishing up my MBA online, so of course my student loans are killing me. But look at how good everything else is! I've got a lot of support in my life. So, yeah, I think I'm finally ready to make a career move."
- **Point B:** "I have a director-level role in the medical devices field!!!"
- **The Plan:** "Work my network, leverage the alumni community, and go to med-tech meetups."

Obviously, this Point B is going to involve a lot of little hops, so there's a whole process to think through. The power of the Life Pie is that it helped our hero see that they're in a good spot to make that happen.

The Life Pie reveals misalignments in life, so that we can clearly see the change we need to make. It reveals Point A—where you are—and Point B—where you want to be—which makes it roughly a billion times easier to know how to make our lives just a bit better. (We'll do a deep dive into this process in chapter ten.)

Workshop with Janice:
ORIENT HONESTLY

Now that we've seen some of the ways we can pull the wool over our own eyes, let's apply that to our project. So far, we've chosen a problem, identified collaborators, and defined Point A and Point B. Here's how we can get a little bit more honest with ourselves:

1. Take a look at the Point A and Point B you wrote up for the chapter two workshop. Read the two statements and identify where you might want to do a Five Whys root-cause analysis.

    Remember that my project is about creating a strategic communications plan for the next six months. It's a critical time (the book is coming out!), and there have been important changes in my business life.

2. Write down your Five Whys question. Take a moment to consider and then write your answer. (See page 57 for examples.)

3. Do it again—ask a why question and answer it. (We're showing how to use the Five Whys solo, but it's easier if you have a partner who can formulate the next question based on your answer.)

4. Keep going until you get to a really solid, telling, "I don't know" answer. Mine looks like this:

Starting Question: Why do I avoid making a strategic communications plan?	Because I like speaking off the cuff.
Why do I like speaking off the cuff?	Because I can tailor my messages to the exact people and situation.
Why do I tailor the messages to the exact situation?	Because more general messages seem less persuasive.

| Why are my general messages less persuasive? | Because the messages all seem good— it's hard to choose and prioritize. |
| Why can't I choose? | Uh. I don't know. Maybe because I'm not a marketing person??? |

5. Now that you've done your Five Whys, you may find you've had some insight that will alter your Point A.

    In my example, I looked at why I avoid doing strategic communication plans. I know all of the steps and have done them before. By doing a Five Whys analysis, I can see that a root cause for this avoidance is my wish to customize the messages to each individual and case. This helps me to see that the real complication I need to resolve is the tension between creating one-off custom messages and having a generalized messaging platform. Given this insight, I went back and refined my Point A to the core situation and complications:

    Due to recent changes in my business focus, my external stakeholders are becoming confused and need clear, simple communications from me. Simultaneously, I'll be going on a promotional tour with strangers. These are different kinds of communications, and my personal strength in improvisational customized communication (how I've handled it in the past) isn't going to cut it.

6. Write simple summary statements for Point A, Point B, and how to get there. Can you summarize your challenge in three lines as I've done below? For my example:

    - **Point A:** *I have a big communications period coming up with two very different kinds of needs, and the way I've handled it in the past isn't going to cut it.*
    - **Point B:** *By two months from now, I will have a strategic set of core messages that I can use consistently, so that all my stakeholders (including new ones) understand my business.*
    - **How to get there:** *Start by choosing the most important stakeholders and the most important changes to the business.*

Chapter 4

WHEN THINGS GET (HYPER)DYNAMIC

J anice has spent most of her professional life working with one type of entrepreneur or another, inside large organizations or in Silicon Valley startups, mom-and-pop businesses, even in the federal government. One hallmark all these people share is that you have to make hundreds of decisions without sufficient information every day. "You're pitching the *Wall Street Journal* in one minute and plunging the toilet in the next." You must be willing to do everything and anything that needs to be done, whether you've been trained to or not, and you can't waste time as you go about doing it. It's not lost on us that it sounds a lot like being a stay-at-home parent.

Keeping your head about you while you make "in the moment" decisions is an important leadership skill. You have to do all the things, and there are emergent things (like real or metaphorical diaper blowouts), and you need to just get on with it without losing your cool.

THE OBSERVE, DESCRIBE, PARTICIPATE TOOL

We each walk around all day, every day with the same deceptively simple Point B: What should I do in this moment?

Should I speak up at this meeting or hold my thoughts? Should I put that employee on a personal improvement plan or give them another chance? Should I take my ferret to the vet or wait one more day? Should I buy a size 10 legging or size 12?

The skill we're about to introduce is drawn from a wing of behavioral psychology called DBT (dialectical behavior therapy). Outside of therapeutic applications, the simple, practical skills developed for DBT can help anyone manage their reactions to everyday situations. These tools provide simple-to-follow instructions for navigating our emotional responses and interactions with others. When Marsha Linehan codified the DBT skills, she was assembling an instruction book for folks who didn't know how to behave around others. Because we're all flawed, it's not surprising that the instructions she created can be helpful to anyone. Who doesn't struggle to find the right things to say or the right ways to react from time to time? Especially in the face of hyperdynamism and endless change? DBT's tools can help us get the clarity we need so that we can respond to just about any situation in reasonable and measured ways.

HOW DBT CAN LEAD YOU TO POINT B

Dialectical behavior therapy (DBT) is a type of talk therapy that was developed in the 1980s by psychologist Marsha M. Linehan to treat borderline personality disorder.[1] Now, you might be saying, "I'm relatively sure I don't have borderline personality disorder, so why should I care about DBT?" Well, because this type of therapy comes with a whole slew of skills and mindset shifts that can be valuable—even transformational—for anyone. And for decades, the skills training embedded in DBT has been used by healthy people outside of therapeutic settings to increase their effectiveness.

These DBT techniques can be particularly helpful when the Point B you're hoping to reach isn't a goal or activity but a state of mind. DBT offers you prompts and tools for Orienting Honestly, defining Point B, and getting there. For instance:

If Point A is, "I'm frustrated because one of my employees is upset with me, even though I made the only decision that was reasonable."

Point B could be, "I'm at peace with the situation, and the employee feels heard, even if they aren't satisfied."

DBT encourages you to recognize that when you're deciding how to interact with others, you must prioritize: you can put the relationship first, your own objective first, or your self-respect first. DBT gives you step-by-step instructions for shifting from one priority to another. In this example, our hero could go in there guns blazing, defend the decision, and insist that the employee stop carping. But that wouldn't really get her to Point B. That reaction prioritizes self-respect at the expense of everything else.

In this example, our hero wants to achieve her objective (helping the employee accept the decision) without torching the relationship. DBT offers a self-management tactic to use when you want to do just that: the acronym is GIVE, which stands for Gentle, Interested, Validating, and Easy manner. When you enter into a difficult interaction, GIVE reminds you to use a gentle tone of voice when speaking, express sincere interest in what the other person is saying, validate their thoughts and feelings verbally, and maintain an easy manner throughout the conversation. Mentally repeating the acronym GIVE can help you keep your cool, listen more actively, and cultivate empathy, even when you're dealing with someone or something that challenges you. If our hero uses this technique to navigate a follow-up conversation with her employee, she has a much better shot at reaching Point B.

DBT works well in work contexts because it offers guidelines for getting along with people, understanding charged interactions, and managing our feelings. The popular mythology that you must "keep your feelings out of the workplace" is ineffective, even if it were possible.

Feelings are signals, which means they reveal our moral compass and our own ethical framework. They tell us right from wrong and allow us to delineate what's good or not good for us as individuals. Feelings guide us in how to choose our next, right, effective actions. So, rather than eliminating them, we want to appropriately engage our emotions while we're at work, and techniques from DBT can help.

A foundational practice in DBT is Observe, Describe, Participate (ODP). This set of steps encourages us to recognize and name what is going on inside our noisy minds before we say or do anything. When examined physiologically, thoughts are merely unbidden neurological events, and many of them happen just at the edge of our conscious awareness. Implementing ODP brings that brain chatter into the light so that we can make effective choices for how to respond in the moment. So, if you're sitting in a work meeting that's not going well, and you have to be effective in that moment, that's when the ODP skill can be your best friend.

There's a universal A and B embedded in the ODP steps that works for any "in the moment" situation:

Point A (What inspires you to use ODP): I'm having a strong reaction to things that are happening, and I want to be skillful in what I do next so that I don't make the situation worse.

Point B (Where you want to be after you've used the ODP skill): I have a clear idea about how to participate effectively in the current situation.

ODP steps help you make quick observations of your own physical and emotional state along with your thoughts and action items. Here's how that goes:

Observe: This first step is noticing (without judgment) that you're having a reaction to whatever is happening around you—surprise, anxiousness, frustration, and so on. It only takes a nanosecond to become aware that you're having thoughts or feelings, and then you move on to the next step.

Describe: In this step, you take a few moments to write down what's happening with your thoughts, physical sensations, and action urges. Resist the temptation to judge yourself for what comes out. This can be short phrases like "head pounding" or "very frustrated," but try to be observational, objective, and focused on yourself. Janice finds it helpful to gain objective distance as she describes her stream-of-consciousness thoughts by starting every sentence with the words "I had a thought that . . ." Put together, it sounds like this:

I had a thought that we should push out the launch by two weeks.
I had a thought that pushing out the launch would be a disaster.
Heart beating fast, feeling warm.
I had a thought that I wish Tom would shut up and let Jin talk.

If you're like most people, you might judge yourself for some of these thoughts. ("It's not nice to say shut up.") So, if you notice that judgment, set it aside. Noticing that you're having feelings about Tom makes it easier to manage those feelings, move past your reaction about changing a deadline, and find the clarity to focus on the task at hand. When you do the first two steps, it can seem that you're slowing down time. And in that space—when you give yourself a moment to recognize and note your thoughts—your mind will provide you with calm clarity.

Participate: In this final step, you bring yourself fully back into the current moment and whatever is happening around you and choose your next action from that place of balanced wisdom.

ODP can be called upon whenever you find yourself in a tense conversation or tricky situation and want to make sure you take the best action possible, as a leader and as a human being. To do that, you need to be in a state that DBT experts call the "wise mind," a place of balance between your reason-based mind and your strictly emotional mind. When you are in a wise mind, you won't take actions that make sense logically if they run counter to your feelings. You also won't take actions that feel right emotionally but aren't fully reasonable. By walking through the steps of ODP, you can leverage reason and emotion in tandem and in balance.

Here's an example. Say you're a graphic designer who has just finished creating an advertising concept for a client. You've gone out on a limb and designed something radical, but you feel like you've nailed it. You sent mock-ups via email on Monday and your entire team is on edge, worried that the client will hate the concept and you'll all have to go back to square one. The week wears on, and finally the client sends your whole team one email about the concepts, which says, "We've been working furiously to get through all the mock-ups you sent. We'll need some time to discuss the new colors you're recommending . . ."

Whoa! What does that mean? What does that ellipsis imply? Is the client omitting key information? Your emotions go into overdrive, and soon you've convinced yourself that the whole project is scrapped. They hate everything about your concepts! You'll probably get fired! It's a disaster! Thank you, brain, for serving up these automatic thoughts that are out of step with the facts of the current situation! Psychologists call this kind of distorted thinking *catastrophizing*. It drains our energy, disrupts our interactions with others, and makes it that much more difficult to act effectively.

This is the perfect time to take ODP out for a spin. Use those simple steps to bring yourself back to center and begin using your wise mind.

Observe: Take a step back from those strong feelings and allow yourself to identify what's happening inside you and around you. This creates a little extra space and can feel like slowing down time. If you could narrate, here's what it might sound like:

"Feeling tension across my forehead. Mind is racing. Worst-case scenarios are bad. Looking at my team members. What are they thinking? The room feels tense and heavy."

Describe: Capture the thoughts, physical sensations, and action urges you're experiencing. Don't judge what comes out—simply note your true observations. When you first start using this technique, it's helpful to write each observation as an item in a list. In our scenario, you sit down to do the Describe step and at first it comes out like this:

"I'm frustrated. I'm so confused and anxious about this client email. Why were they so vague? It makes me feel out of control and worried that I've done everything wrong."

But then you remember to write out thoughts, sensations, and action urges as a separate item. This very short sentiment unpacks into a dozen or more statements.

My thoughts are racing.
My breath is tight.

My face is hot. (Oh, I'm feeling fear!)

I feel a little queasy.

I had the urge to send the client an angry email. (Yeah, let's not do that.)

I had a thought that my client is being vague.

I had a thought that they hate the design. (Maybe they're just arguing with each other?)

I had a thought that I don't know what to do next.

I had a thought that my work is out of control.

I had a thought that I've done everything wrong.

You took three minutes to write, and as you wrote, thoughts that were lurking on the edge of awareness became clear. (Thoughts like "I've done everything wrong.") Now you can see that your thoughts weren't accurate, and that much of what you wrote is untrue and unkind to yourself. Your work is not out of control, you won't get fired, and you haven't done everything wrong. Objectively, you can see that you're just afraid, and it becomes easier to know how to proceed.

Participate: Give yourself wholly to the events that are occurring. Stay present in the moment as you experience all the things you have just observed and described. This might look like:

- **Point A:** I need to validate and support my client's decision-making process even if I don't like it. But I also want to accelerate getting specific feedback.
- **Point B:** The client thinks I'm a good, professional partner, and I will get some insight about their opinion sooner rather than later.

So you send an email: "Thank you for your message, Andi. Take the time you need to discuss the design. We know it's a big departure from where you are now, and at the same time we believe it could take your brand in a powerful new direction. I'd be happy to get the team together to talk about the risks and advantages of this strategy. I'll give you a call this afternoon to touch base."

Since it's impossible to get real clarity until you talk with the client, you send the email then shift gears and focus on other work. Since your mind is now clear, you can release yourself back into the flow of that other work and put this issue aside until it's time to discuss it with the client.

ODP is a skill that's been helping people Orient Honestly for decades, even in the face of intense emotions and strong physical reactions. We believe it will become increasingly important as the pace of change in our world continues to accelerate. As with all skills, though, ODP takes practice to master and implement seamlessly as an individual and a leader. If this skill appeals to you and has clear applications in your life, make a goal of incorporating it regularly. At the same time, give yourself some grace. Keep trying. It will get easier, and when it does, having ODP at your disposal will help you be a more effective leader in your workplace, community, friend group, and family.

LIFE IS NOT LINEAR

As 2020 was drawing to a painful close and COVID-19 vaccinations were *finally* rolling out, a new variant of the virus emerged. The vaccine couldn't always knock it out of our systems, and people who had mistrusted the vaccines claimed that this proved that the science behind them was faulty. In fact, it wasn't at all surprising to scientists that a resistant variant emerged.

It's not that the science was wrong; it's that science can't anticipate every future possibility.

A new variant had entered the system and wasn't stopped by the existing vaccine. That's how science works: You form and test a hypothesis, act on it as far as you are able, and then adjust when new information becomes available. You revise both your hypothesis and your action plan based on what you've learned.

Life is the same. It's seldom linear, much as we might wish it to be. If we were able to describe Point A, envision Point B, and work our way from one to the other without any setbacks, that would make everything so much easier.

But not necessarily better.

Because the setbacks are what force us to learn, to undertake crucial self-reflection, to attack problems with fresh creativity. That's frustrating, we know. Setbacks feel utterly infuriating in the moment. But if you simply plow through everything that you do—hoping that everything will be setback-free—you're going to fail again. And again. Especially in our dynamic world, you need tools for when stuff gets messy.

And perhaps more importantly, you need the optimism to carry you through difficulties. You need to train yourself to be resilient and hopeful so you don't get thrown off course when circumstances shift.

HYPERDYNAMIC MADNESS

If we're being honest, we need to be prepared for continuous change. That's just the world we live in now. Back in the 1980s, we thought the world was moving fast. Technologies were emerging, economies were shifting, walls were coming down. It felt like everything was accelerating, and we all had to scramble to keep up. In 1987, legendary business consultant Tom Peters proclaimed, "**To meet the demands of the fast-changing competitive scene, we must simply learn to love change as much as we have hated it in the past.**"[2]

It's almost cute that people hated change so much back then.

We've mentioned this already, but we're echoing it here again because we truly want to drive home this mind-bending point: Given the pace of change and transformation we've witnessed in just the past few years, we can safely say that our world is moving more slowly right now than it ever will again. Acceleration may have been happening back in the '80s—when we had to send paper memos or talk live on the phone to get anything done—but it's picked up steadily ever since then. And as far as anyone can tell, it will continue to speed up.

Not just the pace of business, but the pace of everything. That ever-increasing pace is fueled by technology, of course, but it's also fueled by the sheer number of humans on the planet. And with compounding factors piling up, we end up mired in circumstances that seem inexplicable and untenably complex. Once upon a time we could focus on the small issues affecting our immediate families and communities, but no more. On a near-daily basis, our lives are being radically affected by the macro forces reshaping our world.

We need a new word. Because it's not just dynamic, it's HYPERdynamic.

Hyperdynamism can make our lives feel fantastically out of control, and that's not our fault. There are truly massive changes happening right now, and they just keep coming. The world seems to be operating by a different set of rules, which means the leadership advice of decades past feels outmoded and brittle. Much of that so-called wisdom never spoke to us anyway, which is why we've spent so much of our careers cultivating a new, more flexible set of leadership practices. We looked for tools, ideas, and practices that could reliably guide us to accomplish more with less effort and far less drama. The Four Leadership Motions offer an approach that helps real people in any context make progress faster and more easily.

Continuous change is the new (new, new, new) reality. If you don't expect the unexpected, you may freeze, deny, or overreact. If you don't learn to improvise when the situation around you morphs, you'll find yourself up to your eyeballs in drama. And there's enough drama in the world already.

What you *do* need are skills and tools. Tools like mindfulness and skills like ODP can help you stay calm and effective. You need to notice when hyperdynamism has shown up and meddled with your situation, changing your Point A or Point B. And if you don't notice that they've changed, you're going to waste time and energy and *still* fail to make progress. If you don't notice that your colleagues or friends disagree about Point A, Point B, or the actions needed to move between them, that will lead to some serious conflict and interpersonal clashes. Cultivating awareness of hyperdynamism, and how it acts on your Points A and B, will equip you to adjust your actions and expectations in real time.

A DYNAMIC POINT A: USE THE OODA LOOP

How can we continue to Orient Honestly in a time of constant change, amidst the seismic external forces impacting our lives?

We start by accepting that Orienting Honestly isn't a discrete, onetime activity. Occasionally you can take stock of your situation, understand your complications, and articulate your true current state, then move on. But most of the time, you'll need to do a quick reorientation periodically. Where you are, who surrounds you, and which resources you have at hand may all shift unexpectedly, impacting your Point A before you can begin moving toward Point B.

Fortunately, you can reassess Point A repeatedly as conditions change using a simple tool invented by a U.S. Air Force colonel. Seriously.

We have worked as occasional advisors to the U.S. military. Those leaders excel at finding ways to make their work and life simpler and more predictable. They excel at dealing with mountains of variables that refuse to remain the same. When you're training people to cope with a wide variety of high-stress, life-and-death situations, you want them to feel confident in the decisions they make. And that means giving them versatile tools for assessing current conditions, monitoring changes in those conditions, and understanding the consequences of possible actions. One of those tools is the OODA Loop.

The OODA Loop was initially developed by Col. John Boyd to help fighter pilots in the U.S. Air Force to make decisions in battle situations. It has since been adopted as a universal self-management practice that makes it easier for individuals to decide which actions to take in dynamic situations. We love it because it's easy to remember and can help anyone summon quick clarity under the most chaotic of circumstances. Chaos is just a situation where your Point A is changing quickly and unpredictably.

OODA stands for Observe, Orient, Decide, Act. It's a four-step cycle for maintaining situational awareness and making a contextually appropriate action. It focuses on absorbing available information, putting it in context, and quickly making the most appropriate decision, again and again as situations unfold. It falls within the universe of 4LM because it is not enough to merely "Orient" Honestly. We need to take meaningful action in order to progress.

It is normal for humans to take in new information as their situation changes. What is sometimes overlooked is **the crucial step of synthesizing new observations within the existing knowledge landscape** before making decisions and taking action. Often people simply leap from observation to action. The expression "look before you leap" should probably be something more like "take a second to process what you've

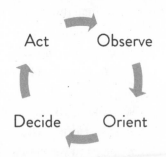

observed and put it in the proper context before you take a risky action," but that's not as pithy.

Here's an example:

During times of conflict, the U.S. Air Force flies missions, called sorties, in the areas where air support is needed. These aircrafts fly multiple missions in a single day crossing hundreds or thousands of miles, so it would be inefficient to have them return to base for fuel. Instead, "tanker" planes, giant aircraft filled with fuel, rendezvous with the combat aircraft to refuel them in midair. Aside from the incredible feat of engineering and skill it takes to pull this off, think about the planning it takes to keep all those planes fueled and active, despite the dynamic conditions of combat. Let's see how OODA plays out in this high-stakes, very dynamic situation:

- **Observe:** Based on many inputs, each day an air mission plan is released that describes what each combat plane will be doing the next day.
- **Orient:** Once the plan is released, a tanker planner team evaluates the needs, assessing where tankers will be needed and at what exact times in order to keep the combat planes on-mission.
- **Decide:** Tankers and personnel are allocated to each of the specified coordinates.
- **Act:** Each morning, a tanker plan is submitted for the day's sorties.
- **Loop Around:** *But*, based on intelligence and changing on-the-ground conditions, approximately 70 percent of the planned sorties are either revised or canceled on the day of flight. So, the tanker planning team looks at the day's revised plans (Observe), they evaluate the changes to the timings and locations (Orient), they re-map the tankers to the new mission coordinates (Decide), and they send the plans to the tanker flight teams (Act). This happens every day, in multiple areas around the world, for all of the Air Force combat operations.

By walking through all four steps, you impose informed logic on a dynamic situation, where taking shortcuts might leave you vulnerable. OODA helps to relieve stress by increasing certainty in your decisions and actions. If we want to reduce the drama, we need to get clear, make a call, and let go. OODA does that.

If we deconstruct the OODA Loop in light of our Point A/Point B framework, you can see why it works:

- Point B is preestablished: accomplish the mission objective.
- In a situation where Point A is changing rapidly, the "Observe" and "Orient" steps help you to maintain awareness of the unfolding situation.
- Situational awareness helps you to decide on a next productive action.

Think about the flight plan illustration mentioned earlier. If you're supposed to fly from your current location to Albuquerque, you must know where your plane is right now. If it's in Denver, you'll need to take one route. But if you made an emergency fuel stop in Omaha, the original flight plan won't help.

One of the things we love about the OODA Loop is that it helps us decide our next right action given the absolutely latest circumstances. By reminding us to continuously assess where we are before taking action—to Orient Honestly —it helps us mindfully cultivate ongoing contextual awareness. How does this make life easier? By providing a solid foundation for smart decision-making during difficult moments, and by giving us a simple framework to calm our minds when life feels chaotic. It's another way to Orient Honestly.

OODA is such a good way to stay cool during emergent situations, and home life provides abundant opportunities to practice the skill. Four weeks before our son was due to be born, we decided to retile the floor of the only full bathroom in our small, one-hundred-plus-year-old San Francisco flat. We owned the flat, so the job was ours alone. Our Point B was simple: use up the stack of tile that had been sitting on the floor of the baby's room. But as Jason dove into the project, multiple complications arose, causing a recursive OODA Loop as each new surprise popped up.

Once he began removing the old tile, he saw that the edge tiles were plastered into the wall of the 1930s bathroom. Removing that trim meant removing the bottom four inches of the horsehair plaster wall (Observe).

Jason saw that the scope of the project would increase if he chose to remove the trim, but it was mismatched and even uglier than the rest of the tile (Orient). It looked like repairing the base of the wall would be straightforward, so he chiseled out a hunk of the bullnose trim. Huzzah! Decision and action!

With the bullnose removed, however, Jason could see that the galvanized hot water pipe was rotted and had to be replaced immediately. Another OODA Loop had begun.

He couldn't access the fragile pipe without taking out more wall (Observe!), and with two weeks left before the baby's due date, the project was now outside of Jason's technical skill (Orient!). We decided to call a plumber (Decide!) and did so the next morning (Act!).

Two weeks before our due date, with only half the plumbing done, no running water, no kitchen sink or shower, Janice went into labor (Hyperdynamism!).

We brought our newborn son home to a happy but un-plumbed home with only a powder room functioning for all the postnatal water necessities. We showered at the neighbor's, heated water on the stove, and ate food our friends cooked (Observed, Oriented, Decided, Acted). And although it was difficult and frustrating and occasionally scary, we have no regrets—we were young, broke, overconfident, and that tile was tragic.

Because we're living in hyperdynamic times, we must be prepared to recalibrate and adjust while still in motion. Even when we know where we want to go, the conditions that are affecting us right now are constantly in flux. With all this uncertainty and change swirling around us, we need easy, fast tools to help us avoid panic and stay centered. The OODA Loop helps us do this in real time, for any evolving situation.

A DYNAMIC POINT B: USE THE PIVOT OR PERSEVERE EXERCISE

Early in his career, Jason had an unspeakably horrible boss—let's call him Dick. This guy made Jason's life extremely difficult and did everything in his power to push him out of the company.

- Dick would invite everyone on the team but Jason to meetings in his glass-walled office.
- He would have Jason create lengthy PowerPoint presentations, and then disregard them.
- He blocked Jason from talking with project stakeholders.
- He criticized Jason for not knowing information that was not shared with him.
- And worst, Dick told other managers in the company that Jason was not worth hiring.

When he first realized what was going on (Point A), Jason's goal (Point B) was to keep his job and stay in that department. He tried everything he could to satisfy Dick, prove his worth, and demonstrate that he was an asset. Jason spent weeks creating well-researched materials, volunteered for important assignments, reached out to partner with colleagues, and requested access to information and people, but he was blocked at every turn.

After a few months, Jason knew that he'd chosen the wrong Point B. Nothing he ever did would align him with this particular leader, and forcing himself to stay in that department was making him miserable. So he changed his Point B. Instead of keeping *that* role in *that* department, he decided to find a role elsewhere in the company. He still loved his work, and he knew he could find a way to continue doing it under a different leader from a different angle. This change had the *expected* effect of getting Jason away from the horrible boss, and the *unexpected* effect of opening up new career possibilities. By accepting that his point B needed revising, he shifted to a different role under a leader who challenged, trusted, and supported him. This improved his situation in multiple, lasting ways.

Most of us have had similar experiences. We set out to lose thirty pounds and eventually realize that what we really want is to be stronger. We decide to get an art history degree, then see that architecture is a better fit. We build a product that we think is brilliant but have to scrap it when users explain the dozen reasons they hate it. The moment of realization can feel like a gut punch. We are sick, sad, and disappointed all at the same time. That's natural and should be honored. But once the initial moment passes, we can begin to move past it by using the Pivot or Persevere Exercise.

This tool comes from a school of thought called the Lean Startup that was developed by our mentor and friend Eric Ries, where it's used to evaluate products and businesses, but it can be applied to virtually any situation where Point B has unexpectedly changed.

Step 1: The first step in a Pivot or Persevere moment is to evaluate and articulate what happened. If things didn't go as planned, don't hide from that. We're Orienting Honestly here.

- What did you expect to happen?
- What was your original Point B?
- What actually happened?
- What does that mean? What are the implications?

In Jason's situation, sticking it out and pleasing his boss was the original Point B. But it became clear that he would never be successful or happy working in Dick's department, even though it was the right department with the right work for the right clients. The implication was that he needed to create a new plan for himself.

Step 2: The second step in a Pivot or Persevere is to ask, "How should I best move forward from here?" (Sounds a little like the Decide/Act in the OODA Loop, right?) Generally speaking, the options break down into four possible paths:

- **Pivot:** It's not having the effect you want, so change your strategy. Maintain elements of your original goal but approach it in a new way. (Jason pivoted by changing his Point B.)
- **Persevere:** Stay the course. Keep doing what you've been doing because it might be working. (If it looked like Jason's boss was responding, he could have stayed in his department.)
- **Double Down:** Increase your efforts and invest more energy in achieving your desired outcomes. (If Jason's boss had responded positively to his efforts to satisfy him, he could have gone all in.)
- **Abandon Ship:** Accept that your current course of action isn't tenable at all and go back to the drawing board. (If Jason had decided to leave the company entirely.)

Determining which of these options is the right one means combining your knowledge of the current facts with an evaluation of your gut instincts. Consider what happened and what it means before deciding how you want to proceed. What do the facts tell you about what you misunderstood, or about how the hyperdynamic world decided to monkey with your plans? And now that you see the situation clearly, what do your instincts tell you? Remember that Point B is a statement of what you want to achieve, feel, or experience after making mindful changes or taking strategic action; it's an end-state and outcome, *not* an output, accomplishment, or discrete goal. Knowing what you know now and feeling as you do now, what should your revised Point B become?

Unfortunately, there's no litmus test for Pivot or Persevere besides your own self-knowledge and surety. You must trust yourself to make the right decision in the moment, and also trust yourself to recognize when you might need to make a different decision in the future. That kind of flexibility and agility will give you strength at all times but especially in circumstances that are constantly in flux.

When you're dealing with dynamic or hyperdynamic situations, whether it's go-to-market product releases during a pandemic or home renovations during childbirth, even the most thoughtful plans can get thrown out the window in an instant. In those moments, having a clear understanding of our Point B is what saves us. Knowing where we want to end up enables us to make in-the-moment decisions about what to do next and, in the next chapter, we'll see how that can be the foundation for an approach to planning that's optimized for hyperdynamic times, the Outcome-Oriented Roadmap.

SO MANY ACRONYMS START WITH "O"

Acronym	What It Stands For	What It Is	Page Number
ODP	Observe, Describe, Participate	A mindfulness tool for keeping cool in the moment, during an otherwise emotional situation	66
OGSM	Objectives, Goals, Strategies, and Measures	A goaling mechanism for keeping organizations aligned that tends to have a "top down" effect	119
OH	Orient Honestly	One of the four key principles in this book	9
OKR (this one is coming up!)	Objectives and Key Results	A goaling mechanism popular in Silicon Valley that tends to have a "bottom up" effect	121
OODA Loop	Observe, Orient, Decide, Act	A behavioral pattern for maintaining situational awareness despite rapidly evolving conditions	75
OORM (this one is coming up!)	Outcome-Oriented Roadmap	An alternative to traditional planning that places the focus on results rather than activities and deliverables	91

Workshop with Janice:
MINDFULNESS AND THE ODP TOOL

We're going to take a break from our project for this workshop, so that we can practice the Observe, Describe, Participate skill. At the core of this skill is the ability to notice and capture your inner voice without judging it. This type of mindfulness practice has lots of benefits, not least of which is being able to regulate your own reactions during rapidly unfolding situations. There are so many circumstances where this really helps, like if your mind leaps ahead six steps and you need to slow down so that others can catch up, or if you've ever suffered from imposter syndrome. Noticing and naming each thought as it arises can slow down time. Plan fifteen minutes for this activity.

1. Find a spot where you won't be disturbed for about ten minutes. Set yourself up with a pen and paper or notebook. Take a deep breath and let it out. Set a timer for ten minutes.
2. Start by noticing physical sensations, including sounds, smells, and body sensations like an itchy nose.
3. For a moment, try not to have thoughts. You may find that when you try NOT to have thoughts, you start to have LOTS of thoughts. (The irony!)
4. Write down every single thought you notice, without judging it or questioning it, until the timer goes off.
5. Read through the list of what you wrote. Do you notice anything surprising?
6. If you see any "should" statements about yourself or others, rewrite those nonjudgmentally.
7. Now go on about your day as usual. That's the "P," which simply means participate fully into whatever comes next.

I'll let you in on a secret: I often use this activity when I'm sitting through a particularly horrible meeting. When I'm getting frustrated or bored and I already "know" that the thing being discussed isn't productive, then I'll check myself by stealthily doing a few minutes of ODP, and I often find that I get so much more out of (and contribute more to) the rest of the meeting.

Part 2

VALUE
OUTCOMES

Chapter 5

FROM PLANS TO OUTCOMES

> *A goal without a plan is just a wish.*
> *By failing to prepare, you are preparing to fail.*
> *Plan your work, and work your plan.*

The best-laid plans of mice and men often go awry.[1]

When the pace of change becomes your greatest threat, plans and predictions can no longer be relied upon. In the stock market, there's always a blanket disclaimer—"Past performance does not guarantee future results," and it's starting to feel like that's true everywhere. Work culture is obsessed with planning—both inside and outside of the workplace. We've been taught that planning will save us from

---

* Adapted from the Robert Burns poem "To a Mouse."

the unknown and will ensure that we get to the finish line. But what if things change? What if you learn something important, say you figure out you can do it in a tenth of the time using an approach that wasn't in the plan? But now consider that success is often defined as on-time, on-budget execution according to the plan's specifications.

The problem is that plans are so very fallible. Planning is not a prediction of value.

The idea that we can write out a series of steps and predict with some certainty that the results will be valuable—that's twentieth-century thinking. That's Henry Ford thinking. And it's not nearly as relevant to our challenges today as we pretend it is. People, especially leaders, have dangerously conflated the act of creating a plan with the experience of being prepared. The reason is that plans usually focus on outputs (concrete, measurable goals) instead of outcomes (valuable end-states), which can create a false sense of security in the hyperdynamic world.

THE PROBLEM WITH PLANS

Typically when people think about planning, they think about making a list of the things that they will do leading up to the creation of an output. If you're a manager planning for midyear reviews, your list might include "collect self-evaluation forms," "review salaries," and "schedule individual meetings." All those sub-tasks definitely need to be completed in order to fulfill the larger goal of finishing midyear reviews. But what's the desired *outcome* of the midyear review process? What are you actually trying to accomplish, change, or improve by executing everything on your list of tasks? Your goal isn't just, "Being done with the midyear review process," right?

When you value planning above outcomes, it's easy to conflate effort with achievement. Having done work or checked things off a list isn't the same as creating value through your actions.

One of the managers on Jason's team was preparing to do midyear reviews and came to Jason with a question. "I'm getting a little hung up on this process," she told him. "The feedback form is kind of rigid. Some of my people are brand new. Do these tools really apply to them?"

"Well, let's go back to what we're trying to accomplish," Jason said. "We want to know if this person is learning and growing. Second, we want to understand the general state of talent in our talent pool. If you don't think the prescribed tools are going to achieve those two things, then do something else."

She was relieved to discard the process steps that didn't serve her, the organization, or the employees she was trying to support. By focusing on the outcome they both wanted, Jason gave this manager the autonomy to decide—based on the unique needs of the person she was evaluating—how she was going to create the impact that both she and Jason wanted. This was an OODA Loop, and the manager learned that she has permission to deviate from the plan to accomplish the outcome.

This mindset encourages creative thinking by focusing people on the "why" (the desired outcome) instead of the "what" (do these steps as specified). As we know, when new information comes to light, you may need to change your plans in order to reach your Point B.

Professional planners frontload the strategic outcome thinking, and then use sophisticated tools like Gantt charts to capture resources needed, time estimates associated with each task, and relationships between tasks. The execution plan they create is essentially a prediction: IF each person stays in their swim lane and does their tasks and deliverables by the date shown, THEN we will have succeeded. The Gantt chart message to the team is, "This is complicated, but we've figured it out for you. So don't mess with it, just do your thing, and we can check in along the way to make sure you are still on-plan." In a desire for efficiency and progress, this planning system isolates individuals and discourages critical reevaluation of the plan's effectiveness.

For complex projects especially, Gantt charts help to ensure on-time, on-budget delivery according to specifications (outputs), but they don't connect individual actions to why that matters (outcomes). And they won't help us know what actual value we will have created through all of that effort, which means the people who are responsible for implementing the steps can't see whether it's likely to deliver the valuable outcome at all. **Everyone takes it on faith that if we execute our little portion of the plan according to the items that were specified up front, then we will necessarily have done the right thing and have delivered the value.** When, in fact, we may just have done some work and checked some boxes. It all hinges on how good the plan was, and whether everything stayed the same in the time it took to do the work.

It's not wrong to make a list of things that you need to do, and then start doing those things. What's unrealistic is believing that the list is right no matter what new information arises as you move through its action items. What's wrong is viewing that list as your work, disconnected from a higher outcome. Countless studies have shown that when people are connected to a higher purpose, they do better work. They're more motivated. They're happier.[1]

Organizations have done it this way for the sake of predictability and stability, but those things don't exist anymore in the context of hyperdynamism. So everyday leaders all over the world need more flexible methods that connect actions to value, progress, and carefully considered outcomes.

FOCUS ON OUTCOMES TO CREATE FLEXIBILITY

Back in chapter two, we talked about the difference between outputs and outcomes. Both then and now, we want to reinforce that of course outputs are important; single achievements and discrete goals have their place. So does praising and rewarding people for their efforts, even if those efforts yield unexpected or disappointing results. But placing greater emphasis on outcomes than on steps, deliverables, or other Gantt chart–type items allows the plan to flex and adapt when new information shows up.

An outcome is a statement that expresses a desired, measurable future state. It describes what it will be "like" if you succeed, and why the work is worth doing. It's the end-state you intend to create.

When you focus on outcomes, you have the flexibility to adjust the plans, steps, deliverables, and approach as you go—in service of creating the best possible result with the resources available. You can evaluate and iterate as you go (OODA Loop) instead of staying wedded to steps or a deadline. You can let go of investments and sunk costs and direct your energies toward accelerating progress. You can create guidelines and checklists to help drive progress, but if they aren't leading toward the outcome, you can recognize that and change them.

Valuing Outcomes—one of the Four Leadership Motions and the focus of this section of the book—means identifying what it is you want to have, change, or be, and setting important parameters around that. When we identify and pursue a single output, we are denying ourselves the vast universe of other possibilities that could also get us what we want to have, change, or be. But when we identify and pursue outcomes, we move organically toward an ideal state with enough flexibility to readjust when we need to.

Knowing this, we have started using Outcome-Oriented Roadmaps (OORM—adding the *M* makes it easier to remember, we have found) with our colleagues at work and family members at home. We find that this technique helps everyone involved release their death grip on task lists and deadlines and operate as an open-minded team working toward a shared outcome.

HOW TO MAKE AN OORM

A solid Outcome-Oriented Roadmap keeps everyone moving in the same direction while enabling them to achieve really big things. It outlines a series of outcomes that, in combination, represent big progress. These outcomes may include multiple parallel tracks in addition to the expected sequential component outcomes.

When we were setting up a new apartment in Minneapolis, we were starting from scratch—we didn't have a single spoon or trash can. A basic sequence of outcomes for that project's roadmap might have looked something like this:

We can sleep there overnight	We can cook dinner	We can have friends over	We can live a full life there	It feels like home

You might decide that "cook dinner" and "sleep overnight" probably can be tackled at the same time on a trip to Target. But probably "live a full life" is more involved than "have friends over," so you might want to sequence one before the other. This example also begins to show you how focusing on outcomes allows for some flexibility when it comes to execution.

Consider the outcome "We can cook dinner." This could mean multiple things—the bare minimum might be a pot of chili. So we would need a pan, a few utensils, a refrigerator, and some paper bowls. But as you think about it, there are other levels to it. We love to cook, and the kitchen is always going to be a focal point of our attention. So you could build out a "cooking" swim lane for the roadmap:

Outcome	We can cook dinner the first few nights.	We are ready for most of our usual cooking and eating.	Our kitchen is fully stocked and ready.	Our kitchen is awesome to cook in!
Wish-For Date	September 30	October 31	January 31	August 31
Activities	Go to Target.	Look at table settings. Find local cookware stores. Shop around.	Shop at secondhand stores for unique serving pieces and used small appliances.	Make appointment to look at wallpaper, choose art pieces at Open Studios in June.
Outputs	A few pots and pans, paper plates and compostable utensils, sponge and dish soap, napkins	Pots and pans, dinnerware, utensils, knives, towels, etc.	Everyday glassware, linens, serving bowls, platters, small appliances, etc.	All of the special things, art for the walls, wallpaper, stools for the counter

As you begin to build out the roadmap, you are sequencing and scheduling the incremental outcomes. The Activities and Outputs sections may look like checklists, but they serve a greater purpose. They can be changed easily, as needed, without affecting the roadmap. No two OORMs are the same, and there's no single "right" way to create one. They are simply agreements about desired outcomes and how those outcomes will be measured, presented in terms that are loose enough to evolve as progress is made. They place focus and emphasis on the result; how you get there is up to you. They can be Word documents, spreadsheets, illustrated storyboards, graphics, or something altogether different. Use whatever format does the best job for you and your team. (You can even put them into a Gantt chart, if that's the language that speaks to you.)

As you dig in, keep these definitions clear in your mind:

If you spend time doing it, it's an **activity**.
The tangible result of that time spent is an **output**.
The reason for doing those two things is the **outcome**.

If you need to get more clarity around how these three concepts relate, turn back to the exercise in chapter two on categorizing activities, outputs, and outcomes.

Let's say you're creating an OORM with your family because you're facing the sudden need for your two kids to be homeschooled. You can start the roadmapping process by allowing everyone in the family to express their hopes and thoughts. After that, you might decide your Point B is, "Both kids will make enough progress on their schoolwork each week to stay at grade level." Here's how outcomes can get more specific and actionable.

- Both kids will make enough progress on their schoolwork each week to stay at grade level.
- Our homeschool will encourage collaboration and independence.
- Kids plan their own classwork and homework.
- Dad will spend only a small part of each day helping the kids with school tasks.

The last two bullet points easily turn into action items, but they're in service to the higher purpose of independence and staying on grade level. Once this is solidified, the discussion can turn to how and when a day's schoolwork will be determined, how to measure progress, and what to do when questions arise (activities). You can schedule check-in meetings so you and the kids can discuss how the OORM is serving you, what you've learned, and any adjustments that need to be made to help you all progress toward Point B together (also activities). And you can create a schedule for reviewing homework and completed projects (outputs).

As this example illustrates, an OORM encompasses multiple outcomes. One recent client had a team working against a dozen high-level outcomes that each addressed different thematic areas. Once we got those dialed in, we revisited them every quarter for several years. The outcomes themselves didn't change too much over time, but the activities and the outputs underneath them did. Some of our plans worked better than expected, others not so much. As we learned more and made progress, we were able to course-correct and ensure our efforts were being poured into tasks that were completely aligned with our goals.

We would never have been able to tease out those high-level outcomes if we hadn't built that client roadmap alongside key decision-makers within the company. Assuming your OORM will be used by a team or group, make sure the relevant stakeholders are involved in creating it. Don't just write it all out yourself. Get the right people in the room to collaborate so everyone is aligned. Regardless of whether the situation is work- or family-related, the people involved in creating an OORM fall into three categories:

1. People with the authority to say yes
2. People who have relevant knowledge
3. People who have to live with the outcome

Keep the group small and use common sense. So, if you need to make an OORM for your family that centers on an unexpected death in the family, your bereaved and confused five-year-old shouldn't be involved. Yes, he has to live with the outcome, but he cannot process the necessary details to contribute to the decisions. If you need to make an OORM for your team that focuses on shifting to a new set of work protocols, your CEO shouldn't be involved. She may have the authority to say yes to anything but doesn't have the right knowledge to contribute meaningfully to the discussion.

Once all the right people are in the room, start discussing the outcome(s) before you do anything else. What changes do you want to make or see? In your business, or in the world, or in certain people's lives? What is the end-state you want to create? What will be different if you make your desired outcome a reality? We like to try and get a list down in about an hour and refine it over a weekend (or no more than a week). We do it quickly because "pretty good" and fast is way better than "ideal" and slow. No matter how much time you spend polishing it up, it's going to be wrong somehow—so get it into action! Then revise and iterate when you've lived with it for a month (and every quarter after that).

As you noodle on it, if people start contributing outputs or activities to the conversation, redirect. Make piles of outputs, activities, and outcomes. To get at the outcomes, ask questions like, "How will our group/business/ life be different if we do that?" Those questions will help your team members refocus on articulating an end-state instead of action steps to take.

Be clear and choose your outcome(s) wisely. If you're clear on that end-state, it can guide everything you do for years to come. For example, we worked with a client whose Point B was, "In one year, we will have adopted a growth mindset." That sounds mighty vague, but it was helpful for their purposes and allowed them to check in on the daily work they were performing. They chose this quote from Carol Dweck's 2006 book *Mindset* to guide them: "The passion for stretching yourself and sticking to it, even (or especially) when it's not going well, is the hallmark of the growth mindset. This is the mindset that allows people to thrive during some of the most challenging times in their lives."[2] Individual people doing discrete tasks could say to themselves, "Am I still stretching myself, or have I slipped back into what I already know?" If yes, they would continue. If no, they would reevaluate and pull in new resources. That kind of self-correcting guidance is absolutely *golden* to team members working within a large organization or on a complex, multifaceted project.

Now, once you've got your outcomes articulated and defined, you'll need to prioritize them. We often get the question of how many. For teams new to the practice of OORM, we like to start with four to six (few enough so you can remember them all, but not so broad that they're completely vague). You can't do everything all at once and may have certain outcomes that are contingent on others. Don't get hung up on delivery dates but do create a loose order based on strategic priority.

Then, with the big picture captured, you can distribute the map to individuals and have them work backwards to create more concrete and executable plans for themselves: ask them to consider what needs to happen within the year, the quarter, the month, the week, and the day—always ensuring that activities map back to the outcome or end state. And remind them to perform that self-check as often as they need to. ("Is this activity aligned with [desired outcome]?")

One of the best things about OORMs is that they help you decide what not to do. With everyone committing to focus their efforts on the same outcomes, they can trust each other to decide on the right activities and outputs to get there with more autonomy. With this type of shared focus, we trust all our coworkers to organize their own work in their own way, using their own language and their own vernacular. OORMs mix the best of self-directed work with the best of collaboration and empower everyone to do their absolute best work. They make progress faster and easier, regardless of what surprises might pop up.

OUTCOME-ORIENTED ROADMAPPING IN A VLO (VERY LARGE ORGANIZATION)

Marcella Xavier (not her real name) is vice president of R&D at a Fortune 100 company that, after a century as a market leader, needed to relearn how to launch new products. Over the past five years, Marcella and her team have transformed the company, implementing new skills, mindsets, and metrics across all levels, geographies, business units, and divisions. Outcome-Oriented Roadmapping was an important part of their success.

People always say to me, "Oh my God, you folks were able to shift the culture in the company faster than we'd ever seen." But it was not always smooth. There were times when we were in danger of not making it.

About three years into the transformation, my team had grown to twenty-five people, and it was never going to get any bigger. When you're ten people, nobody expects you to cover a ninety-thousand-person company. But by the time we reached twenty-five, we needed to support all the business units. We were spread across all functions and levels, and we began to struggle.

One of the company's really fantastic planning people, Rashaad, joined the team to help and I remember him saying to me, "You have a really special thing going here. It's amazing, but you have no operational discipline." He said, "Marcella, you're not a team anymore—you're an organization."

We needed to operationalize in order to get to the next level, to fully infiltrate the company. And you wrote down for me, "We've hacked through the jungle and now we need to pave the road." And I thought, "Oh my God, that's exactly right. The only way to get more people to come through the jungle is to give them the road." How can we make it easy for others to do all of the training and coaching that we've been doing ourselves?

Rashaad sat down with me to make a plan. He asked the normal planning questions, like, "What are your deliverables?" "What are you going to be measured on?" "What's your ninety-day action plan?" Planners use what they've learned in the past to help you figure out what to do in the future. But when you're in this land of uncertainty, that approach doesn't actually help. There was nothing from the past to help me figure this thing out. His questions weren't helping me; they were just making me feel bad. I didn't know what I would be measured on. And I wasn't sure the company understood what they should be measuring me on, either.

So I decided to try using Outcome-Oriented Roadmapping to either supplement or replace our regular planning process.

The overarching outcome we landed on was "Instead of doing the work, we need to enable others to do it for themselves." Basically, stop hacking through the jungle, and pave some roads. Under that, we identified four focus areas that would be important: talent, structure, growth-stage projects, and democratizing the process. Once we had the four focus areas, then we could orient people toward them. We could create roles and responsibilities much more easily. We figured out how we could measure. And I could answer all of Rashaad's questions.

I would say the Outcome-Oriented Roadmap accelerated what we were doing by 10x. I attribute this to two things:

1. **Every hour was spent in places that had a better chance of success.**

   We had to figure out how to be, how to maximize productivity with an organization that just wanted to say yes. Our team came for the mission and they felt that in order to deliver the mission, they had to say yes to anyone who reached out to us. What we realized is to actually deliver the mission, we had to be more selective with where we said yes. And the Outcome-Oriented Roadmap enabled everybody to make those decisions by giving them something to align their efforts to.

   We decided that every hour we spent had to deliver 5x or 10x the value. And we knew by then what the conditions were that enabled every hour we spent to actually deliver for the company. That was the big unlock—every one hour has to be worth ten.

2. **Every person on the team could now make their own decisions every day.**

   Before that, they would always come to me, because "Marcella sees everything." It had gotten to a place where I made all the decisions. Democratizing the process took so much pressure off me. Any phone call to my team members got handled. They knew how to say, "You know, we have to prioritize the organizations that we handle personally. But there's a helpful video you can watch." We enabled others versus doing everything ourselves.

SIX TESTS TO BULLETPROOF YOUR OORM

Our friend and product leadership expert Aloka Penmetcha wrote a fantastic article titled "Do You Have a Good Outcome-Oriented Roadmap?" that helps people reverse engineer their OORM by putting it through a series of tests. Whatever form the roadmap may take, it is likely to enable success if it passes all six of her tests.

Test 1: Are the Outcomes Clearly Articulated? A well-articulated outcome describes the value a team intends to create, and for whom; it says more about the impact and less about the actions you may take.

- Clear outcome: In one year, our company will have created a self-driving unicycle.
- Unclear outcome: We will explore autonomous tech opportunities.

Test 2: How Good Are Your Metrics? In other words, do your chosen metric(s) actually measure whether or not the outcome has been achieved?

- Valuable metric: Positive user reviews and feedback
- Unhelpful metric: Uncontextualized sales

Test 3: Have You Articulated Risks and Mitigations? You can never predict everything that might go wrong, but you *can* understand the assumptions you're making and discuss how you might cope if those assumptions lead you astray.

- Assumption: There is significant market appetite for self-driving unicycles.
- Risk: Ours will be the first on the market, so we are not certain it will sell.
- Mitigation: We will perform consumer testing to determine if people are actually interested in this offering and do so before we invest significantly in production.

Test 4: Does Your Roadmap Represent an Aligned Viewpoint? Since an OORM is a way of capturing and communicating priorities that are shared by a range of stakeholders (team, leadership, family, etc.), they (or their representatives) should be involved in its creation.

Test 5: Is Your Roadmap Easy to Discover and Consume? This communication tool must be accessible to everyone who needs to use it and crystal clear in how it expresses outcomes and priorities. Don't bury it on a hidden drive somewhere; ensure all stakeholders have access to both the roadmap and any supporting documentation that might help them gain context.

Test 6: Do You Have a Systematic Approach for Reviewing and Iterating Your Roadmap? OORMs must be living documents! And those who use them must be willing to update, revise, and recalibrate them as more data comes to light. Create a regular cadence for checking in on your OORM and editing it as necessary. Every six months works for most workplace roadmaps.

If your OORM passes all of Aloka's tests, it will free up leaders to lead effectively, instead of micromanaging. It will create shared accountability among team members and increase individual autonomy. All while instilling everyone with a shared sense of purpose by keeping that all-important "why" front and center.

And, perhaps most importantly, it will help everyone avoid the tension that comes when something inevitably "goes wrong" (i.e., changes the plan) and you have to make adjustments.

NAVIGATING FROM POINT A TO POINT B

Let's go back to our navigation analogy from chapters two and four.

Let's say you're planning to drive from Denver (Point A) to Albuquerque (Point B). We've already walked through handling changes to A and B, but what if the *route between them* is what shifts? What if there's a jackknifed semi on I–25? Or what if you lock your keys in the car at a remote rest area and have to smash the window (true story, involving a caged rabbit and a long-haul trucker). When the path from A to B is forced to change, it can feel like a crisis, unless you're prepared to adapt your plans on the fly. OORMs offer us the flexibility to help us stay nimble as individuals, focused as leaders, and united as a team when circumstances force us to adapt the plan. Because outcomes aren't prescriptive about how we might get to Point B, we can stay cool and adapt when things don't go as planned.

So, if you're driving from Denver to Albuquerque and encounter that jackknifed truck, you won't just sit on I–25 until it's cleared off the road and be inexcusably late in arriving; your desired outcome is arrival in Albuquerque, so you can start investigating alternate routes that will lead you there. If your alternator gives up the ghost, you won't cancel your trip and let down your friends and family: your OORM allows you to consider alternatives like buses, trains, and rental cars. With a flexible roadmap, you know you have options even when the unexpected pops up.

In the homeschooling example from earlier in this chapter, your OORM states that the kids are mostly in charge of their classwork and homework planning, but what if they start shirking their duties? You can use one of your check-in meetings to discuss what's going wrong and make some changes. Maybe it would be easier for them to handle this responsibility if they had a chunk of time each week to plan for classwork and homework. Or created a rough schedule for classwork and homework each week, then reviewed it with a parent. Whatever the solution turns out to be, the family will discuss and settle on it together. No one will panic, progress won't grind to a halt. When an unexpected detour or roadblock arises, everyone will feel equipped to adjust the route as a team.

Where a traditional plan or map or route locks you in, an OORM lets you be nimble in the face of unexpected changes. And that's something that everyday leaders desperately need in this unpredictable, fast-moving, decidedly hyperdynamic world.

Workshop with Janice:
MAKE YOUR POINT B OUTCOME ORIENTED

Focusing on outcomes gives us the flexibility to change the things we're doing if those things aren't actually moving us forward in the ways we thought they would. For this workshop we're returning to our projects. In the chapter three workshop, we ended with clear statements for Point A and Point B, and we had the beginnings of how we might get from here to there. Today we're going to work on refining Point B to make sure it's an outcome, rather than an output or an activity. We said earlier:

> If you spend time doing it, it's an **activity**.
> The tangible result of that time spent is an **output**.
> The reason for doing those two things is the **outcome**.

In my example from the chapter three workshop, my Point B said I would have "a strategic set of core messages" by a certain date. That sounds like an output to me! It's time to look at how to transform it into an outcome.

Grab your Point B (and your team if you have one), and we'll check to make sure that it's not too confining.

1. Pull out your Point B and answer these questions:

    a. Is your Point B something that you would spend time doing? (Digging a hole.)
    b. Is it the tangible result of that time spent? (We have a hole!)
    c. Or is it the *reason* you did the others? (We can keep our bone safe from other dogs.)

2. If your Point B is an activity (1a) or an output (1b), describe why you will do that activity or create that output. What will be different once this is done?

3. Adjust your Point B to reflect this new understanding.

It's okay if you still believe that your previous Point B (the activity or output) is necessary to achieve your outcome, but in many cases, you'll find that being specific about *why* you wanted to do that activity in the first place allows you to open up to other possibilities for how to get there.

4. Check your new Point B. Does it feel really big? Try breaking it up into smaller component outcomes.

5. Try putting these smaller outcomes in order, with the bigger one at the end. This is the beginning of a simple Outcome-Oriented Roadmap.

6. Try to fill in with other small component outcomes that would be needed to achieve the bigger one. Add these to your OORM in the order that feels appropriate.

7. As you do this work, you may naturally find yourself circling back to previous steps and making changes. These refinements are "iterations," and that's great, as long as you don't get stuck iterating in a perfectionist loop. After a little refinement, set down your work and move on to the next chapter and workshop.

So here's my project. Take a look at the Point B that I had coming out of our last project workshop:

> By two months from now, I will have a strategic set of core messages that I can use consistently, so that all my stakeholders (including new ones) understand my business.

When I ask myself the question "Why do I want the core messages?" I can realize that stakeholder understanding isn't really the problem. I'm great at having one-on-one conversations with them and connecting their needs with my business. Underneath all of this marketing focus is a very real problem: I expect a busy season coming in a few months, and I need to be ready to get in front of people I don't know. (I know, all of you marketing people out there are slapping your heads, thinking, "Of course you need a messaging platform for your customer and marketing roadshow!" What's obvious to one person is a flash of insight to another. Don't judge—I'm good at other things.)

From this point of view, I think a refined Outcome-Oriented Point B might be:

By two months from now, I will be able to describe my current business priorities clearly and briefly, without the benefit of context, for instance during a podcast interview.

Of course, having stakeholders understand my business is important, but it's not the heart of the problem that I need to solve in my specific situation. The heart of the communications problem is that I'm great at knowing what to say when I'm with a person and a context I know. Where I need strategic preparation most is with new people in an unknown context, and that's why I have anchored it in a podcast interview. This would *never* have occurred to me if I hadn't been doing this workshop alongside you.

Now I have to figure out what to do to make my first outcome actionable. That will come in the next chapter.

Chapter 6

MAKING OUTCOMES
ACTIONABLE

O rganizations are basically throngs of people gathered together
for collective purpose. In the capitalist business world, we tend
to believe that the purpose of the organization is growth and
profit, colloquially known as "shareholder value." That pervasive belief started
with Milton Friedman in 1970 and is called the Friedman Doctrine. This fla-
vor of economic and moral philosophy is controversial to say the least, and if
you've made it here, you probably find this kind of thinking cringey at best.
For the most part, individual humans don't live for wealth accumulation and
power accumulation alone; people crave higher purpose and belonging. The
best leaders, therefore, authentically and truthfully connect the day-to-day
activities of work to larger, more meaningful purpose.

**"People who live their purpose at work are more productive than peo-
ple who don't. They are also healthier, more resilient, and more likely to
stay at the company."**[1]

"LIVES THEIR PURPOSE," NOT "MEETS MY EXPECTATIONS"

In this chapter, we're going to introduce a handful of goaling mechanisms that are used in work environments to ensure that everyone across an organization is aligned to accomplish a collective outcome. One way to ensure that those goals get adopted is to relate them to purpose and passion. A study published by *Harvard Business Review* found that companies with a clearly articulated purpose that was widely understood experienced more growth than companies without one. Specifically, 52 percent of purpose-driven companies saw high growth (10 percent or more) compared with 42 percent of *non*-purpose-driven companies.[2] Deloitte links workplace purpose as a solution to the problems brought on by hyperdynamism, pointing out, "Smart machines and cognitive technology may boost efficiency, but humans who work with them say they feel more isolated, anxious, and burned out than ever. It's critical now to focus on strengthening your employees' sense of belonging and on the satisfaction, purpose, and pride they feel in doing good work that supports your organization."[3]

People may mistakenly believe goal-setting tools exist to help them create accountability to set and meet expectations, but most people don't just want to check boxes. They want the things they do to be important and meaningful. They want to feel like they're contributing to something worth doing that is larger than themselves. When used mindfully, goaling mechanisms will tie work to an individual's internal purpose that connects them to the organization as a whole. This can ignite the natural human passion for the work they're contributing. They make small tasks feel more meaningful because they feed upward toward an outcome that everyone believes to be valuable.

You get the picture: purpose is the new black. If you're a leader, you've got your work cut out for you because Valuing Outcomes is harder than focusing on activities and deliverables. It's challenging to rise above the urgency of daily to-do lists, and even more challenging to convince people to exchange old mindsets for new ones. The top-down and bottom-up frameworks and goaling mechanisms that we share here can guide behaviors and choices toward a bolder outcome. They offer operating models that allow leaders like you to present a higher order objective in a way that people at all levels can understand, embrace, and enact. And if you can gently but insistently remind your people to relate their own passion and purpose to the objective, you will motivate them in an effective and organic way.

This flow of "purpose" up and down and across an organization is closely related to the concept of cascading intent.* Cascading intent describes how every person can act, independently or together, in alignment with an outcome that has been identified. It helps leaders transform agreed-upon outcomes into intent and action, which is helpful since a whole lot of things have to happen to bring those outcomes to fruition. Cascading intent enables people at various layers in your family, organization, or group to use their own locally informed judgment to choose which activities they'll do to deliver on those outcomes.

And it has its roots in the most hyperdynamic circumstance that humans can experience: war.

HANNAH JONES: LEADERSHIP THAT MOVES MOUNTAINS

For most of her career, Hannah Jones was one of the leading Chief Sustainability Officers in the world. For sixteen years as Nike's first Chief Sustainability Officer, Hannah took a leading role in stewarding the transformation of its supply chains, turning them into models of innovation and industry change. Today, Hannah is the CEO of the Earthshot Prize, an environmental prize founded by Prince William and dedicated to spotlighting and supporting the scaling of solutions that could repair and regenerate the planet in this decade. Throughout her career, Hannah has always been drawn to epic challenges—distributing millions of condoms across Europe in the early days of the HIV/AIDS crisis, founding Nike's first digital new business incubator, cofounding a coalition of businesses

---

* We'd like to disambiguate our use of the word *cascade*. In modern business usage, the term *cascading* has frequently been applied to a rigid, top-down approach to business metrics. In this and following chapters, our use of the term *cascading intent* derives from other sources and encompasses a wider variety of activities and mindsets.

supporting a strong Paris Agreement, and sitting on the boards of Method soap and Oatly to help these sustainable-first businesses scale. And she did all of this as a single mom of two kids, one of whom lives with type 1 diabetes. If anyone can teach us something about connecting work with purpose, both personal and industrial, it's Hannah.

Purpose moves me. I have a deep existential sense of impermanence, about having one life and living it richly and fully and being unafraid of making it a story that is uniquely mine (which is probably a privilege in itself). So there's a kind of fearlessness that comes from that. Certainly for me, change is not frightening—it's almost a little bit thrilling and exciting. (I'm probably in the 1 percent of people that feel that way.) I have felt terror at times from what I've had to do, and that's when purpose has really given me the fortitude to do those things. But if you combine fearlessness with purpose, then the need to be in the "transformational change agency" business, well, it's just clear, isn't it? "This is what you have to do."

I've never been motivated by a title or by power in itself or by money and things like that (going back to that old patriarchal model). I've always been motivated by change for good. As Spider-Man's uncle would say, with great power comes great responsibility, but also a greater ability to effect change. And if you can be an agent of change for good, whether that's in people's lives at a micro level or at a macro level, then isn't that a life worth living?

I have done things that didn't fit in with a steady progressive career, and I think that may come from my mom who, after having been a stay-at-home wife, then went on to wear multiple hats—from an artist, to a writer, to a corporate lobbyist. Watching that made me believe, "Well, even if it all goes wrong, I know I'm a really good barmaid, so I can always pull a good pint and earn enough money." I now have the privilege of wealth and stability, but I also know that I can live and be happy on quite a small amount, too. That's part of where the fearlessness comes from.

Having studied a lot of systems' changes, I see things in systems' maps. So going from Point A to Point B doesn't really feel like white space because I visualize the map. It doesn't feel like I'm going off into the unknown. It feels more like, "Oh, if we pull this lever here and then we pull that lever and if we move to this place, and then we pull that lever, this could probably happen."

The advice I would give people undertaking to change an organization is to understand motivation. Understand what motivates people to keep things as they are, and what might motivate them to change things toward the future you want to help craft. Motivation is at the root of most human behavior—and most people are pretty entrenched in what their motivations are and pretty easy to read. If you truly embrace these motivations, and you're not critical or judgmental of them, then you can start to meet people where they are and bring them with you as allies, as opposed to combatants.

So, for example, in the early days, sustainability was very much couched as a kind of female, hippy dippy, angry activist movement with no rationality on the economy or numbers. You know, "hug a tree," "save the polar bear" (with respect to trees and polar bears). I spent years turning sustainability into a question of math, a question of logic, and a question of business rationale. And then I spent another number of years framing it as a growth and innovation opportunity. And in doing that, I met the CFO where he was, and I met the head of innovation where he was, and I met the CEO where they were and the board where they were.

So sustainability as "hug a tree" wasn't getting us anywhere. But once we framed it as a risk mitigation effort for the board, a financial benefit to the CFO, and a growth opportunity to the innovator and the CEO, we could start to pull levers with far greater power than when I had remained entrenched in my own language or the language that I was expected to use.

So my advice to changemakers is, know your place in the system, but know other people's places and benefits and why they are in the system, doing what they do. Then figure out how to make their worlds feel better to them. "Make everybody else the hero in the story" was one of my mantras.

I'll give you an example. Working on labor rights, it was very easy to demonize people in the supply chain operation or indeed factory owners with comments like, "They don't care," and "They're not doing what they should be doing." And also "I'm on the side of the justice for the young woman worker in Vietnam," or wherever. That could become extremely divisive and confrontational. Many times, across the world, that has happened. And it became clear—to me at least—that as long as the team I was responsible for was acting as the police, then change was not going to happen very easily.

How could we make this something that the actual factories and the supply chains and teams could own, and feel pride and accountability around? And with that mindset change in ourselves, we went from a place where it was pretty combative between the head of the supply chain and myself to a place of real partnership, where people called us "brother and sister." We presented Harvard case studies together. He owned the accountability for the performance in the factories, and the factories were incentivized; the better the performance, the bigger the orders and the longer term the orders would be. I became his thought partner and occasionally could say, "Come on, let's try doing something even bigger and better."

I go back to the idea that "there is good in everybody." Even the people you're backed against the wall with. How do you find that good in them? It comes back to, "Can you bring compassion into this? Can you bring compassion into how you understand other people's motivations?" I'm not motivated by status and money, but many people are. I can be derisive of that or I can recognize it for what it is. I'm not motivated by stability, but many people are. How do you meet them where they are, and allow them to bring out their best? Because they bring something really important to the world—the world does need stability.

As a change agent, an innovator, or an entrepreneur, you're not always going to be in sync with where the world is, and if you're okay with that, there's a moment where it can flip and people can say, "Hang on, that idea I thought was ridiculous and insane or irritating has suddenly become valuable and helpful and important!"

Know what you believe in, know what your purpose is, and stay the course. It's the journey of any entrepreneur. It's the journey of anyone doing something that feels out of kilter with what the world thinks is normal and normalized. You're always going to have that idea, and it's always going to be too early, and most people will ignore you until they decide to invest in you. And they'll wish they'd invested earlier.

PROVIDE JUST ENOUGH DIRECTION

In 1982, the U.S. Army officially codified the concept of "Commander's Intent" in a pamphlet titled *US Army Field Manual (FM) 100-5, Operations*,[4] but the principle had been leveraged by both American military forces and other nations for hundreds of years before that. Our modern understanding of commander's intent originated with Prussian field marshal Helmuth Karl Bernhard Graf von Moltke. He championed *Auftragstaktik,* a military philosophy that empowered individuals to take initiative and make autonomous decisions in complex and shifting situations. *Auftragstaktik* stemmed from von Moltke's experience on the battlefield. He knew that detailed and meticulously planned orders fell apart once fighting commenced. In his words (with our added emphasis):

In general, **one does well to order no more than is absolutely necessary and to avoid planning beyond the situation one can foresee**. These change very rapidly in war. Seldom will orders that anticipate far in advance and in detail succeed completely to execution.

The higher the authority, the shorter and more general will the orders be. The next lower command adds what further precision appears necessary.

The detail of execution is left to the verbal order, to the command. Each thereby retains freedom of action and decision within his authority.[5]

Expecting people to follow a prescribed series of steps in the chaos of battle is unrealistic and dangerous. Leaders are better off training and trusting their team, so they can make informed choices as conditions change, while staying aligned with overall goals of the mission. This is what we mean when we use the phrase *cascading intent.*

Unlike top-down, Capital-L Leadership, **cascading intent assumes all participants can be trusted to make the best use of their time and resources** to achieve an outcome. This means telling the people under your command the result you want them to focus on; in the military, that might be capturing an opponent, or cutting off an escape route. The outcome is clear, but the means are intentionally vague, in order to give the people pursuing it the flexibility they need to make real-time decisions in the face of unpredictable circumstances.

An example of commander's intent unfolded during D-Day in World War II. The naval and airborne invasion of France on June 6, 1944, had been planned for years and rehearsed for months in advance of the actual military action. The world's most accomplished generals had formulated a precise series of glider plane and parachute landings to secure bridges, crucial road intersections, and other strategic points. This would pave the way for a successful ground invasion. When the day arrived, virtually everything went wrong: parachuters and gliders landed in the wrong spots, and thousands of soldiers connected with the wrong units. And yet, individual leaders and soldiers kept the outcome in mind: "Above all, seize the bridges." They understood that no matter where they landed, they needed to work together to seize the bridges and key terrain. The years-in-the-making plan—with its meticulously choreographed actions—went right out the window, but commander's intent allowed the mission to proceed, and ultimately be successful.[6]

Let's explore how cascading intent can be used in workplaces and homes.

CASCADING INTENT CONNECTS ACTIONS TO OUTCOMES

Let's say you're working in a large corporation and have been tasked with starting a new team that will take on a new project. You won't have a chance to meet anybody on the team before the work begins, so how will you decide the best way to divide the work?

Traditional leadership advice might recommend that you learn about the strengths and weaknesses of the individuals, research the problem space, and create a six-month roadmap with deliverables and tasks for each team member. You solicit feedback from your leadership and your new team. Your plan assigns tasks to the employees who seem best suited for them, and everyone gets started knowing what their job is.

No matter how good you are, how thoroughly you prepare, your assignments will probably be flawed, because your insight into the team will be incomplete. The people on your team certainly will have more current knowledge than you do. When everything goes sideways—as it always does—you'll only have yourself to blame. This traditional leadership approach might allow you to focus the group's efforts on outcomes, but it certainly doesn't utilize your most valuable resource—the insights, thoughts, and mental horsepower of your team. Cascading intent is a way to Leverage the Brains of your team. You may have asked for their input once you had a fully formulated plan to present, but you've done all the thinking and planning, in advance and all alone! You've deprived them and yourself of the collective mental power inherent in any team.

If, instead, you approach the project with cascading intent, the team can develop an outcome-based roadmap and let the detailed planning fall to the appropriate level, as von Moltke described. Cascading intent promotes trust and efficiency, and it unites people in their efforts. It creates alignment across a team and offers a reminder to individuals that they're participating in something bigger than themselves. Your group feels valued and seen because you are actually seeing and valuing them. And, as a bonus, if you're wrong, you're all wrong together and you'll figure it out together.

Cascading intent allows leaders to nudge people toward creativity, problem-solving, and surfacing solutions independently. A fantastic example

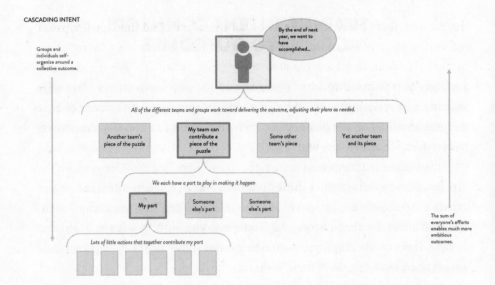

CASCADING INTENT

comes from the most unlikely corner of leadership—rock stars. It won't surprise you that we've had to anonymize the story. But apart from the names of places and people, it's all true. And no, it's not Kurt Cobain.

SMELLS LIKE TEEN SPIRIT

Monika moved from her native Kansas City to Seattle in 1993 to work with a legendary recording artist. She started out doing marketing but moved up quickly and was consulting with the artist himself in a matter of months. It was a tumultuous time, with the artist embroiled in multiple lawsuits, and cash flow was drying up.

"To be clear, this was a cash crunch for the business, not for the artist himself," Monika explains. "He kept his personal fortune separate from the company. So when we needed extra cash from that separate pool of money, the leadership took turns going in to tell him."

This time, she drew the short straw: she had to break the news to him that the company needed about $500,000 to make payroll and cover costs. Monika was not looking forward to the conversation.

"The artist was a man of very few words," she says. "So when I went and I told him, he looked at me and he said, 'I play the guitar,' in that raspy voice that he had. Just, 'I play the guitar.' So that threw me. And then he dismissed me with a wave of his hand, like 'we're done here.' I went back to my office to mull this over, and a couple of hours later he called and asked me, 'Have you figured it out yet?' I hadn't." Monika had to figure out a strategy from his somewhat cryptic statement of intent: 'My contribution to revenue is to play the guitar.' Which meant she needed to turn that into money. So she started to consider what else was brewing in the company that might be harnessed to generate immediate profit.

In addition to her other duties, Monika was overseeing the build of the artist's official website. The mid-'90s was a time when most musicians were just starting to use the internet. "We were building out this website so that he could sell his music directly. I started to ask questions about how many email addresses we had in the database. It turned out we had a couple hundred thousand; he was way ahead of the curve. We also had hundreds of songs in the vault that had been recorded but never released, so I started thinking we could take some unreleased music, package it up, and sell it to his email list."

A brilliant idea that cascaded from the intent of, "I play the guitar."

"A couple of days later, I went to his office and asked him for two original songs that no one had ever heard," she says. "Then I asked if he would be willing to do a chat with fans on AOL to see if we could sell the tracks over the internet. He asked, 'Well, what kind of songs would you like?' And I said, 'Anything that no one has ever, ever, ever, ever heard.' I explained that this could be both a revenue-generator and a way to road test new music with the fans. He said, 'Let's do it. When do you need the records?'"

She gave him a tight deadline knowing that the company needed that money. The fans were thrilled, and Monika's idea generated enough revenue for them to get through another full month.

The lesson in cascading intent went beyond just creative revenue ideas. He wanted Monika and his whole team to make sure a budget crisis like this didn't happen again. "He said to me, 'We need to understand how we eat. And as long as I can play the guitar, we will never be broke.' He wanted me to understand the value of talent and creativity and also find ways to be productive without overburdening that talent with extra information."

Even the best leaders tend to cling too tightly to control when they're conveying their vision for eventual outcomes. It's awfully tempting to tell people what you want them to achieve and then give some (hard-to-ignore) recommendations on how they might achieve it. But cascading intent means managing that instinct. It urges everyday leaders to express their intent in terms of what they want to achieve and why, then offer genuine autonomy (with guardrails) around what to do and support when it gets difficult.

THE CASCADE: BREAKING A LARGER OUTCOME INTO SMALLER BITS

Even when a group is aligned around outcomes, in most circumstances it's hard to take action until that outcome is broken into smaller tasks. Individuals need to have enough autonomy to execute in the face of hyperdynamism, but they also need some actionable, day-to-day guidance within the larger outcome. To create that specificity, we can divide broad goals into narrower component goals, and divide big leap-forward goals into incremental-step goals.

Researchers have found that large decisions can be made easier by breaking them down into smaller increments,[7] and the same is true for goals: large goals are more manageable when broken down into smaller component goals. A shared outcome statement like, "As a family, we will collaborate to make our home life less dramatic and more peaceful in the next six months," is wonderful, but it may be too vague for individuals to act upon. Dividing it into goals that each person can address on their own reduces that overwhelmed feeling we've all had enough of.

In the workplace, we[†] have had plenty of experience helping clients formulate meaningful outcomes and find ways to define smaller goals that bring those outcomes to fruition. We recently had a client whose initial outcome statement was, "Our customer has a simpler, more efficient supply chain because of our software." The team itself had seven people, and although they all contributed to visioning the higher-order outcome, they struggled to map their individual work back toward it. So we led them through the following

---

† To maintain confidentiality, multiple stories were combined to create this example.

exercise, which you can also use to break up your desired high-level outcome into smaller outcomes or goals.

Step 0: "Groom" the Original Outcome. We call this step zero because we want you to consider attaching it to the front of any process you do with your Outcome Roadmap. Grooming in this context means refining. Think of it like this: you're not completely reshaping your eyebrows (or beard), you're just making them a little less pointy. Grooming means making small adjustments to match the current, more advanced understanding of what "good" looks like. You should groom the outcome routinely. In our example: "Our customer has a ~~simpler,~~ more efficient supply chain because of our software."

In this case, we decided to remove the word *simpler* because they cared most about efficiency, which for them meant faster, less error-prone, and fewer delays. With this understanding, we realized that adding steps might be fine, as long as it represents better throughput and less effort. This was a small change, made in a conversation that lasted about ten minutes, and it avoided the inevitable debates about "steps" vs. "efficiency." By taking out one word, the team avoided the bickering that can squander people's time, patience, and goodwill.

Step 1: Ideate Component Outcomes. Ask everyone on the team, "What are ten outcomes that, if put together, will accomplish the higher-order outcome?" Ten is an arbitrary number that we like to use for ideating. Since this is an ideation step, don't worry about whether they're "right" or "good." If this is group work, we would get three to four people together and have them write down all the ideas (of course on sticky notes with a Sharpie, because that's how we roll), ten per person. Then cluster them thematically. It doesn't matter how many clusters you end up with. Based on the contents of the cluster, write your component outcomes.

If the discussion ends up producing outputs instead of outcomes, that's fine. An output might be "finish building the new search results page." You can reframe output statements by asking the question "If you had that deliverable, what would be true and different that *isn't* true today?" or "How would things have changed if you had that deliverable?"

Step 2: Check the Whole Picture. Are the Components All Necessary and Sufficient? "Necessary and sufficient" is a concept in formal logic. First, check to make sure each thing is needed in order to create the outcome. If not, take it out of the picture. When that refinement is done, ask, "If we do all the things we've identified, are we likely to have accomplished the larger outcome?"

Step 3: Divide the Work Roughly. Look at each of the ten component outcomes and ask, "How might these things map to the people available to do the work?" The act of trying to connect actions to people will likely inspire you to break your outcomes into even smaller components. This is good! It allows you to begin understanding what's really needed to do the job. I want to make a special note about division of labor, especially in the home. This is a case where social factors like biases, gender norms, and past experiences can skew how work is divided, so we try to be mindful of equitable divisions and appropriate allocation of labor.

Step 4: Confirm Alignment. Before execution begins, however, the team formulating those mid-level outcomes should do a quick check on their work. A simple and effective way to do this is to ask, "If we did all of the things we've identified, would we have arrived at a good place?"

These four steps are just one way to create micro-goals within the larger, shared outcome. Depending on your context, you may want to try a variation on this process, or something entirely different. But do try something, because defining sub-outcomes helps individuals see their connection to a larger whole. Instead of focusing solely on their narrow, siloed work tasks and churning out outputs, they see their contributions in context. Their accomplishments thread up toward a result that matters.

All of our work with founders, CEOs, commanders, and presidents has shown us that leadership in general—just like the Four Leadership Motions—is fractal in nature: each subunit has the same shape as the larger whole. As leaders, what we do one-on-one impacts what we do in meetings and groups. How we think and behave on a micro level is reflected at the macro level. If we are intentional and mindful as individual leaders, that intentionality and mindfulness will reverberate throughout our companies, families, and entire lives. We can be more effective and more deliberate across situations and relationships.

GOALING MECHANISMS BRING ACTION TO INTENT

Last night we were visiting with our good friend Huiqing. She's a group product manager at a software company. As GPM, her job is explicitly to align the projects undertaken by the software teams to the strategy of the company, and in turn to the company's purpose. The company is experiencing massive growth, which means she must take into consideration conflicting priorities and a constant stream of dynamic challenges. We asked her about which goaling tool she prefers, and her answer was beautiful. She said, "It doesn't really matter to me. Whatever works for the teams in their specific context." As long as the teams are able to connect their day-to-day activities with the outcomes on the roadmap and purpose of the company, then things will move forward. For her, letting go of control and perfection enables more of the right thing to happen.

There are a host of business frameworks for defining actionable goals that are compatible with outcome-based planning and cascading intent. It's a confusing coincidence that so many of them begin with the letter *O* (outcome, objective, output, oh boy!); we will try to keep them straight for you (see "So Many Acronyms Start with 'O'" sidebar, 82). Adopting a well-documented framework helps organizations coordinate outcomes across teams, levels, and departments. If you work at a larger company, there's a good chance you already use one of these frameworks. For you, the descriptions below can help you connect those practices to what we've described in this chapter. Or, if you're looking for a goaling process to adopt, any one of these can be used to implement the things we've talked about. There are excellent books and online resources for each, so this is presented as an overview to help you find one you like. You're welcome to skip to the next chapter if this isn't a match for your needs right now. It's here for you when you need it.

OGSM (Objective, Goals, Strategies, and Measures)

This framework is the one you're most likely to know about before cracking open this chapter. It is believed to have originated in Japan's car factories during the 1950s,[8] and is designed to help teams translate statements of vision and strategy downward into day-to-day work. Generally speaking,

OGSM tends to be used in a longer-term, strategic context. Therefore, it can tend toward a top-down approach and can fall short when it comes to individual goal-setting.[9]

First, the acronym describes a series of steps to be taken that cascade downward from high-level ideas to daily activities. Objectives are defined first, then goals are described and nested beneath them, then strategies are formulated to make the goals possible, and measures are chosen to track the progress of the goals.

Once top leadership has formulated their higher-order objective and their goals to support it, those goals become the "objectives" for the next level down. Once that level has generated their own goals based on their narrowed objective, *their* goals become the objectives for the next level down, and so on. In this way, everyone's day-to-day tasks connect to each other and help move the organization toward the high-order objective defined by top leadership.

Soren Kaplan, an affiliate professor at USC's Center for Effective Organizations, created this template to help teams of any size build out their own OGSM approach:

Objectives
Clearly define the team's overall objective, which should be linked to the team's ultimate purpose. For example: Create an engaging customer experience that drives repeat sales.

Goals
Break down the objective into smaller, more attainable goals. Each goal should be defined in a way that it can be clearly tracked and recorded. For example: Update website to include useful content that enhances the customer experience.

Strategies
Create strategies to accomplish each goal by considering what it will take to achieve the goal, your available resources, and your timeline. For example: Use articles to engage customers in learning about new technologies, including our products.

Measures

Define specific, quantifiable metrics that allow you to compare where you are today with what you will achieve in your defined time frame. For example: Write six new articles this quarter to publish on our website and promote through social media.[10]

The challenge with OGSM is that the *G* and the *S* are often guesses, and the *M* is usually an activity metric. So your GSM may or may not actually deliver the *O* you're looking for. With OGSM, you're being asked to think through how you "would" approach something, but there is no circular mechanism for learning whether it's having the correct effect, and no way to adjust course as new information or context comes to light. So, if you use OGSM as your goaling framework, put into place sensing mechanisms to help you see, as you move forward, whether your *G* and *S* are having the desired *O*. Think of it as an OODA Loop.

OKR (Objectives and Key Results)

Created by Intel founder Andy Grove and codified in Christina Wodtke's book *Radical Focus*, this framework ties the objectives you want to achieve to the key results you'll use to chart your progress. Generally speaking, an OKR framework is used as a quarterly planning tool, building a picture from the bottom up and emphasizing rapid revisions and flexibility. This has made OKRs beloved in Silicon Valley startup circles, where flexibility is essential and organizations are smaller. On the downside, OKR can sometimes fall short on strategy and long-term vision.

To implement OKRs, most companies start by identifying an objective at the top, then mapping out three to five supporting key results below it. Defining objectives means putting simple and descriptive language around what is to be achieved. These objectives shouldn't be vague in any way, but instead should be significant to the organization, factual, and tied to action. If formulated as outcomes, they'll help you stay on target and avoid spinning your wheels.

The key results you select should reveal your progress toward the objective. Helpful KRs are both specific and time-sensitive, leaving no room for doubt as to whether or not they've been met. And, of course, they must be measurable and verifiable.

All of this information can be captured by writing a version of the statement:

I will (Objective) as measured by (Key Results).

For example, "I will grow my landscaping/snowplowing business as measured by a 10 percent increase in gross revenue in the coming year."

V2MOM (Vision, Values, Methods, Obstacles, and Measures)

Of all the frameworks out there, the one you can pick up today and use yourself and on your team is V2MOM. We like it because it scales well, with relevance for a whole organization, a team, or an individual. And, like the best facilitative frameworks, it guides you through a thought process that connects the big-picture strategy to the small actions. Salesforce chairman and CEO Marc Benioff created this planning framework to maintain alignment across his growing company. V2MOM has cascading elements since it communicates the company's overarching goals first, then ensures they're aligned with managers' and employees' goals and expectations. As you can see, one way this framework differs from the others is by incorporating "values," an addition that some leaders feel helps them to influence behavioral norms within their organizations. Benioff outlines the five-step framework as follows:

1. **Vision:** What do you want to achieve? (*This is where you put the high-level outcome.*)
2. **Values:** What's important to you?
3. **Methods:** How do you get it? (*This is where you put the component outcomes.*)
4. **Obstacles:** What is preventing you from being successful?
5. **Measures:** How do you know you have it?[11]

To the "values" portion, we'd add a bit more detail, like, "What ideals and beliefs can help your company fulfill the vision?" The values shouldn't just sit there in the queue apart from everything else; they need to link back to the vision to make themselves useful.

DIY Cascading Goaling

There's a lot of overlap among these frameworks, so any of them can help you put structure to OORM and cascading intent. Depending on your desired outcome and team makeup, it may make more sense to create your own goaling mechanism instead of borrowing someone else's. Feel free to mix and match.

If you're shopping for a goaling framework, know that it doesn't really matter which one you choose, as long as you embed it into your daily operation. The goals have to guide the team's daily work and priorities if they're going to contribute to a meaningful outcome. When they're used as directed, they connect actual work to important outcomes, and provide mechanisms to check that the work is having the effect that you want it to. These are elegant systems that help people organize and communicate through the disparate layers of an organization. And perhaps most importantly, they create alignment, which is priceless in a group of people working toward a shared outcome. It doesn't matter how big or small the team or company may be, it's consistent alignment that has the most impact. A team of three may argue endlessly if they lack alignment, and a global enterprise with one hundred thousand employees may function seamlessly if it promotes alignment. Leaders who recognize and leverage this truth can accomplish the impossible.

Successful companies, healthy families, and vibrant communities can all operate that way. All they need is a compassionate leader who understands the value of genuine alignment, and a goaling mechanism to build a flexible work plan around. And it truly doesn't matter which mechanism you use. It only matters that you find a mechanism to align your team for collective impact.

Workshop with Janice:
FROM OUTCOMES TO ACTIONS

We left off last time with a Point A and a Point B, and we had refined both, so that we got to the heart of the problem and the soul of what a resolution looks like. For me, it's:

- **POINT A:** I have a big communications period coming up with two very different kinds of needs and the way I've handled it in the past isn't going to cut it.
- **POINT B:** By two months from now, I will be able to outline my current business priorities clearly and succinctly, without the benefit of context, for instance during a podcast interview.

This is a good time to try an OGSM.

You may remember back in chapter five we showed this example of an Outcome-Oriented Roadmap (see opposite page). This is very similar to the OGSM format, and you can look at each column here, each outcome, as a nearly complete OGSM. So if my first outcome is "We can cook dinner for the first few nights," we can call that an objective. Having a few pots and pans, etc., that's my goal. Going to Target and shopping for those things is my strategy—it's what I'll do to achieve the goal. And in this case, measurement is easy: I can check off each item on the shopping list as I acquire them (hopefully by the date I need them).

This might be a good time to start involving one or two other people from your team. Choose someone who has insight into the problem and pull out your work from where you left off last time. Here's how you're going to make it actionable.

1. On a big surface that your whole team can see, write the first outcome from your OORM that you did in the last section. You can make a grid like in the OORM example on the opposite page if that helps (it probably will).

2. Under that, make a list of things you need to get done, at least to a certain degree, in order to achieve that outcome. These are your goals. It's

OUTCOME (Objective)	We can cook dinner the first few nights.	We are ready for most of our usual cooking and eating.	Our kitchen is fully stocked and ready.	Our kitchen is awesome to cook in!
OUTPUT (Goals)	A few pots and pans, paper plates and compostable utensils, sponge and dish soap, napkins	Pots and pans, dinnerware, utensils, knives, towels, etc.	Everyday glassware, linens, serving bowls, platters, small appliances, etc.	All of the special things, art for the walls, wallpaper, stools for the counter
ACTIVITIES (Strategies)	Go to Target	Look at table settings. Find local cookware stores. Shop around.	Shop at secondhand stores for unique serving pieces and used small appliances.	Make appointment to look at wallpaper, choose art pieces at Open Studios in June.
WISH FOR DATE (Measures)	September 30	October 31	January 31	August 31

worth taking a few minutes to look at these and see which ones you might be able to cross off, but still achieve your objective.

3. Under your goals, write the activities you'll need to do to get them done. If you can't think of any activity you could do that would achieve the goal, you probably need to rethink your goals. These activities are the strategies you'll use to achieve the goals.

4. Finally, under that, how will you know that you're achieving your objective? What things can you measure? In the case of being ready to cook in our new house, it's easy: we can check off the goodies on our shopping list. Some things are more nuanced, though, and are measured as a percentage rather than a binary (done vs. not done). Think about what kind of measurement you need and how you'll get it. A metric that you

don't have the tools to measure is not going to help you, so make sure it's something you can get at.

Now you have an OGSM to work with. You might be tempted to go through the other outcomes on your OORM and do the same with them, but I'd advise you to wait for now. Do this one first. See where it's easy and where it's hard. Learn from the process. You can go back and work on the others once you're comfortable that you know what you're doing.

Finally, don't put too much pressure on yourself to "get it right." This is not easy, and it takes practice to get it all just right. What's important is that it's "right enough," so that it informs what you're doing and helps you move forward.

So, now I need to take "*I will be able to describe my current business priorities clearly and succinctly, without the benefit of context, for instance during a podcast interview*" and turn it into this format. Here's what I did:

First, immediately when I started writing down things to be done, I went off-script and they ended up in a big jumble. I immediately wished I'd done it on sticky notes on a wall. I found that I really needed the grid with headings (see below), which helped me know how to organize the items from the jumble.

I found huge relief just getting this out of my head, especially once I had my objectives clarified. Everything else slots in underneath one of them, which brings a sense of calm, and I can imagine moving through this project without freaking out. Even though it's a tight time frame and a complex piece of work that I'm not expert in, I can hold it all in my head now. And, even better, I can see how involving a team would help me to build out the plan and execute on it.

It can be a bit fuzzy sometimes when you're looking at goals versus strategies versus metrics. Don't worry about this too much for now. You'll learn how to refine it as you do it. The most important thing is that you measure each week and you actually *do* the activities in your strategies. Keep a log of your measurements and hold yourself accountable for executing on the strategies.

OBJECTIVES (Outcomes)	I feel confident explaining my business to strangers (e.g., on a podcast).	Current stakeholders understand the changes to my business.	I can respond quickly to inquiries and questions during the roadshow.
GOALS (Big activities)	Make a messaging platform.	Identify what's confusing stakeholders currently.	Have assets readily at hand.
STRATEGIES (Smaller activities)	Gather outside resources: Find the messaging guides from marketing projects. Reach out to consultants from last year. Build a one-page messaging hierarchy: Define key audiences and messages. Revise products and services for next year. Practice with friendly podcasters and journalists.	Prioritize existing stakeholders. Define points of confusion. Create custom messages where needed.	Create or update assets: Websites Email sign-up Messaging cheat sheet Social calendar Rate card
MEASURES	By September 30, have done ten practice interviews.		

Part 3

LEVERAGE
THE BRAINS

Chapter 7

TINA FEY VS. ELON MUSK

As head writer for *Saturday Night Live*, Tina Fey had to lead (and leverage) some of the sharpest brains in comedy. The *SNL* writers team is notoriously competitive, with meticulously workshopped sketches often being cut at the eleventh hour, wounding egos in the process. As head writer, Fey urged her team to collaborate with and support each other. In an interview with *Variety*, she said, "You're taking other people's sketches, and you don't take them away and manhandle them. You try to sit there with them to figure out, 'How can we help you make the best version of what you were hoping to do?'"[1]

But if you ask a group of people "who's the greatest leader of the past thirty years," they will instead often point to business leaders like Steve Jobs and Elon Musk: lone geniuses who built massive empires. Even those who admit that these founders had help often go on to imply that the primary drivers of their success were their unique perspectives, ideas, and abilities. It's a myth. Truly. The idea that a single person can do it all, have all the right answers, and make all the right decisions is fiction. Jobs did tons of user research and the company threw away the majority of its prototypes before he made his (in)famous proclamations. Musk cofounded PayPal with a host of other people by merging his year-old banking startup with its largest rival, a move that involved at least eight "cofounders," two of whom led attempts to unseat Musk as CEO within the first year. The second coup succeeded.

So even these famously individualistic founders all Leveraged the Brains (whether they wanted to or not). It's just that we love a good hero story, so let's call that "The Myth of the Infallible Leader." The Myth of the Infallible Leader is toxic. Like, "actually makes people ill with stress" kind of toxic. "Unrealistic and crazy-making" kind of toxic. After all, if skilled leaders are expected to have all the answers regardless of problem scope or complexity, how will they feel when they can't find solutions on their own? How can they ask for much-needed input and support if asking questions will make them look like failures?

Great leaders know that they are only capable of seeing the world from their own, limited perspective and that pulling in a range of people will make their original ideas better and more enduring. People who have had varied life experiences see situations from different angles and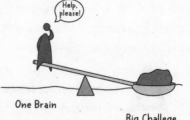

One Brain

Big Challege

are able to offer different solutions to the same problem. If you want to create or improve something, the best way to do it is to build a diverse team and explore the possibilities as a group. You get more and better understanding of the problem when you view it from multiple angles. You access more and better solution ideas. The team will be more invested in the solution idea you choose and be better equipped to execute because they were there when you examined the problem.

Regardless of the outcome you're aiming for, the best way to get there is together. Leadership is about bringing people together to share their insights and perspectives and doing great things in collaboration.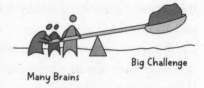

Many Brains

Big Challenge

HOW DO WE LEVERAGE THE BRAINS?

When there's a challenge, gather the right people around you and invite their ideas. We know this sounds reductive, but it truly is that simple. Just get yourself in the habit of reaching out whenever you've got a new idea or unexpected hiccup. Ask, "Have you ever had this problem? Know anyone who has? How did you solve it?" Or even, "Can I get your insight on this concept I've been kicking around?"

Here's why we want to make Leveraging the Brains easy to do and impossible to avoid: it's because we're continually indoctrinated to believe in the ego-driven Capital-L Leadership style. While writing this book, Jason took a Harvard executive education class. All the students were asked to take a survey about their leadership practices that included the question, "You've been given a challenge. What is the first thing you would do to begin addressing it?" The answer options were:

1. Come up with an answer and tell people to deliver on it.
2. Assemble a cross-functional team to look at the problem and create a solution together.
3. Escalate the issue that you're confronting to the senior leadership team and see what resources they can apply to it.

In a global class of 570 students with a decent spread of gender and racial diversity, most believed that answer two was correct. Jason nearly did a spit-take when the instructor later defined the leader's job as "getting people to deliver on tasks." Five hundred and seventy people were told that their natural instinct toward collaboration and Leveraging the Brains was misguided.

But, in today's world, **you can't possibly know everything**. New challenges, new vocabulary, new context pops up like pimples on a teenager. Devising the solution isn't your job. Your job is to gather, equip, align, and activate your team to deliver great solutions to bold and pressing problems. Leaders don't need to have the answers; they need to know how to frame problems in ways that inspire their people to be imaginative, innovative, and collaborative. A good leader formulates a clear and honest Point A and frames Point B as the desirable outcome, then brings it to colleagues to leverage their ideas and experiences.

This is what we mean by Leveraging the Brains: when you work with other people, you gain the ability to create exponential power, way beyond your own capability or insight.

DIVERSITY, EQUITY, AND INCLUSION (DEI) IN LEVERAGING THE BRAINS

When we talk about Leveraging the Brains, we're suggesting that carefully involving more people can drastically improve the speed and effectiveness with which you move forward toward your outcomes. In part it's the adage "many hands make light work." But beyond that, a diverse group will solve problems faster and will foster a more dynamic culture, marked by growth mindset and creative abrasion. Study after study has shown that diverse groups of people create genuine diversity of thought, which in turn fuels better business decisions.[2] A homogeneous group of young men or wealthy white people or folks who all share the same worldview will not get you the range of thought you should now be seeking as a leader. Hiring and empowering people of different backgrounds, orientations, and experiences quite literally makes it more likely that a team or a company will succeed.

It's worth noting, though, that the word *diversity* has become contentious in recent years. When it first became common language in workplaces, the idea of tokenism was still new and companies assumed that it was enough if

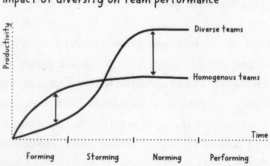

Impact of diversity on team performance[3]

Productivity

Diverse teams

Homogenous teams

Time

Forming   Storming   Norming   Performing

you included one woman or one person of color. More recently, companies have begun to hire and promote more people from historically marginalized groups, but far too many do so to create an appearance of action rather than from an understanding of its value.

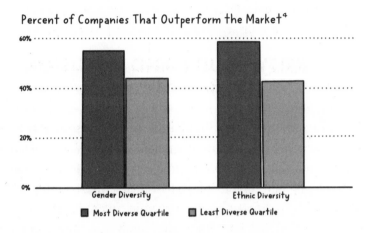

Percent of Companies That Outperform the Market[4]

This is borne out in the numbers. Six years after their first diversity reports, Alphabet, Apple, Facebook, Microsoft, and Twitter have seen low single-digit increases in their percentage of Black employees.[5] A recent global survey by McKinsey & Company revealed that more than a third of the companies in their data set still have no women at all on their executive teams.[6] And a large body of research has found that hiring managers continue to display bias against underrepresented minorities.[7] So while companies make stirring public statements about their commitment to hiring diverse workforces, they struggle to deliver on those promises, because it's not enough to bring together people who have varying life experiences and perspectives.

After hiring for diversity, companies must foster *inclusion*, which means making sure they are valued and their voices are heard. If you assemble cross-functional teams with diverse members but only a few of them feel comfortable making contributions, you've missed the point. Creating an equitable environment goes a long way toward helping people from underrepresented groups bring their voices and authentic selves fully to the table. The majority of tactics and tools we describe in this book are designed to foster equitable participation, right down to encouraging team members to write ideas on uniform sticky notes. Even minor considerations like ensuring everyone's brainstorming outputs are the same size and shape contribute to an overall sense of equity.

The concepts of diversity, equity, inclusion, belonging, and justice (sometimes abbreviated to DEIB or JEDI) are integral to the other ideas we share in this book. Please find one of the many excellent books and videos on the subject to increase your awareness and make it part of your leadership conversation.

Jason leads a team of about sixty people in a competitive field where recruiting new employees is known to be very difficult. His company had set a goal of employing 50 percent men and 50 percent women by the year 2030, with 14 percent underrepresented minorities by that same year. By partnering effectively with his HR, recruiting, and interviewing teams, Jason's group hit that goal by the end of 2021, nine years early (we think perhaps his company should be a bit more ambitious!). Here's what worked to hire and retain a diverse team:

1. Jason set a nonnegotiable expectation that the hiring pipeline include candidates from underrepresented groups and stood firm when recruiting partners had trouble finding enough qualified applicants with their existing sourcing strategies. (The hiring manager's commitment is critical here.)

2. Screening criteria for each position were set in advance and consistently applied. These needed to be adapted to allow a wider range of educational and professional backgrounds.

3. To ensure fairness, the process was run the same way for every candidate. Nobody could fast-track a preferred candidate or skip steps.

4. Recruiting materials and interview guides were checked for bias and edited for inclusion.

5. Interviewers were given clear assignments to evaluate for specific characteristics important to job success, using a standardized process.

6. Multiple interview types were used (behavioral, take-home, etc.) to get a broader picture of all candidates and avoid behavioral "gotchas" like Stereotype Threat.

7. Attrition continues to be tracked carefully to ensure that new employees feel welcome and valued, and don't jump ship.

The team maintains its inclusion goals by setting clear expectations and engaging each other in solving the problem. The company works closely with the U.S. Department of Defense, and its customers are largely enlisted personnel. Many of those are young, many come from families that aren't wealthy, and many are people of color. We believe that when you're making products, the only way to truly serve your customers' needs is to know their perspective. It also builds trust when the people you serve can see folks they recognize working behind the scenes.

This team now has a phenomenal group of viewpoints to include, ideas to incorporate, and brilliant brains to leverage, support, and promote. As leaders, we're enriched when we can collaborate with others. It helps us make good decisions and build better offerings.

That applies to your groups and teams, too, of course. The people on your team were hired *instead* of other people who applied for those jobs. They were hired because they are valued *over* others for the role they play. They were hired because somebody (or several somebodies) thought they were *smart*. You should use that. **It's literally your job to use that.** Make use of the other brains that are available to you. It's the absolute best way to get where you need to go.

LEVERAGING THE BRAINS IN THREE STEPS

This is a little bit more complex than just training yourself to ask for help and get input from others. Some leaders rely on their height and charisma (you know who you are), a few are bullies (albeit charming), but our kind of leader gains leverage using three techniques.

Step 1: Frame the Problem

Essentially, Frame the Problem means describing Point A and declaring an ambitious Point B. Orient Honestly around the current situation, describe both the situation and the complication, and be succinct. You may be tempted to tackle this step on your own, but run it by a few folks first. The people around you will observe and value different elements of the current situation, which means they can help you describe it more comprehensively and accurately.

For Point B, find a future state that's ambitious enough to inspire, but realistic enough to be achievable. Review chapter three if you're hazy on defining a solid Point A and Point B.

Step 2: Get the Right People in the Room

As we mentioned in chapter five, there are three types of people who should be involved whenever you're making an important decision: those with the power to say yes to whatever solution is proposed, those with subject matter expertise, and those who will be affected by the decision itself. This group isn't just great for decisions. This is your go-to invitation list. When you leverage those specific brains and capture their best thinking on the question at hand, you'll have the best shot at making progress.

Including the three types of people is just as important in personal and family situations as it is in work situations. If you're debating whether to host an exchange student for a year or add a garage to your property, you might think your seven-year-old doesn't need to give her input—but she probably does. Within a family, children have to live with the consequences of big changes or impactful decisions. They may also have subject matter expertise and firsthand data, depending on the situation. Your seven-year-old may not always get her way in these conversations, but seeking out her opinions and concerns will give you insight into what she's thinking and how to make even unpopular decisions work for her.

Step 3: Respect Your Collaborators

One of our all-time favorite management books is *Extreme Programming Explained, Second Edition* by Kent Beck and Cynthia Andres (but only chapters one through seven; after that it's all software practice details). Reading this book for the first time was a watershed moment for both of us. In a book that's mainly about creating agile software, Beck and Andres also write extensively about principles vital to collaboration, and the values required to be successful collaborators. Those values are trust, feedback, courage, simplicity, and communication.

"The courage to speak truths, pleasant or unpleasant, fosters communication and trust. The courage to discard failing solutions and seek new ones encourages simplicity. The courage to seek real, concrete answers creates feedback."[8]

This passage describes a work environment in which interpersonal respect is paramount. Respect is the value that sits under the surface to motivate and regulate so much interpersonal behavior: In order to create disproportionate value (i.e., "leverage"), you have to respect each other. Likewise, lacking a foundation of respect, attempts to involve others will fall short of their potential and may backfire. You must deliberately choose to notice and set aside judgment in group discussions, and work to maintain open relationships with the people you involve.

The opposite of respect is contempt, and as our cofounder Kate Rutter once taught us, "contempt is the one relationship dynamic that cannot be repaired." If you have a negative experience with someone and have the courage to give them simple feedback, you can repair that relationship. But if you or they sink into contempt, that relationship is done. There's no way to include them that will leverage their brain power in a productive way.

One of the best pieces of advice we can offer around respecting your collaborators is to always work *with*, not *at* them.

WORK *WITH*, NOT *AT* PEOPLE

Team leader Sasha came to Jason recently to get support and advice. Sasha sat down and unloaded: "We're doing all this work to help the teams understand what the real priorities are, and how that affects what they should be focused on. We send them the priorities list, but they don't listen to what we have to say."

This is a fairly common complaint, and Jason gave his usual reply: "Have you involved the project teams in contributing ideas and developing solutions? If you do all this stuff and then hand it to them and expect them to implement it, you're working *at* them, not *with* them. And when you work *at* people, they have a natural tendency to push back. They're the folks who have done all the research into the problems they're working on, so they will have a lot to contribute."

Most of us have experienced being worked *at*, feeling like a partner or colleague is trying to sell us something they've cooked up on our behalf (but without our input) and now they want us to "buy in" to it. When we work *at* our partners and colleagues in the name of speed or efficiency, it's prone to backfire. If you don't consult the person/people you're creating for, you're unlikely to have the best and most complete perspective on the problem you're attempting to solve. You're not even pretending to Leverage the Brains, and by the way, you're sabotaging trust in the process.

This issue can arise frequently in charity, nonprofit, and community organizing work. Well-meaning organizations swoop in with resources and solutions they believe will benefit the people they're serving but do so without talking to those people. Often this results in frustration, disappointment, and wasted resources.

A great example of this was reported by Delaney Hall for the podcast *99% Invisible*. For a story on the architecture of Santa Fe, she spoke with artist and builder Roxanne Swentzell whose mother, Rina, had organized an effort to stop the building of HUD-subsidized housing. Back in the 1970s, the government unveiled a plan to build affordable housing in the Santa Clara Pueblo area, but the homes they wanted to build were prefab single-family houses with fenced-in yards and hard boundaries. This conflicts with the Pueblo people's way of living and doesn't support how work, family, and home care are approached.

"The houses had nothing to do with our cultural ways of life or values; the way the houses were designed had to do with a lifestyle that was foreign to Pueblo lifestyle," Swentzell told Hall. "The way [a Pueblo] village was structured portrayed that kind of community thinking, in that there would be the main central ceremonial house, the kiva, in the middle, with the outdoor spaces that everybody used, and then these individual spaces for storage and sleeping that surrounded that."[9]

Although Rina Swentzell fought hard to convince HUD to create housing that reflected Pueblo community culture—and fought to convince her neighbors that preserving their heritage through traditional village-style housing was important—the single-family homes were built. For a while, the residents did their best to improvise around these new homes, but eventually people began to drift away.

"It's kind of like a ghost town of sorts," Swentzell said. "So it broke. It fragmented."

If HUD had talked to the residents of Santa Clara Pueblo and had developed a clear picture of their needs and social structures, they could have built affordable housing that would have supported this community. Instead, they poured money into homes based on their own ideas and perspectives. The ill-suited homes virtually destroyed a group of people who'd been living together in a certain way for thousands of years. HUD had the best of intentions, but they failed to Leverage the Brains. They worked *at* the residents instead of *with* them.

Collaborating effectively means acknowledging that you are just one brain in the pool. It means setting aside your ego, and accepting that "leader" is a role, not a status level. It means never concerning yourself with having the "best" ideas, since competition like that is irrelevant and can kill cooperative ideation. Share your best thoughts, but also release yourself from attachment to your own ideas as best you can. Don't get invested in how much support your contributions receive; just surface them, then listen as others respond.

Create and maintain an environment where the collaborators actively seek to understand each other, rather than trying to persuade. Remember that when persuasion starts, people instinctively react with Stop Hands.

They feel sold-to, unconsciously mistrustful, and inclined to defend.

 They start looking for flaws in the ideas instead of remaining receptive. This is a natural, biologically mandated reaction. The human brain registers persuasion as a kind of threat, in which the persuader may have placed self-interest above the interest of others or the greater good. The neurological response immediately begins to assess whether the case being presented will harm them in some way. People naturally push back when they feel like someone is trying to convince them to believe, do, or support something that is not in their

best interests. They want to investigate until they feel certain enough to allow themselves to be persuaded.

If, instead, participants give each other the opportunity to consider the options and formulate questions about them, they'll relax their defenses. Make sure people listen with the goal of understanding and ask their own clarifying questions. They'll react with Open Hands.

They'll engage, collaborate, and participate to the best of their ability knowing that you are valuing and seeing them. They'll know that you're seeking to work *with* them, not *at* them.

ALEX WEST STEINMAN: BUILDING A RESILIENT ORGANIZATION

Alex West Steinman is cofounder and partner at The Coven, an online and in-person gathering and coworking space centered on the experiences of Women, trans people, and nonbinary people. Classic startup wisdom says, "Don't have too many cofounders," but these founders attribute their resilience and success to a four-person founding team. By leveraging the strengths of the different founders, their business has endured through the pandemic, racial reckonings right outside its doors, a recession, and various life changes. Alex provides us with a model of what it takes to Leverage the Brains and explains why that has been the right approach for The Coven.

All four of us came from an industry that was cutthroat, fighting tooth and nail, one woman at the top. And so now to have four women at the top, we had to unlearn a lot of things that maybe helped us get ahead there, that we now see were toxic and unhealthy. That kind of change takes a lot of "self" work, and a lot of "soul" work, and a lot of "soul of the business" work. Obviously, we haven't solved it all, but we've come a long way in learning to live our values as friends and business partners.

My mantra this year has been "Arrive from a place of curiosity." In my younger years I was much more headstrong, thinking I had to know everything, have the answers. I might come to the table not even interested in what other people had to say, but more of "I need to just get off my chest what I think, and don't challenge me or I'm gonna be super defensive." That made it hard to get anything done. I've learned that coming into a conversation with curiosity gives you a different kind of power and position. By asking the right questions, you direct the conversation and facilitate resolution.

You know, having four cofounders isn't easy. In some respects, it's been really hard. The easy (or easier) part is our commitment to the business and the vision. The harder part comes with relationships—navigating life changes, having empathy, supporting each other emotionally. People have babies, people get married or break up, a parent needs care, or their house gets broken into. People have complex lives. And to be in relentless pursuit of the mission and vision of the organization requires us all to remind each other why we're doing this, why these hard times are worth it, and why we have each other's backs.

Our investment in empathy and care for each other has made business decisions easier. Our relationships are good enough that we can go to each other and say, "Hey, I don't know how you're gonna feel about this, but here goes nothing . . ." We have this phrase with each other, "Unpopular Opinion!" Which means, "I know I'm about to say something y'all aren't gonna like." Nine times out of ten, we all say, "Great! Go do it." And that tenth time, we have the curiosity, respect, and trust to say, "Okay, tell me more about that."

We recently decided to stop development on a major piece of software. There were a lot of silent pauses in those conversations between the four of us, thinking, "Oh, crap! That was such a waste of time." But our relentless pursuit of the mission allowed us to have that unspoken agreement that this sucks and we have to do it. And we have to move forward, and we're going to take the lesser product, but it's going to end up being just fine. It was nice, having that energetic telepathy between the four of us. It's so different from environments where you're jockeying or lobbying or whipping the votes.

My curiosity comes straight from Bethany. She asks the best questions.

My ability to slow down comes directly from Liz. She's a shower thinker and an overnight processor. I'm more like, "I've already sent the email. What, you're still thinking about this?" But then she'll come back with "What if we did this another way?" And it's better.

And Erinn has such deep empathy for humans. She has given me an ability to think about how the other side might be feeling in a situation. Being able to pause and feel that person's feelings can help us to move forward in a really productive and caring way.

And they would probably say that my ability to move fast and *not* break things (we're not breaking things!) rubs off on everybody else, you know?

We're all operating with each other's DNA. Having that diversity of mindsets is so helpful. It's a process of learning and unlearning. It's made me a better leader.

THE ACCIDENTAL BULLY

For humble leaders to Leverage the Brains that are available to them, they must walk the line between leading and participating. That can be trickier than it sounds. When you're in a position of authority and you're also a participant in the process, you may inadvertently skew discussions.

Let's say you convene your cross-functional team, but then during those meetings, you keep summarizing or offering your personal take, saying things like, "So what I'm thinking about this is . . ." You may have shut down all those people that you just went to great lengths to include. Be aware that as the convener of those people and the leader of that group, your words and opinions hold extra weight. This is how many well-meaning leaders become accidental bullies.

If you are in this sort of leadership position, we recommend holding off on advocating for a position. You have authority, either situationally or structurally, so you don't need to say a lot. Instead, focus on asking great questions, keep meeting participation active and productive. Make sure you're getting what you need from each person. This makes room for others to float their ideas and express their opinions so you can truly Leverage the Brains instead of just going through the motions.

We know it can be hard to do, especially if you hold a position of high authority or can claim abundant social capital. Many of the military leaders we work with struggle mightily to sit back and listen, only chiming in when they can do so without stacking the odds. We have struggled with accidental bullying in our own roles.

In 2020, Jason planned a trip to Austin, Texas, for some one-on-one meetings with the junior staff. Given that COVID was raging out of control at the time, he didn't make these one-on-one meetings mandatory but instead offered them as an option to employees living in the area. He figured he was doing the right thing until one of his managers set him straight. This manager pointed out that everyone in Austin would feel pressured to meet with him simply because he'd traveled all that way during a pandemic. And also because saying "no" amounted to a professional faux pas—you don't say no when your boss's boss comes to town to meet you. Jason hadn't been thinking in those terms, but once he realized how his invitation to meet might be received by the team, he reframed it so it was abundantly clear that there was no expectation, especially if anyone was worried about risk of infection, and he booked remote meetings with everyone who wasn't able to see him face-to-face.

The fact that one of his managers felt comfortable alerting Jason to this dynamic is a sign of a healthy and collaborative environment. Leaders should empower their people to give them feedback if they run off course. When collaboration and Leveraging the Brains is your strategy, they should create an environment where the people they've gathered are comfortable speaking their minds, as well as prompting and inviting contributions from their colleagues. Leading with integrity means inviting and welcoming respectful contributions, and focusing more on steering, listening, and knowing when the team needs to hear from you. Leaders who are actively Leveraging the Brains must contribute judiciously, knowing their contributions carry additional weight.

Workshop with Janice:
IDENTIFY YOUR COLLABORATORS

Up until now, we've had you working on your projects alone. But we can now see that one really can be the loneliest (and least bold) number. You don't need to go it alone, and you shouldn't have to try. So let's find you some co-conspirators.

1.   Let's make a list. Write down all the people you have talked to recently about this problem or challenge. As many as you can think of. Some of these people have given opinions or advice. Some may be complaining or expressing a need to solve the problem. Some might be empathizing with you, providing a sounding board or shoulder to cry on. If you can't think of anybody, brainstorm your closest collaborators who just might have anything to add or contribute.

2.   From that list, circle anyone who is a subject-matter expert (SME). My list has several marketing experts.

3.   Now circle anyone on the list who needs to live with the outcome. For me, it would be my marketing intern and several freelancers.

4.   Finally, is there anyone on the list who must agree to whatever solution you might come up with? That is, if they say "no," you can't move forward? Who can veto any solution you might propose? Circle those people, if any. I don't have any circles. (I'm the ultimate decision-maker for my project.)

5.   How many people are circled? Is it more than three people? If yes, you're going to need to get that number down.

   •   Who's the best collaborator in each of the three categories of people (SME, Live with the Outcome, Can Say Yes)? Can each of those people represent the interests of the others? Do they care enough to dig into the project? If yes, that's your team. Everyone else is on the sidelines for now.

- If there are people who "need" to be involved for whatever reason (e.g., they're super enthusiastic, or they're going to make life difficult if they're not involved), then you can give them jobs to do. These should be jobs that don't involve making the final decision on your behalf or being invited to the collaboration sessions.

Chapter 8

EXTERNALIZE, ORGANIZE, FOCUS

This might be the most useful chapter in the whole book. We're going to show you that you're already a master at the skills you need to Leverage the Brains. Leveraging the Brains means slurping out the insights and instincts of a few well-chosen co-conspirators. Theoretically, you could make the important decisions alone, but why would you want to? It's less interesting, less effective, and you won't have anyone to celebrate (or cry) with.

You may feel like convening a group is time-consuming and inefficient. Perhaps you know that certain people will clam up and make you *drag* their contributions out of them. Or maybe the opposite, maybe they're guaranteed to hog the mic. You may have tried in earnest to Leverage the Brains in the past and ended up with a messy, formless, open discussion that led to exactly zero progress. It's bad enough when this happens live and in person, but even worse when it goes on for weeks via email or in shared collaboration documents.

Open discussions among groups can be profoundly unproductive. The absence of structure means people feel free to pontificate, pursue tangents, and pass around extraneous information. But perhaps most importantly, open discussions really *don't* Leverage the Brains. Group dynamics play out predictably, with a small number of people dominating the conversation, while others lurk quietly. People in the latter group may be shyly withholding truly genius contributions and the people in the former group may feel the pressure to do all the thinking. It sucks for everybody.

Leveraging the Brains means making use of *all* the brains in the metaphorical room—not just the boldest, loudest ones. Leveraging the Brains means making the most of the skills, talents, insights, and knowledge that each person brings to the table. To do that effectively, you need tactics that equalize power differentials, while also aligning people around a shared outcome through their active participation. In Part 1, we talked about framing the problem, setting up Points A and B for the people you've brought together. So what do you do to get from Point A to Point B quickly and effectively? You need a tool that makes the most of everyone's time and energy. It should focus them on a well-framed question or topic and give them a framework for generating information together and winnowing it down to the essentials.

And guess what? We've got that tool.

EOF IN A NUTSHELL

In our experience, one of the easiest ways to Leverage the Brains is to use a three-step approach: Externalize, Organize, Focus (EOF). This process is useful for any professional or personal situation that feels murky, confusing, or packed with too many options and unspoken opinions. It's the "order out of chaos" tool. It's reliable to use solo or with a group, in real time or over a longer period, in-person or remote. Here's an example to show you how it works.

Let's say you're the manager of a busy coffee chain store. Your goal is to make sure customers get their stuff quickly and accurately. Each time a server at the counter takes an order, they write it on a paper cup or bag. That's the E—Externalizing. It wouldn't help anyone if the server kept the order in their head.

With two cashiers taking orders, the morning rush gets hectic fast. So they make a single line of cups and bags according to the sequence in which the orders came in. That's the Organize step. It creates meaning from the externalized data—if a cup is first in the line, it's the next one the barista should fill.

The final step is Focus. As the manager, you assign one barista to hot drinks, one barista to food, and one barista to cold drinks. Your food barista doesn't have to worry about the hot cups in the line, or the cold cups. They just scan for the first food bag and get that order started. By creating Focus, each barista can execute on their part more effectively, reducing errors in the process.

That was a simplistic example. So let's add some complexity and look at an office situation, where the chaos that needs to be wrangled is opinions, data, thoughts, consequences, and feelings rather than coffee orders. For this example, let's say there are four managers who work for you and twenty-seven people in total who report to them. You've been given a fixed budget to allocate performance increases for everybody. That's a whole lot of feelings, facts, and opinions. Every manager, every employee will have something to say, and if you get it wrong, people will be mad and some might quit. It's happy news that you get to give people raises, but if you handle it wrong, it could still be a disaster. What do you do?

Externalize: The first step is putting as much of the situation as possible into physical space, so that people, in this case your managers, can literally see what's going on in each other's heads. In most cases, "externalizing" means writing down our thoughts or ideas where others can see and understand them.

In our example, your first job as leader is to figure out what needs to be externalized. You decide that first you want to externalize the scope of the problem—how many people should get raises and how much of a raise they need. You have each manager list their employees by number (to avoid managers nit-picking each other's recommendations), and how much of a raise each person should get. The total of all the desired raises together is $310,000 more than the allotted budget for raises that year. It's in a shared space, so all the managers can see that it's too much.

In other situations, Externalizing could take the form of voice memos, creating diagrams, whiteboard drawings—anything sharable. Most of us externalize collaboratively all the time without realizing it: We make whiteboard drawings, schedules, outlines for projects. Externalizing helps everyone to see and *understand* the wide range of thoughts and ideas within a group. As long as thoughts and ideas are trapped inside our skulls, they can't benefit the rest of the group. Externalizing also helps us to remember without having to do all that hypervigilant concentration to keep all those items in active (prefrontal cortex) memory.

Organize: Next, we work to make sense of the undifferentiated mess of items we've just externalized.

In our compensation example, we have a list of twenty-seven people who altogether are currently allocated a lot more money than you have to give. So, you need to Organize. You ask your managers to sort their people into three piles: those who are below pay scale and therefore must get a raise, those who are fine and don't need a raise, and those who are somewhere in between. When you look at the "must get a raise" pile, everyone can see that it eats up most of the budget, leaving only $70,000 left for everyone else. For the sake of simplicity in this example, let's assume that these are all fair assessments.

This is the most common approach to the Organize step: grouping items into logical sets (by type, urgency, cost, or any other criterion), sometimes using a sorting tool or grid. Placing the externalized items onto a grid or into clusters imbues them with meaning, which we can interpret in the next step. This reduces our cognitive load by narrowing the original list of undifferentiated items down into a much shorter list of related ones: people have an easier time mulling and discussing three categories of things than twenty-four individual things.

Focus: Based on the grouping we've done, we need to decide what matters. That means interpreting the significance of each grouping and letting that guide a batch decision.

In our example, the managers have all contributed to making three piles.

First, let's consider the people who don't need a raise. These people were just hired, or promoted, or gave notice, or are not performing up to standard. We can disregard them for now, obviously.

Next, we look at the pile of people who are below pay scale and need a raise just to bring them up to an equitable level on par with their peers. (This is part of the Equity in Diversity, Equity, and Inclusion.) Each one of these is an immediate Yes for a raise. We have to do these first. Note that we have now resolved almost everyone with very little effort.

With that all sorted, we can focus all our discussion time and attention on the eight people who are in that last group: those who *might* need a raise. We can have a full and deep discussion right where we need it. The managers and I get together and talk about these people, by name, one by one, allocating the final $70,000 in about one hour.

The idea of EOF is to make it possible to spend time where it's needed, by making broad and easy decisions wherever you can. Ideally, the tools you used during the Externalize and Organize steps provide simple clarity about where to focus. Focusing means attending to one set of items and disregarding the rest for a time. Choosing a focus allows us to point all our cognitive resources at one shared target. This helps to reduce the chaos so much! We promised to reduce drama and hopefully you can see how much less drama there would be in a raise cycle with this type of approach.

We think the best tools are the ones that take existing patterns and extend them into new situations. Even though this is likely the first time you've heard EOF described, you have almost certainly used it in your life. So we suggest starting with the most common, simplest EOF situation, building awareness of why it works. Then, you can apply the lessons to more complex situations. Start with a trip to a grocery store (or maybe Home Depot, Target, or Menards—something you would do anyway).

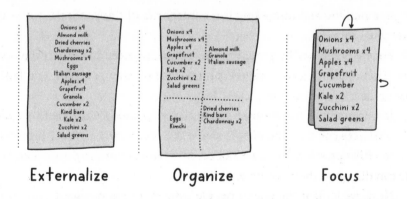

Externalize   Organize   Focus

At the beginning of the week, set out a piece of paper and a pen in a community location. This is an invitation for yourself and everyone else to Externalize. During the week, ask anyone in your home to jot down whatever needs to be purchased, in whatever sequence it shows up. As you run out of paper towels, or realize you'll need cream of tartar to make a certain recipe, you put it onto the list. That's Externalizing—shared, visible, available to everyone.

Next, before you go to the store, rewrite the list. Divide the new paper into four sections that roughly indicate the order in which you walk the store. For us, it's produce first, then dairy, then meat and the aisles, then things on the far side of the store. Voila, Organized.

Finally, at the store, fold the paper into quarters, so that your list matches the current section of the store, and cross off items as you put them in your cart. That's Focus. It's easy to see everything, miss nothing, and catch duplicates.

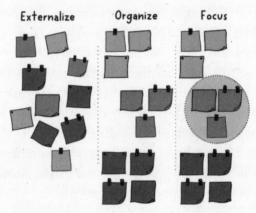

You remain focused and move easily from each chunk of the list to the next, without missing items. When you go to check out, you have confidence that you haven't missed anything. At home, you are fully stocked for the week.

This everyday use of EOF illustrates why this tool is so effective across situations. Each of the three steps helps dispel overwhelm in its own way. When we dump information out of our overcrowded brains and into a shared and visible space, we reduce the stress and worry over forgetting important details. When we find ways to group and arrange that information to help us make sense of it, the organized state of the items holds some of the work for us. It provides a schema, a shortcut, and sometimes even a rough plan of action. And when we are able to use what we've done in the previous two steps to focus our work, we can do so confidently, knowing that we've been mindful and thorough as we explored our options. Nearly any project of any size feels simpler once it's been viewed through the lens of EOF.

And although EOF makes comprehension and prioritization feel much easier, it isn't just about simplifying. Especially in work contexts, this strategy prompts us to deliberately identify and consider *more* concepts, options, or ideas than we would naturally. When the two of us facilitate EOF, we typically ask participants to externalize all their ideas on a topic and put each one on a separate sticky note. We've found this single step to be incredibly valuable because it allows everyone to externalize everything they're thinking, without judgment, interruption, or interpersonal politics getting in the way. It's also valuable because our best ideas aren't always the first, or the most obvious ones. We want to exhaust our creative thinking capacity, to uncover insights that might be lurking in the background. Then, we can look more objectively at the options and make a smart choice.

And this brings us back to Point A and Point B, our guideposts for Orienting Honestly. As we encounter increasingly challenging situations, simply nailing down those A/B statements won't be enough. We need to take action to get from Point A to Point B. We need mechanisms to help us get started when we contemplate questions like, "How will we get our kid ready for college?" or "What can our team do to become more innovative?" Before your family or team uses this mechanism, you may feel like all you've got is a desired outcome and the will to bring it to fruition. Afterwards, you'll be able to envision the first few steps and divide the work among key players. Using EOF can create clarity within any complicated question, and once we have that clarity, it will propel us toward taking informed, decisive action to move toward Point B.

In addition to Leveraging the Brains within a group, EOF is also an absolutely stellar tool for leveraging your own brain. It's a self-management strategy that helps us categorize information and distill options that are already floating around in our minds. As we mentioned back in chapter seven, scientists and researchers have found that large decisions can be made easier by breaking them down into smaller increments.[1] But even though tackling a series of micro decisions can make macro decisions easier, sometimes just identifying those micro decisions feels overwhelming. Luckily, the Externalize, Organize, Focus tool can help us manage both micro and macro without allowing us to get distracted or bogged down.

We've relied on EOF to help us choose our next steps on everything from planning family vacations to making investment decisions, and we've used it with countless clients over the years. It's a process that has proven helpful and effective in creating clarity regardless of the setting, players, and circumstances.

Now that you've got the gist of EOF, let's look more closely at each step in the process. Each of the three activities merits a deeper dive since each has its own benefits.

EXTERNALIZE: GO WIDE

So, we've already Oriented Honestly to get Point A and Point B formulated, right? Why not just dive in and take action? Do something? Anything at all that feels like it might move us toward that carefully envisioned Point B.

Well, for starters, taking action without developing a clear understanding of our thoughts is often counterproductive. In fact, that kind of damn-the-consequences action can make life harder and more confusing, especially when working with a group whose input you need. Since 4LM exists to make life easier, we're steering you away from that. A little bit of structured thinking can help. Take a breath, see a bigger picture, and you'll be able to leap forward.

With A and B defined, we need to take the jumble of thoughts and ideas about the problem out of our heads so we can understand them and focus on the parts that matter. Then we can deal with the whole situation more deliberately. **Your mind is an abundant place**, so when you start dumping all these thoughts out on the conference room table, you're going to understand *why* you were muddled in the first place.

What does that look like in real life? How do we move ideas or issues from our mental space—where our ideas swirl around in circles and push each other out of the way, vying for more attention—to a place where they can all be seen and addressed? Here are a few ways this looks in a range of real-life contexts.

Business Example

At the start of a new consulting engagement, we spend a bit of time examining the risks of a potential new endeavor and discussing how to mitigate those risks. Risk is scary and discussing it in a group setting can make it feel even scarier, since people feed off each other's emotions. So we use an externalization exercise to guide the work. We create a prompt around the endeavor being discussed, something like, "What's going to cause the biggest problems for us when we try to pursue this?" Then we give everyone in the group three to five minutes to come up with ten ideas, ten potential pitfalls that could jeopardize the effort.

The magic of this is simple articulation. We can't take action on any of those risks or do anything to mitigate them unless they're known, unless they're out there, and unless we decide they're important. As long as the possible risks are floating around in people's heads, they'll cause anxiety and stress. But once a risk is written down and shared, then we can decide as a group how to cope with it.

Artistic Example

Jason is a bass player. He may compose a bassline and play it over and over for a year. And as long as that bassline remains inside his head—as long as the only thing he does is sit down with his bass and play it whenever he wants to—it's unlikely that he will ever move forward and make it into a song. However, once he records it, it exists outside of him and he can examine it from new perspectives. He will pick up other instruments and begin experimenting with accompanying parts. As long as he ruminates over that one lick, the other ideas don't flow. Once it's recorded, his brain has more space for other thoughts and ideas. It's as if his brain is a stage, and that lick is Björk and Lady Gaga swanning around in meat suits—it's the only thing he can see or hear. Once it's recorded, the divas can leave the stage, and other parts take the spotlight. The recording is an externalization of the bassline that allows him to develop it in a way that he couldn't before.

Personal Growth Example

Another example comes from the world of twelve-step programs such as Alcoholics Anonymous. Step four in these programs asks participants to create "a searching and fearless moral inventory of ourselves." This involves writing a very careful list of character assets, strengths, and weaknesses that have led them to this stage in their lives and then reading that list aloud to someone else. As you can imagine, doing this is *hard*. It's a dreaded part of recovery. And that reveals one of the other benefits of externalizing. You see everything differently when you write it down. But it's an important part of the recovery process because recovery goes beyond putting a stop to drinking or getting high or any other addictive behavior. To move on, you have to look at yourself, understand yourself, and be willing to do deep work on yourself. You have to know why you fell into addictive patterns so you can avoid them later. The "moral inventory" is part of that deep work. Twelve-step participants are asked to write down their moral inventories because just thinking about them keeps them in that nebulous mental realm. Those character assets, strengths, and weaknesses need to be externalized—written and spoken aloud—before they can be addressed.

You'll note that two of these examples (and, if we're honest, all three) involve externalizing *our own* stuff, alone. How is that "Leveraging the Brains"? Isn't this part of the book just about collaboration with others? An important aspect of the EOF tool—and the whole 4LM approach—is its ability to reveal quickly and efficiently what's *in our own mind*. These are shortcuts to know ourselves better and get the best of ourselves. When we grab a pack of sticky notes and ask ourselves the prompting question "What's going to cause the biggest problems for us when we try to pursue this?" we come up with a lot more information and insight than we would otherwise. In this way, treating ourselves as a participant in a collaborative endeavor yields the same benefits we can expect when we use these tools on others.

We've said before that the Four Leadership Motions work alone and together in any combination. This is one of those moments where you can see the interplay. Although these three examples sound very different from each other, they all involve Orienting Honestly. In order for Jason to begin the real work of songwriting, he needs to externalize a bassline into a recording and be honest with himself about how it sounds, what should change, and how it can fit into the larger context of a song. In order for a group of business leaders to effectively address a complex decision or problem, they need to externalize all of its elements and be honest with themselves about any roadblocks. In order for an AA participant to continue the work of recovering from addiction, they need to externalize the traits and behaviors that caused that addiction to become an impediment to their lives and be honest with themselves about their own role in their addiction. Externalizing often involves Orienting Honestly, including the scary, unpleasant, messy aspects of what's going on inside us.

That level of insight and honesty is crucial if we, as leaders, want our actions to be effective and our decisions to be durable.

To get the most out of externalization writing, it helps to do it with pen and paper rather than a computer. Writing longhand activates different parts of the brain than typing, and EEG scans show that longhand writing produces optimal neurological conditions for learning.[2] Multiple studies have shown that taking notes with pen and paper helps us process and remember the information more fully than typing it into a laptop.[3] And a 2017 study found that "Sensory-motor information for the control of (pen) movement is picked up via the senses, and because of the involvement of the senses, they leave a wider mark on establishing pathways in the brain, resulting in neural activity that governs all higher levels of cognitive processing and learning."[4]

Bottom line: Your externalization will feel better and be more helpful to you if you do it longhand.

ORGANIZE: NOW, DECIDE

Now that the contents of our brains are all written down (or captured in some other way), we need to begin the process of grouping them. This allows us to consider fewer ideas by bundling them in meaningful ways. It's a way of gently down-selecting from the entire array of options.

Organizing is neurologically advantageous because it reduces the number of items your prefrontal cortex must manage. When you group items together in categories, your brain no longer concerns itself with remembering the individual items; it shifts to focusing on the categories. You may start with two hundred items, but after they're organized into seven categories your brain releases the tension around the full list and actively manages the categories. Neurologists call this phenomenon "chunking," and it's a strategy that humans use for everything from learning to memorization to language acquisition.[5] Our tendency toward perceptual chunking is the reason behind the dashes we use in telephone numbers. It's easier for our minds to see and memorize 212-555-8947 than it is to make any sense at all of 2125558947.

By grouping the numbers, we ease the brain strain. The same thing happens when we take everything from our externalization and organize it. After processing, the information feels instantly more manageable.

Our role model for the Organize step in EOF is Wanda Brown, who you met back in chapter one. She taught us that sales is the process of helping a customer make a decision in resolving a problem or need. (*Note that any foolishness here is our own, not Wanda's.*) The process must begin with considering a wide range of options. Once the options are in view, the customer feels overwhelmed and it's the salesperson's role to provide a sensible structure for that landscape. This concept has been adopted by IDEO and Stanford's d.school as "flare and focus," but we like to call it Go Wide, Then Decide.

The evaluation and selection process proceeds in stages:

1. **Look at Options:** The customer needs to explore the landscape of options, so help them take a look. This relieves pressure. Without that sense of full scope, the customer will eventually worry that she's overlooked something important and begin to doubt any choices she's made.

2. **Develop a Mental Model:** This organizing step is the part that helps the most. By dividing the array of options into discrete chunks, the customer moves away from the overwhelm and begins to identify which chunks are best aligned to address her needs.

3. **Eliminate Options ("Down-Selecting"):** Once the customer has begun to identify which chunks are for her, she can throw the rest overboard. At this point, she has turned the corner from "Going Wide" to "Deciding." From here, most folks will be comfortable eliminating options that don't suit their needs.

4. **Choose:** The choice is made confidently because the customer was able to evaluate a wide range of options, understand the landscape, align categories to her needs, and eliminate options that didn't fit.

What does that look like in real life? How do we create meaningful groups of the items or ideas we've externalized?

Janice was hired to help a large company improve its decision-making processes, and her first experience was observing an executive-level decision meeting. On the agenda was a proposed partnership. The meeting began with fifteen minutes of quiet time, so that participants (all VPs and C-level executives) could read the twelve-page "preread" document that had been distributed the day before. This was her first red flag. Then it was a Q&A session. Attendees would ask the presenter a question, and he would respond, taking an average of fifteen minutes to reply to each question. The meeting was meant to be an hour long, dragged on for ninety minutes, and did not result in a decision. In fact, the CEO ended the meeting by asking, "Why is this even in front of me? It's not strategic at all, just a bunch of tactics. Someone else could have made this call."

This was an extreme example but fits a common pattern: Externalization has happened already (or takes place during the meeting), but no one provides the framework for understanding, and the group gets distracted by discussing a wide spread of possibilities and concerns until time is up.

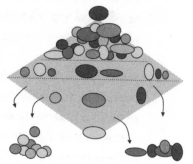

WILLIAM DONNELL: FACILITATION MAKES HARD THINGS EASIER

William Donnell is the founder of Sodium Halogen, a product design and development firm. What makes him special, though, is his work as a community leader in Jackson, Tennessee. In the time we've known him,

William cofounded theCO and has developed STEM and innovation programs that have elevated thousands of people in Jackson and across the rural western Tennessee region. His calm, cheerful, relentless leadership takes our breath away.

My wife Jill and I find ourselves in leadership roles at my company, Sodium Halogen, but also at church and here at theCO. I think there are a lot of similarities in how we lead across all of those different places.

One of the leadership behaviors I'm working on this year is leading by asking questions. So, rather than saying, "I think we should do this," I ask the team, "What are some ways we could accomplish this?" I want the input of other people, I want more ideas to choose from, and it turns out that I don't care whose idea it is. If you have more ideas and more voices to choose from, then you're going to be able to make a better choice.

Here's an example about helping my family figure out how to run our family farm after my dad passed away last year.

My dad had run the family farm for many years, and his style was always, "I make the decisions and whatever someone else thinks is gonna be 95 percent wrong." Now, I've been away from the farm for a long time; it's not been my job. So that leaves my brother, who is forty-five, and my mom, who is seventy-three. They're the ones left to run the farm, but they don't always see eye to eye. So, with my dad gone, there's a huge decision-making vacuum.

I knew I wanted to help them, but I didn't want to jump in like big brother fixing everything. Instead, I had them come into a conference room at theCO on a Saturday and we just said, "OK, what are the big things that we need to figure out?" I didn't have to give any ideas. They came up with all the ideas, and I just helped walk them through a framework of getting it all out and organizing it.

They wrote down their one-, five-, and twenty-year goals, and we adjusted those together. Then we said, of those one-year goals, what are the most important things that we need to figure out immediately? Then, what do we need to figure out in three months?

Many of the things that I think they really had been butting heads on did not even make it onto the list, because they just weren't important enough. It turned out we all kind of agreed on the most important stuff. These things didn't make the final list, but they did make it onto the table, and seeing them there is what made it possible to discard them (psychologically) and move forward.

One thing I love so much with an Externalize & Organize approach is, when you pick the ideas that you're going to move forward with, you can pretty much throw the other ones away. Recently, my business partner Chance pointed out that this gives you permission to focus on the important things and not be distracted by the less important things. The way he said it "gives you permission to focus" really clicked for me.

It also helped my brother and my mom avoid a lot of friction, saying, "You know what, those things are really not that important."

FOCUS: PREPARING FOR ACTION

If you do externalize and organize well, it's easy to focus on the things that matter, and that's usually the hardest part. In fact, most decisions aren't really decisions if you externalize and organize first. Once you've completed those two steps, an obvious choice will present itself. From there, it becomes exponentially easier to act with alignment to create impact.

That said, after your team has organized, you may still have several strong contenders for your first phase of action. Or you may disagree about priorities. If this is the case, the focus phase should consist of sequentially taking passes at eliminating options. Your goal at this stage is to prepare for coherent action, and to do that mindfully, your team or group needs to winnow down the remaining information and agree on what matters most. Reduce the number of options until it becomes crystal clear what you're choosing from, then take the time you need to discuss the remaining options and make an aligned choice to take action. Here are two examples.

Business Strategy

One of the focusing frameworks that we've used is based on the work of Michael Mankins, a leader at Bain & Company. It starts by scheduling two meetings that will be attended by all of the decision-makers. Let's say your organization wants to invest $5 gajillion to expand internationally. The first meeting is called "Facts and Options," and the sole purpose of that meeting is to look at the facts and consider the options. At this meeting, the presenter hands out a summary called "Issue on a Page," which highlights the most salient facts and context on a single page. The group then agrees, yes, these are the facts and those are the options we should consider. Option 1 is English-speaking countries first, option 2 might be Asia-Pacific first, option 3 could be high-growth economies first. Each strategy has an obvious advantage. The point is not to debate the options in this meeting, it's to agree that these are the options to debate. Once that's resolved at the first meeting, you have achieved focus!

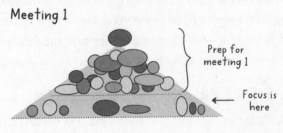

Meeting 1

Prep for
meeting 1

Focus is
here

·"These are the options to debate"
·"These are the salient facts"

A lot of hard work goes into preparing for this meeting. Researchers, strategists, and executives have to find the facts, choose which ones are important, examine and frame up options. This is the magic of the decision-making process that Mankins developed: it forces the group to focus and commit.

The second meeting is Decisions and Commitments. It's scheduled for about two weeks after the first, which gives everyone ample time to discuss options offline, explore questions and concerns, do additional research, and decide how they want to proceed. How will resource allocation take place? Who will lead each team? What will the first milestone be? By the time both meetings are done, the company has clear direction and a good idea of how to begin the work.

Meeting 2

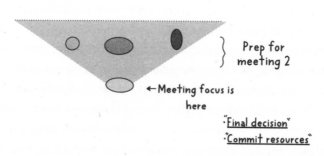

} Prep for
meeting 2

←Meeting focus is
here

·"Final decision"
·"Commit resources"

Retirement Planning

Several years ago, we hired a financial planner who gave us a truly massive list of things that she wanted us to do. We were overwhelmed. She'd externalized on our behalf, based on the information we gave her about our financial situation, but nothing was categorized or prioritized. We were so spooked we put the list aside and ignored it—for six months! The next time the planner reached out to see how we were doing with our action items, we ghosted her. But she didn't give up on us, and we're grateful.

It's so embarrassing looking back on it, but that's the human struggle, isn't it? Finding the courage to face our fears head-on. We needed to externalize and organize to defeat our own overwhelm. So we made a spreadsheet that created a framework for the focus we needed to get started. We knew that we would need to have a list of no more than five things to do between calls with the planner, and the ability to ignore everything else. The act of ignoring all but the most urgent things keeps us focused on making a little progress, continuously, for a long time. It has been four years, and we're still using the same list with the same planner. The list is ugly, and messy, and the focus it provides has absolutely transformed our financial confidence.

There are neurological benefits to this final step in the EOF process that both examples take advantage of. Narrowing options helps free up prefrontal cortex real estate, but focusing *at this stage* is especially helpful to our brain because it helps it reset and prepare to be creative again. That may sound confusing, so here's the backstory.

Externalizing is a form of divergent thinking; it's basically generating ideas, moving them from passive half-thoughts in your mind into a tangible space. Organizing creates meaningful groupings that can be labeled, and focus is a form of convergent thinking.[6] In most cases, groups of people working together on a project will cycle through the divergent and convergent processes several times, refining the solution in the process.

Let's say your company needs to move its headquarters, and the executive team begins discussing what they want from a new home city by externalizing all their ideas. Those criteria get organized into groups, possibly by geographic location, real estate price ranges, or proximity to customers. The team talks and determines that they want to keep the headquarters in the Midwest, so they throw overboard a whole slew of options. And now that they have agreed upon a new guardrail (Midwest), the group can go back to externalize once more to make sure *all* Midwest options are on the table. Then, when they shift to organizing again, they can use convergent thinking to hone in on a smaller group of Midwestern cities. Perhaps this discussion surfaces the executive team's desire to be near an international airport, so they eliminate all cities that don't have one and ask if there are any midwest cities with international airports that they've missed. It's an iterative process in which each round of consideration clears out the less-good choices and reveals the options that are better. After a few rounds of moving in the right direction, **when all the options on the table are solid contenders, then it's time to make the call**.

We've given you a handful of examples where EOF has been used in personal contexts, but we know it may still seem like a tool that belongs in a conference room. So we want to share one more story about the power of externalizing, organizing, and focusing outside of the workplace to encourage you to bring this tool with you everywhere you go.

KANBAN AT BRIGHTWORKS

During his seventh-grade year, our son, Evan, attended a school called Brightworks in the San Francisco Bay Area. This was only their third year of operation, and they had decided to make some changes in the physical layout of the building. About a month before the school was going to open for the year, leadership realized there were still a boatload of things that needed to be done to make this reorganization of the space possible.

Fortunately, they had lots of volunteers who wanted to help out. Unfortunately, managing an ongoing rotation of twenty to forty drop-in volunteers was beyond chaotic. The Brightworks staff wasn't sure how to organize or divide up the work among the people who were so eager to do it.

So the two of us met with school leadership. We talked through their biggest needs and discussed what the school could provide in order for all the work to get done. We saw that they weren't in a position to designate a volunteer coordinator to assign out and track the work being done, so they'd need a self-running system. We set up a Kanban board. Nothing fancy, but super effective.

A Kanban board is a project management tool that has EOF built in. (In fact, it was one of the tools that helped us really see the EOF pattern more than a decade ago.) Kanban helps teams visualize work, limit work-in-progress, and maximize efficiency. By using sticky notes and columns to organize various tasks, Kanban boards enable large groups of people to manage complex work together. Here's what a simple board looks like:

In the Brightworks situation, we asked the school leaders to write down on sticky notes every single thing that needed to get done before the school year began. We created the Kanban structure on a wall using blue painters' tape to mark off the columns and told the leaders that the key to using this tool was to always limit the number of things in that middle column—the "in progress" column. So, if they were using the board on a daily basis, as most teams do, they'd tell any volunteers they could select any task/note from the left-hand "to do" column and place it in the "in progress" column. If they completed the task, they'd move the note to "done," and if not, they'd put it back in "to do."

The school leaders writing down all the work tasks was externalizing. Creating the Kanban board was organizing. And the WIP (which stands for work-in-progress) area created focus. It allowed anybody who wanted to see what was happening to walk up and instantly understand what was being done, what was accomplished, and what work still remained.

Not only did this system enable the decentralized group of volunteers to complete all the layout changes to the building, but Brightworks leadership found the Kanban methodology so valuable they still use it in the school to manage projects, even many years later.

PUTTING EOF TOGETHER

When you put EOF together, you can have massive impact on just about every aspect of business and collaboration. Remember that abysmal executive meeting, where the top brass of a publicly traded company spent more than ninety minutes discussing a topic only to have the CEO wonder aloud, "Why is this even in front of me?" If Janice could hop in her time machine and give this meeting a makeover, here's what she'd have the various players do instead:

- At the start of the meeting, give note cards to the participants and encourage them to write their questions during an opening presentation (Externalize).
- The presenter should use the opening time to establish the Point A and B for the meeting. ("At the end of our time today, we will have made a concrete decision about which way to go.") (Externalize)
- Instead of sharing the whole twelve-page document (no doubt well-researched), the presenter hands out and talks through a two-page summary that includes a short list of facts that are necessary to make an informed decision and a simple framework for understanding the viable options ("Generally speaking, there are four ways we could go with this partnership . . ."). (This step includes all three: Externalize, Organize, and Focus.)
- The presenter talks for no more than fifteen minutes, during which the participants have been writing down their questions (Externalize).

- He closes by reiterating the meeting-specific Point B and offering a prompt: "Please choose one question that gets to the heart of the decision" (Focus, then Externalize).
- He goes around the room and writes down one question from each person. A few people probably pass. A few people probably add support to a previous question. There are seventeen people, so that takes another ten minutes. We're now halfway through the hour, and we've surfaced the primary concerns of the group (Organize).
- He chooses four questions to answer that get to the heart of the decision (Focus).
- In the last ten minutes, he asks the CEO if she would like to make the call herself or delegate it to a smaller group. This leads to a short but clear discussion (Focus).
- They leave knowing which direction to pursue.

In this example, the EOF helps to establish a shared understanding, focus the discussion, and becomes light-years more productive. It's orderly and participation is equalized. A group this size probably can't reach consensus in an hour. But, having heard the high-level summary and targeted answers to clarifying questions, they have contributed significantly to the quality of the decision.

COMPUTING HORSEPOWER

Frameworks like EOF that allow us to Leverage the Brains are all about efficiency. Although Leveraging the Brains is a process that involves collaboration and alignment of people, its main function is to harness the simple mechanics of computational power. Leveraging your group or team is like hooking up supercomputers on a local network. If you can think of our brains as computers, then connecting them increases our processing power, available memory, and data in the database. That's great, but it could just be chaotic. EOF channels it by sequential rounds of expansive thinking and narrowing. Diverge, then converge. Go wide, then decide. EOF helps us see the most worthwhile paths by Leveraging the Brains in a productive and efficient way. When you consider that many of us spend thirty hours per week or more in "meetings," reinventing the meeting becomes the number-one priority for getting more done in less time with far less drama.

Workshop with Janice:
MAKE A KANBAN WITH A WIP LIMIT FOR YOUR PROJECT

This is so exciting. Kanban is one of my favorite tools because it aligns everyone and makes progress visible, and it's simple to set up and manage. This is the first real workshop with your team, though, so give it an hour. If you aren't ready to involve your team, just gloss over the group-collaboration steps. I did mine alone, and you can, too.

1. Set up your Kanban board with three columns titled: To Do, Work in Progress, and Done. Name the board with your first "Outcome" from the OGSM Workshop in chapter six. If you will be doing this workshop with a remote team, use an online collaboration tool like Miro or Google Slides, which are what we use at the time of writing.

2. Gather together the people you identified as your collaborators (in the chapter seven workshop) and ask them to set aside an hour for this collaborative session.

3. Have everyone in the workshop brainstorm all the things that must be done in order to deliver on that outcome. Don't share them on the Kanban board yet.

4. Instead, ask everyone to divide their items into two piles: things that are absolutely necessary and things that could perhaps wait.

5. Now, we want to share all the items that everyone created together (not on the Kanban board yet). Ask everyone to post their items on a blank area of the Miro (if you're collaborating remotely) or the wall (if you're in person). And ask everyone to quietly read what everyone has put up.

6. While you're reading, begin to make clusters. Using the OGSM model, each cluster should represent a Goal, and the items within the Goal clusters are Strategies (they're probably activities or deliverables).

7.   Number the Goals in the order that you might want to tackle them.

8.   Take the items from the Number 1 cluster and put them in the first column of the Kanban. They can be in any order. If there are items missing in order to accomplish the chosen Goal, add them to the Kanban To-Do column.

9.   Each person chooses one item that they want to tackle first, and they move that into the "Work In Progress" (WIP) column.

10. Now you can all get to work!

Here's my project Kanban. Because I'll be traveling, I can't put my Kanban on the wall in my home office, so I made it using an online collaboration tool called Miro.

Outcome 1:
I Feel Confident explaining my business to strangers (e.g., On a podcast)

To Do | 3	Work in Progress | 1	Done | 2
Choose a framework for the messaging hierarchy	Define key audiences	Find Messaging Guides from last year's marketing project
Determine which audiences are high-priority	↑	Reach out to consultants from last year
Determine needs per audience	Remember: Only one thing in the WIP section at a time.	

Chapter 9

REINVENTING
THE MEETING

Modern meetings are often a disastrous waste of time. There, we said that out loud.

We believe that the number-one best practice for meetings is that they should not consist of *talking about* work. Meetings should be spent *accomplishing* work that can only be accomplished together. Otherwise we're wasting time and energy.

And money. Lots of it.

And yet, we are all constantly forced to schedule and attend meetings where talking about work is all that ever happens. In some companies, workers are expected to spend thirty hours or more each week in scheduled meetings, and people are free to take someone's time just by putting a meeting on the schedule. Work culture reinforces the idea that anything important cannot possibly be handled through a chat, email, or phone call; that gathering people together and talking "about" a set of topics is the way to make progress. Sometimes that's true, but often it's not.

Here's an example from our own experience. A senior leader at a very large organization was given a fifteen-minute chunk of time every month during the CEO's executive staff meeting, with more than twenty participants.

With all good intentions, she chose to use that time to give a project update. Before each meeting, she asked everyone who worked for her to submit project updates, assembled those updates into a report, and then wrote a script for herself describing what was in the report. She used her fifteen minutes to read the script aloud, and afterward, she sent the script out to the participants as a follow-up. It has been argued that this use of time created transparency across departmental silos. But I wonder what other valuable work could have been accomplished in that time.

As this anecdote proves, terrible meetings aren't just annoying, they're consequential. If we're *running* terrible meetings, we risk putting ourselves and our teams in the same situation as our client. If we're *attending* terrible meetings, we may lose respect for colleagues, mentally check out and miss key details, or even get so fed up we consider leaving the company. Bad meetings can be that bad.

MAKING MEETINGS BETTER

In the United States alone, an estimated $400 billion is wasted each year on unproductive meetings.[1] We estimate that most people spend four hours per week, fully 10 percent of their work time, just preparing for status update meetings. That's four hours of prep time to spend fifteen or twenty minutes telling someone what you've been working on. And you're doing this primarily so that you can maintain that leader's support. If everyone in your organization spends four hours each week getting ready for one meeting, how much time do they spend preparing for *other* meetings? How many millions of dollars of your own company budget are spent on meeting attendance?

And how many of those meetings are effective? Executives polled considered 67 percent of meetings to be failures,[2] and our own research supports that finding. Jason once spoke to a room of about one hundred people one evening in Singapore and asked them how many had been in a meeting that day. About sixty of them raised their hands. He then asked them how many of those meetings had been productive. A grand total of two raised their hands.

This is, in no small part, because we don't actually *do work* at meetings. Sometimes we learn something valuable, but often it's too late to do us any good. More often than not, project updates or check-ins devolve into stakeholders asking why you did things the way you did them. How come the logo isn't bigger? Why did you send that report to the client? Why did you decide to use Postgres instead of SQL? And they ask these questions because they weren't there with you while you were making your decisions, so they don't trust that they are the right ones. They have no context. You end up justifying your decisions and rehashing arguments that you already had, with others or in your own head. And that's a terrible waste. No one is working; everyone is just sharing information and explaining choices.

To be fair, information sharing and building understanding both qualify as "work," and sometimes understanding can only be accomplished in real time. Especially when the attendees are C-level execs or four-star generals who simply cannot read all of the emails or briefings they receive and need to be told about crucial topics. However, we've found it helpful to attach a goal or outcome to information-sharing meetings so that they, too, can be spent accomplishing something that we can only accomplish together. That outcome may be something like, "We will have a deep and aligned understanding of the relationship between coffee brewing temperature and acidity."

Does that sound like a "Point B" to you? Because it totally is.

WHAT *IS* A MEETING ANYWAY?

To understand how business culture got so complacent with our time, we tracked down a seminal work on the subject of meetings. In a renowned 1976 *Harvard Business Review* article, "How to Run a Meeting," author Anthony Jay wrote, "A meeting is the place where the group revises, updates, and adds to what it knows *as a group.* The simple business of exchanging information and ideas that members have acquired separately or in smaller groups since the last meeting." He called for meetings to have invited guests (sure) and an agenda of topics to discuss (aha!). In 1976, this made sense. We didn't have computers, email, text, or video. Our options for communication and collaboration were limited, so this format for sharing was actually an efficient choice for creating transparency across people and teams. Today, having a meeting is hardly the best or fastest way to create transparency, and talking *about* work is far less useful than *doing* work. So let's talk about how *not* to run a meeting like it's 1976.

The first thing we do to address this with our clients is switch up the language. Instead of *agenda*, which is about "topics to discuss," we make a *work plan* for the time together. We try to avoid "meetings" altogether and instead schedule *decision sessions* or *work sessions*. This small language tweak sets different expectations for how the time will be spent, and people show up ready to take action. The titles we give to our interactions impact the energy and intensity of those interactions.

We also create efficiency for our time together through collaboration. For a weekly staff meeting, for instance, folks on the team build the agenda, much like we build a shopping list—when something comes up during the week, they put it onto a shared agenda document. Any team member can access the shared document, throw a topic onto the agenda, add an estimate of how much time it will take to resolve it, and initial the item. When it makes sense, we add another layer to team-contributed agenda items: a label that indicates what action is required on the topic. Does it need answers to questions, a decision made, or is it just information to be shared?

These are the first baby steps that you can replicate pretty quickly. What's tricky is making these adjustments in a way that sticks. There are dozens of checklists packed with "meeting best practices," like "set ground rules" and "invite feedback," but they're like using a Band-Aid when you need a tourniquet. Meeting culture needs a more comprehensive makeover. In the remaining sections of this chapter, we're going to take the tools we've covered in the book so far and apply them to the specific context of "a meeting." When you use this approach, it will no longer feel like you're "leading a meeting." Instead, you'll be *facilitating a workshop*. And it will feel more like work to the people who participate, because it is. And that's the goal of Leveraging the Brains: to get much more usefulness out of our time together. And then take a nap.

Frame the Meeting with an AB3

We have permanently traded in the meeting agenda for a tool we call the AB3. It's a comprehensive tool for quickly framing the meeting and establishing ground rules to keep everything on track. When we decide to have a meeting, we start by defining Points A and B for it, just like we learned about in Part 1 of this book, Orient Honestly. We kick off the meeting by going over it all with the participants. It's a fantastic way to convene a gathering that starts by Orienting Honestly, Leverages the Brains all the way through, and Values Outcomes instead of allowing for endless, circular discussion.

The 3 in AB3 stands for the *Three Agreements*. There are things we ask the participants to agree to at the start of the meeting. They vary from meeting to meeting, and cover anything that might slow down progress, distract participants, or derail the meeting. Outlining these ideas at the start helps you avoid falling down conversational rabbit holes, which wastes everyone's time. The three agreements also help further define the path the meeting should follow; they're guardrails and instructions for how the group will use this time, and may include things like, "We agree not to reopen that discussion about bitterness in the coffee," or "For our purposes today, we agree that acidity in coffee is neither good nor bad."

In plain language, the AB3 says, "Here's where we're starting from, here's where we want to get to in our time together, and here are our guardrails to stay productive.

To maximize our use of AB3, we write Point A, Point B, and the three agreements on a whiteboard to keep the meeting on track. If we've agreed we're not going to talk about a certain topic even though everybody knows it's a big deal, and someone pipes up about that topic, we can simply point to the whiteboard and say, "Remember, that's a topic for another day." It's incredibly powerful.

It can be helpful to engage the group in five minutes of collectively editing the AB3, particularly when you're dealing with something that is controversial or contentious or fraught. Discussing where *not* to take the conversation gets the group in alignment from the start. But on top of that, it provides leaders with the opportunity to ensure team members are engaged and invested in what they're trying to achieve together. If a leader begins the discussion of the three agreements by saying something like, "I'm not sure I've got these exactly right, and I'm looking for this group to help me fix them," it shows that this isn't some perfunctory exercise. The leader is authentically inviting feedback, an action that models vulnerability. In many

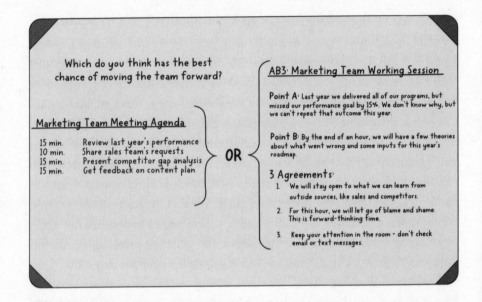

Which do you think has the best chance of moving the team forward?

Marketing Team Meeting Agenda

15 min.	Review last year's performance
10 min.	Share sales team's requests
15 min.	Present competitor gap analysis
15 min.	Get feedback on content plan

OR

AB3: Marketing Team Working Session

Point A: Last year we delivered all of our programs, but missed our performance goal by 15%. We don't know why, but we can't repeat that outcome this year.

Point B: By the end of an hour, we will have a few theories about what went wrong and some inputs for this year's roadmap.

3 Agreements:
1. We will stay open to what we can learn from outside sources, like sales and competitors.
2. For this hour, we will let go of blame and shame. This is forward-thinking time.
3. Keep your attention in the room – don't check email or text messages.

corporate cultures, that's a radical act. In one stunning meeting involving two teams that had become (very politely) adversarial and antagonistic, that five minutes of editing the AB3 turned into ten, then fifteen. At that point, Janice called for a break to have a side conversation with the two team leads. We decided that it would be most productive to let the conversation happen, and that nothing else mattered. So we let it take three hours of our eight-hour off-site and considered it a victory when the issues were resolved.

AB3 gives us a mechanism for keeping conversations on track, but how do we know where that track is or how to follow it to its end? Even if we've got A and B articulated, we still need to chart a way to move from A to B—and, fortunately, you learned one in chapter eight.

Plan the Motions to Get from A to B

To move the group from Point A to Point B in the time allotted, you need to *do* something. Usually in a meeting, the only verb involved is *talk*—talk about this, talk about that. That's the 1976 approach. We're not satisfied with that because it doesn't accomplish enough work. We want something more useful, concentrated, and effective.

To plan the activities that will move the group from Point A to Point B, we turn to our friends Externalize, Organize, and Focus. In this setting, EOF is extremely tactical; it's used to extract knowledge from people's heads, organize that knowledge in a meaningful way, and decide together what patterns have emerged and what next steps they indicate. Using this method equips even busy and overwhelmed groups to eliminate things that don't matter and pay attention to the parts that are most salient.

In a professional environment, especially when you're just giving these methods a try, we recommend designating a facilitator, which creates a different dynamic—one that ensures equal participation and a fairer outcome. There's a subtle but important difference between leaders and facilitators in this context: the leader of a meeting is the person who called the meeting in the first place, the person who most needs the group to accomplish the work that the meeting represents. That person needs to participate. The facilitator, by contrast, does not participate. They provide structure and frameworks to make it easier for the group to get from Point A to Point B. A skilled facilitator works in service to the meeting leader: the meeting leader is more like the facilitator's client. The leader participates in the meeting, but we believe that the facilitator must remain objective and focus solely on helping the group accomplish the work at hand.

Now this may make it sound like the facilitator should be a hired consultant or outside party. They certainly can be but don't have to be. Any leader within the company (or even within the team) may serve as facilitator, so long as they're comfortable stepping out of their role as stakeholder to guide the meeting on behalf of the rest of the team. They must be willing and able to focus their energies entirely on making it easier for the group to get from Point A to Point B. Because of this, it's very common to borrow somebody from another team to facilitate; they will have some context, but no personal involvement or investment and can therefore concentrate solely on helping and guiding the other participants.

Let's say you're going to be facilitating a planning meeting. All twenty participants have already spent time thinking about possible upcoming projects and will be gathering to align on work for the coming quarter. Before the meeting begins, your first job will be to draft a Point A and Point B and create three agreements. (You need to do this even though everyone knows this is a "planning meeting" because it will set the stage for effective collaboration.) But before you even arrive, you need to have a plan for how you will get everyone to Externalize, Organize, and Focus so they can agree on which projects to pursue. And you do that by creating prompts and filters.

Magic Tricks for Getting the Best from People

Facilitators are like magicians, but instead of pulling rabbits from hats, they pull decisions from teams. Their "pay no attention to the man behind the curtain" secret: prompts and filters. Both prompts and filters are simple, clear instruction statements spoken by a facilitator to a room of participants. Prompts help participants *think things up*. These are for externalizing and getting all the thoughts out on the table. Filters help participants *weed things out*. This is for bringing focus to a set of options. Prompts and filters are neurohacks; a neurohack is a technique that helps us access our best thinking abilities quickly and seamlessly. Prompts and filters light up specific pathways in the brain, engaging our massive subconscious to constrain or enable thinking, so the right things get externalized, organized, and sometimes eliminated in a useful way.

A facilitator uses a prompt to get participants generating productively. A *prompt* is a way to assemble thoughts around a focus area that may prove useful for moving a group toward Point B. For example, a PTO fundraising meeting prompt could be, "What types of fundraisers have you ever seen or heard of?" Using general prompts allows the group to generate a wide, diverse set of ideas. Narrowing the prompt creates a more focused inventory. Either might be the right approach depending upon context.

So, after you've established AB3 for your planning meeting, you might say, "We have an hour to get from our Point A to a clear set of fifteen possible projects for the quarter." Then the participants get black Sharpies and yellow sticky notes. (See "Sharpies and Stickies" sidebar on page 182.)

You'd start by saying something like, "I'm going to give you five minutes to come up with ten ideas guided by this prompt: What are the most important projects our team should focus on in the next quarter?" This puts the team into the Externalize step of EOF. The prompt you've given serves to focus participants' thinking in a way that progresses them from Point A to the meeting's Point B. It provides important constraints that help people generate a fairly large number of relevant ideas.

To give you another example, in March of 2020, just as the world was considering how to handle the emerging pandemic, our family had to decide whether to send our son, Evan, back to his isolated Massachusetts college campus after spring break. Things had not yet started to lock down, but a few places had already declared a state of emergency, including our hometown of San Francisco. It seemed dangerous to think about traveling, and we could imagine him getting stranded thousands of miles from our home in San Francisco for an unknown duration. We called a family meeting in which everyone was given a Sharpie, a set of sticky notes, and four prompts (this bi-directional pro/con technique is borrowed from behavioral psychology—it's cool; you should try it):

- What are the pros of Evan going back?
- Cons of going back?
- Pros of staying home?
- Cons of staying home?

After each prompt, we gave everyone three minutes to dump out all their thoughts, one per sticky note. The prompts constrained our thinking in such a way that we could examine the question from multiple angles. (Our daughter's thoughts leaned heavily toward "stay home," while our son's favored "going back.") And the process enabled every person to be heard equally with no shouting, no interrupting, no hiding, no sulking, and no drama.

A *filter*, on the other hand, is designed to down-select, allowing a group to prioritize and winnow down quickly and collectively. At the PTO meeting, an example of a filter would be, "Good fit for our school." So "Christmas wrapping paper" would be a bad fit for a Jewish education program.

We ask participants to "self-edit" with a filter, such as, "Choose five of your ideas you would like to move forward with and five to let go of." This filter is one of our favorites because it accomplishes multiple things at once: it prevents participants from subjecting the room to every single idea they've generated, it allows participants to give some thought to what they truly want to share, and it highlights the importance of only surfacing suggestions that are going to be the most useful.

If you're facilitating a planning meeting and "top five" isn't specific enough as a filter, you might try instead, "Choose five that you think are *more important* to move forward with and five to let go of." This reminds participants that a filter's function is to make progress and releases the pressure for being "best" or "most important."

Once every participant has filtered their original group of ideas down, you can ask them to share their winnowed choices with the group. Everyone will bring their five project ideas up to a blank wall and stick their notes to the wall. From there, everyone's ideas are once more filtered, but this time by the group. This can be accomplished in several ways.

SHARPIES AND STICKIES

Equity is a pretty abstract concept, but it's also one that can have very concrete applications. When the two of us facilitate meetings, we always bring a truckload of identical Sharpies and yellow sticky notes because they create visual equity as participants generate ideas. Think about it: If most people have yellow stickies, but two people have blue ones, the blue ones will stand out visually. If most people use a ballpoint pen but one person uses a felt-tip marker, that person's writing will have more physical weight and boldness to it. We'd like to think that we can overlook these factors, but the reality is that our brains naturally weigh certain visual cues. The items that stand out will be assigned more meaning, consciously or unconsciously.

People will have different styles of handwriting and print their letters larger or smaller, so some visual diversity is inevitable, but forcing everyone to use the same writing implements and pieces of paper does a decent job of creating visual equity. This allows us to evaluate the content of those sticky notes more objectively.

This is crucial. Externalizing needs to be an activity that allows everyone—loud and quiet, introverted and extroverted, leaders and followers—to get equal airtime and consideration. Giving everyone the same tools levels the visual playing field in one fell swoop.

Meeting Activities: Organize

Now that everyone has generated some project ideas, filtered their abundant thoughts, and shared some of them, it's time to let the group make choices together. This needs to be done efficiently and thoughtfully, so that all voices are heard and all participants feel valued.

Having thoroughly Externalized, the next step is about Organizing. If you'll remember, the most important part of the Organize step is to put items together in a way that reveals something important. We call this "finding patterns in the data." To do this, we *sort* the items. Unlike filtering, sorting is not about eliminating items (at least, not yet). It's about identifying ideas with similar properties and grouping them together. We use a handful of sorting frameworks to make this work simple and self-evident. We will sometimes go through a few rounds of sort-and-reduce. Usually, we have people do this work on a bare spot of wall, in groups of three or four. Yes, there are sticky notes all over our kitchen on a regular basis.

The simplest kind of sort is called "affinity mapping." With this approach, you group "like with like," and often what emerges is an organization by topic or theme. If your ideation prompt was "what do you like to eat for dinner," then an affinity map might have meat dishes in one pile and vegetarian in another. Or you might have ended up with "fast and easy" in one cluster and "make ahead" in another. As participants begin to place their sticky notes on the wall, the facilitator prompts them to cluster related items and give each cluster a name. This involves asking questions like, "What unites these ideas?" or "How would we define this group?" If a certain item doesn't group naturally, the team needs to determine if giving it its own category will have a meaningful impact on the work they want to do together.

Affinity mapping is particularly useful if the meeting goal includes understanding a nebulous problem, such as "what are the biggest barriers to growth in the next fiscal year."

There is a second tool that we use for sorting, called the 2×2. We will devote the whole next chapter to it.

Meeting Activities: Focus

Once you've sorted and chunked and reduced the number of "things" in consideration, you need a way to choose which ones to focus attention on. There are a couple of good ways to approach that, and the one you choose will depend on how many items have what you want to do next.

Dot voting and stack ranking are both simple methods that work by engaging the group to eliminate options to direct attention and time on the few options that are worthwhile.

Dot Voting: If you are starting with more than seven items and you want to reduce that number, use dot voting. Let's say we're still on the "what to eat for dinner" example, and a cluster analysis has resulted in eight clusters of items that include pasta, breakfast-for-dinner, salad, slow-cooker, grilling, and so on. For this method, we explain the mechanics and then give the prompt.

The mechanics of dot voting work like this: Using a pen or dot-stickers available from an office supply store, each participant will place three dots on any clusters they wish. They can place multiple dots on the same cluster, or one dot each on three different clusters. In this way, dot voting shows enthusiasm as well as popularity.

For our example, the prompt would be something like: "Please place your dots on the cluster (or clusters) that are your favorite dinner option."

Once the participants have placed all three of their dots, we count the dots. Clusters with the most dots are discussed in more depth, and the rest are eliminated from consideration.

Stack Ranking: Choose the stack ranking method if you have fewer than seven items, and want to end up with a sequenced, priority-order list. Stack ranking involves ordering the clusters by importance from most critical to least critical. We like to start by writing the cluster names on their own individual sticky notes and arranging them arbitrarily into a vertical column. As with dot voting, we explain and then provide a prompt: "This sequence is currently out of order. Your job is to fix it. To do that, compare each item to the ones above and below, and adjust the order until it's correct."

For our example, the prompt sounds like this: "We want your favorite dinner options at the top, and the less good dinner options at the bottom. So keep making adjustments until it's right." We start with the default order because it's easier to react to something that's "wrong" than to prioritize from scratch.

After using these meeting activity tools, the group is likely to be quite close to arriving at your Point B with strong support. This is because EOF is an exercise in alignment. As the group moves through these steps, they're asking questions, explaining their point of view, and working out small mis-understandings along the way. Having conversations about the items that are on the board naturally drives alignment across the team. Just talking about how to sort and how to filter creates clarity and sharpens focus for individual team members. And once you've finally landed on the ideas you're going to pursue, everybody on the team is more invested in results, and the results themselves are more likely to be durable. You've Leveraged the Brains in the room, not only to generate the ideas, but to process those ideas through your set of filters to ensure those ideas are both useful and meaningful.

One of the things that we hear pretty often is that people feel bone-tired at the end of a facilitated session. You might be surprised to hear that we think exhausted participants are the sign of a successful session. It shows that they've actually been doing work together. They've worked harder than usual in the same amount of time, which is mentally taxing but also efficient.

If you were to adopt the practices we've described in this chapter, you'd be getting people to do work rather than just talk about doing work. The only good reason to have a meeting is to take on work that can only be accomplished together. Gathering live, in person, at the same time is one of the most expensive things any company can do. And when people are your greatest expense, you need to make sure that you're using them as effectively and efficiently as possible.

There's one more tool in our tool chest to help with that, and it's the most powerful: the 2×2. Like the tools presented in this chapter, the 2×2 lets you Leverage the Brains through facilitation, strategic focus, and equitable tactics that produce meaningful results in record time.

Workshop with Janice:
MEETING MAKEOVER

Hopefully you're making progress on your project, filling up your Kanban board, and moving tasks from the left column to the right as you get them done. For this workshop, though, we're going to pause on our project.

Instead, we're going to do a makeover of an upcoming meeting. First, you need to choose a meeting. Ideally, it's one that needs a makeover—perhaps it's a routine meeting that's not very productive. Or it's a meeting that you'd like to be really productive. Whatever you choose, make sure it's a meeting that you have the authority to set the agenda for.

1. Determine Point A for the meeting. Remember that Point A should include two components: where do things stand right now and what's complicated about that. Sometimes it takes a little digging.

    Here's my example. Next week I'm helping to kick off a professional development program for one of my clients. Our final planning meeting for my session is on Monday. Point A for Monday's planning meeting is:

    - **Point A:** Thirty projects were submitted, but most of them aren't really what we need. We don't have time to get new submissions, so we have to make these work.

2. Determine Point B for the meeting. By the end of the time together, what will the group have accomplished? What will be different or resolved? Say that in a sentence.
    Here's mine.

    - **Point B:** At the end of this hour, we will have selected ten projects and have provided feedback for how to revise them so that they're better suited to the job.

3. Now we need to prepare to write the three agreements. Spend a few minutes thinking about the types of dynamics that are likely to erode

the productivity of your meeting. Perhaps certain people will dominate, or some will be reticent. Perhaps there are old issues that could cause unproductive digressions or debates. Or maybe there are sexy topics that people will want to jump to. Jotting down anything always makes meetings like this go off kilter.

4. Choose the three things that are most likely to crush the productivity of the meeting. If everyone would just agree to avoid those things, then the meeting would be so much better.

5. Write down the three agreements you just imagined. Here are mine:

   - *We're not going to waste any time talking about how we had better options to choose from.*
   - *We are going to choose very quickly so that we can use most of our time crafting feedback.*
   - *This is going to feel rushed, and we're not going to get any more time, so we can only spend a couple of minutes talking about each of the projects.*

Chapter 10

ONE TOOL TO RULE THEM ALL: 2×2

In 2016, Janice was invited to visit the Navy Special Warfare Center in Coronado, California, where all basic and advanced training of Navy SEALs takes place. The commander at this facility had recognized a need to make strategic improvements, and Janice was asked to run a workshop to help them. She was given one unusual caveat: she couldn't be told exactly what those improvements might be.

So she was put in a room with five groups of Navy bigwigs—each representing a type of work or aspect of training—but wasn't told who did what. All she was able to do was to lead those groups through a facilitation using everything from chapter eight, and adding one tool, which we call the 2×2 (two-by-two). She couldn't dig into the details of their projects, questions, or challenges, but she could teach them how to use a 2×2 to prioritize and make decisions. Their comments reinforced the power of the tools we used:

- "We saw huge mission value from the workshop."
- "Throughout the day, numerous SEALs approached me to comment on how impressed they were at the relevance of the workshop."

- "They made meaningful progress and accelerated the change journey of their particular initiative or project."

These are people who do really hard jobs. Failure is literally not an option for them, and they don't have time to mess around in "meetings" that deliver scant results. After just three hours, the 2×2 helped all five groups make tangible change and create lasting mission impact.

WHAT IS THE 2×2?

The 2×2 is a sorting grid for the purposes of making a decision. It's a decision support tool we use almost daily in our professional and personal lives to help us implement Externalize, Organize, Focus (EOF) quickly, understand complex situations clearly, and make informed choices. It allows us (and our teams and families) to consider various options, then understand those options as they relate to separate selection criteria. You might recognize our 2×2 as a variation on the Eisenhower Matrix, which is specific to deciding on, prioritizing, and selecting tasks by urgency and importance. The version we favor is more flexible and provides a nearly foolproof mechanism for leveraging EOF across a variety of situations.

To use it, you'll need a set of sticky notes, a black marker, and masking tape. Use the tape to create a vertical axis and horizontal axis: basically a large plus-sign. The axes are labeled with relative terms describing your selection criteria, with one end representing a higher or "better" value of the term and the other end representing a lower or "worse" value. We do not use superlatives, only comparatives, for these labels. So, if your horizontal axis represents "level of difficulty," one end would say "easier" and the other end would say "harder." If your vertical axis represents the gamut of "value," one end would be "more valuable" and the other would be "less valuable." Here's what that would look like:

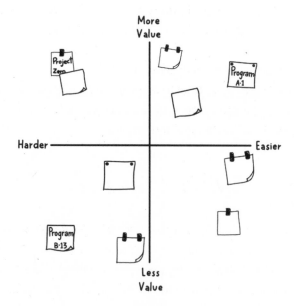

To use it, each idea or task is written on a separate sticky note (External-izing) and placed within the grid according to how it relates to the two axes (Organizing). If you're a team manager and you're using the grid above, a task like "create social media content calendar for Q4" could go in the lower left corner, indicating it could be postponed. A task like "address harassment allegations with Employee X" would go in the top right, indicating it needs to be dealt with ASAP. In this way, the 2×2 helps you manage a large number of tasks or ideas by ordering and categorizing them. The physical arrangement of items within the grid creates Focus.

WHY IS THIS TOOL SO POWERFUL?

One of the things that makes the 2×2 unique as a decision support tool is that it allows you to consider two decision criteria simultaneously. The way it's laid out creates a physical space where you can arrange your options rela-tive to both criteria, and that type of concrete, visual organization empowers you to make rapid progress on choosing which options you're going to pur-sue. In other words, the 2×2 forces you to organize your thoughts into four buckets, then those buckets dictate your focus. Once you've placed all of your thoughts in their appropriate buckets, your focus will become obvious and you can more easily take action.

This tool has nearly infinite applications in the workplace and outside of it. Here's a 2×2 we used to help us decide which restaurant we wanted to go to in celebration of our twentieth wedding anniversary:

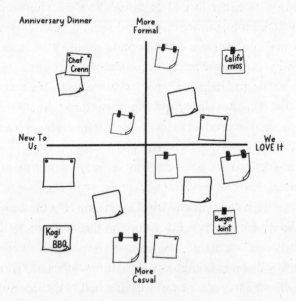

We live in San Francisco where there are an awful lot of restaurants to choose from, and we were struggling to land on a choice that felt perfect. Since this was a very special occasion and we wanted to consider a few fancy options, we made one axis represent "level of formality" (from casual to formal). And since we wanted to increase our chances of having a wonderful and memorable experience—something that's much harder to predict if you eat at a restaurant that's brand new to you—we made the other axis represent "familiarity" (from "new to us" to "we love it"). So, while we love Blind Butcher, it's in the "casual" quadrant and therefore not really in the running. Californios is a formal restaurant that we know we love, so it's a low-risk option and a real possibility. We also threw Dominique Crenn's restaurant into the mix, but we'd never been there. She's a creative chef who we have followed on cooking shows, but it's a *seventeen-course* tasting meal. Not only that, but the "menu" is just a seventeen-line poem describing what each course will evoke for the diner in the vaguest of terms. (Course three might be "Clouds on a rainy day in Florence," and course nine "Regret.") So while it's a formal choice and one that we were curious to try, the menu and the expense were much riskier.

The advantage of structuring our discussion this way is that it allows us to discuss and make small decisions around our options, gradually creating alignment. Our criteria are relatively objective: we either know/love a restaurant or we don't; it's either formal or casual. So we know which quadrant each option will fall into, but we may spend some time discussing where on the casual/formal continuum a certain option should go: Closer to the center? Farther away? And those micro-negotiations that happen naturally as we place options on the grid help us align on what we want. The first superpower of the 2×2 is that it creates clarity and alignment throughout the process. No drama, no arguing, just productive, on-topic, useful discussion and hammering out of definitions and details together as a team.

Its second superpower is its capacity to batch-eliminate options, thus narrowing focus. For our restaurant example, anything that fell below the "casual" line is eliminated immediately. Doesn't matter how much we love it, since we're aiming for a formal experience on our anniversary. Items in the "formal"/"new to us" quadrant and "formal"/"we love it" quadrant get our attention, but the 2×2 organization reduces the number of items we have to talk about in detail. Any time we can wipe out half of the inventory of possibilities, we've acquired more focus and bought ourselves lots of time to have good, deep discussions about the things that matter.

To a great degree, the 2×2 makes the decisions for you. If you're sticking to the rules you've set for yourself and placing your options in the grid squares you've created, you'll know what to do with each sticky note. The obvious choice will present itself. (In the end, we decided to have our extended family over for a backyard COVID-times Thai banquet. We'll go to Atelier Crenn next year for a belated anniversary date.)

SETTING PRIORITIES WITH A 2×2

When we first started using the 2×2, it was to help people to set priorities; everything from software features to budget allocations to vacation destinations. To do this, we use our "base case" 2×2 grid, which we showed you on page 191. If "more value" and "less value" don't resonate for you, replace them with "more important" and "less important." Regardless of which set of words you choose, you may spark some discussion with team or family members around what makes something "valuable" or what makes something "important," since both terms usually describe some subset of other characteristics. In a business setting, "more value" may really mean "makes us more money." In a community service setting, "more important" may mean "has the most impact on the people we're helping." If you can be more specific, do it. Label the axes with those words. Defining what these relative terms mean in the context of your discussion is *good*. Having that conversation with the meeting leader is an important part of preparation.

However, if you're facilitating a group and simply need them to make choices using their gut instincts, digging into definitions will just lead to tangential discussion. If getting more specific will be problematic, just use the "base case" grid as is.

JEANA ALAYAAY: THE REAL CHOICE IS "WHICH 2×2?"

For over a decade, Jeana Alayaay has been a leader and partner in refining the methods included in this book. She is Director of Product at VMware, and has led 2×2 workshops for the National Security Council, the Obama Executive Office of the President, countless consulting customers, and the team she leads at VMware. She's a close collaborator, a masterful facilitator, and, full disclosure, our daughter.

The challenge of leadership is that 99 percent of your problems are people problems. I've found that team members are more impacted by their experience of how we (the decision-makers) arrived at a decision than by the substance of the decision itself. Did people feel like they could follow along with the decision-making process? Do they understand the logic being applied in that process? I've found that people are

ONE TOOL TO RULE THEM ALL: 2×2

often fine with somebody in an authority position making a call, but they want to be able to see the sausage being made.

Generally, people can more effectively engage with visualized ideas than they can with verbalized ideas, especially when the material is complex. That's why tools like the 2×2, where you're visualizing multiple dimensions of a complex idea, can be so powerful; they become something concrete that can be pointed to. Working through a 2×2 has a democratizing effect on decision-making, even if the final authority on the call is a single person. I think this is a by-product of how human beings interact with things they can see. A 2×2 process feels more real for people than someone verbally describing the logic behind a decision, especially in a crowded room where other social and power dynamics are at play.

In software product management, we often use 2×2s for determining priorities. I've seen a lot of folks struggle with what it means for something to be a priority—which is to say that one thing must precede something else. You'll ask them what their number-one priority is, and they'll earnestly respond with fifty things. On a 2×2, those line items are represented as objects and you more easily see the relationship between one object and another.

The 2×2 transforms the concept of a "priority" from a nebulous thing that you have feelings about into a two-dimensional picture we can point to. It's powerful because it visualizes the complexity and makes it plain to see—that can be powerful for people in a shock-and-awe kind of way. Some people revel in it and others are threatened by it.

This year, my husband and I bought a house and we're planning for a lot of renovations. Having many things you'd like to do, in any partnership, can easily lead to arguments, especially about which things on the list are higher priority, what comes before what, etc. That hasn't been a problem for us, though.

We both use 2×2s at work, and we set up several of them to drive out the "roadmap" for evolving our home and the property. Given any session, the first question we ask is, "What's the appropriate 2×2 for the decision in front of us?" Which tool do you pick for the outcome that you want? That's where the fruitful conversations are for us—placing the items on the 2×2 is the quick thing that happens after the hard work of choosing the right 2×2 to use.

For example, last year, our main 2×2 for building a roadmap of priorities was "contribution to our family experience" (rather than "high ROI for resale," for example), so we renovated the bathroom situated between our two offices, remodeled the laundry room, painted, and changed out hollow core doors for solid core. Solar was on the list—we knew that we wanted it, but in terms of our primary 2×2, installing solar was not a high priority. We placed it in the five- to ten-year time horizon.

But then the political and environmental context changed (California wildfires and the war in Ukraine), and this prompted us to take a different look at our priorities. We decided that a much more relevant 2×2 for reprioritizing our roadmap would be "protection from public utility risk" and "wildfire or natural disaster impact in the next five years." That brought solar right up to the top of the list, along with an energy-saving roof treatment, and getting an estimate on a hillside retaining wall. (At the time of writing, the energy-saving roof and solar installation has begun.)

VARIATIONS ON THE 2×2

We used the 2×2 you see on the next page with the founder of a startup you've probably heard of, so we're changing her name. Let's call her Prati, and her story shows how effective this tool can be at creating clarity.

Prati's company had already raised several million dollars in capital and was growing at quite a clip in many cities across the United States. Although the company was progressing quickly, Prati herself was overwhelmed and miserable. She was being pulled in a million directions, constantly asked for input on minor decisions, overloaded by meetings, and unable to catch her breath. When Janice arrived at the office one day, she could see that Prati was underwater. They went into a conference room, and Janice asked Prati to take a pack of sticky notes and use each one to write down every single thing that was weighing on her mind. (This is Externalizing: getting ideas out of your brain and into the world.)

Then Janice created the 2×2 grid below on a whiteboard and asked Prati to place each sticky note in the appropriate spot on the grid. (This is Organizing: making sense of the information that's been Externalized.)

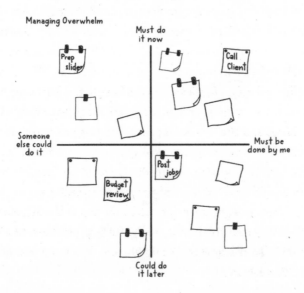

Once everything was up there, Prati was able to set aside everything in the "Could be someone else/Could be done later" quadrant entirely, as well as everything in the "Must be me/Could be done later" quadrant. What remained were items that needed delegation ("Could be someone else/Must do now") and tasks that she truly needed to tackle immediately herself ("Must be me/Must do now"). She had relief and clarity after months of nonstop stress. She also found that this exercise helped her make a key decision. She'd interviewed a man who she really wanted to hire but didn't have a specific role for, and her 2×2 helped her see that he could take over nearly everything in the delegation quadrant. (This is Focus: deciding what matters and directing your energies toward it.)

Although Janice walked Prati through the 2×2 process this first time, she was able to re-create it on her own moving forward and found it to be an invaluable practice for calming her periodic overwhelm and deciding how to spend her scarce time and energy.

Another variation, which we referenced earlier in the chapter, is the Eisenhower Matrix:

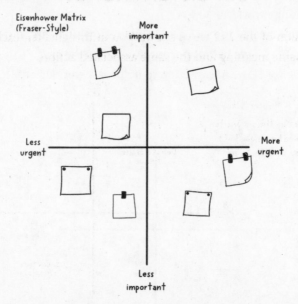

If you are already familiar with 2×2s, you've probably seen this version. Janice was first exposed to it back in the late '90s at a company that had a multilayer 2×2 process that involved ranking items by importance to the business on one grid and ranking items by importance to the consumer on another grid, then merging them. It was an overwrought system that could take weeks to decipher. But we loved the core idea and have continually refined and simplified it on our own until the entire 2×2 process, including ideation, can be completed in just an hour.

Nonetheless, we think it's worth revisiting the original Eisenhower Matrix because it captures our core philosophy: do *first* the things that are most important and most urgent. Interestingly, though, the original Eisenhower Matrix is laid out so that "urgent" falls on the left side and "less urgent" falls on the right. Here's why we chose to flip-flop them.

SETTING UP YOUR 2×2S FOR CONSISTENT ACTION

In every version of the 2×2 we've shown you in this chapter, each quadrant has had the same meaning and the same associated action:

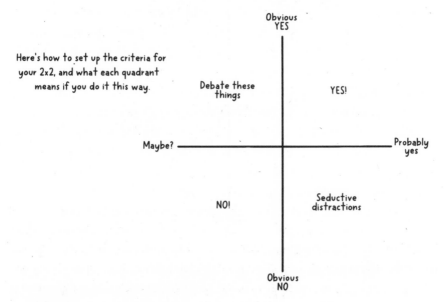

Since we want the 2×2 to be useful across cases and situations, we worked out exactly how to make the quadrants mean the same thing every time. The labels you put on the vertical axis would give you a hard yes/no answer: items you place above the midline will remain in discussion, below the line will get eliminated. The horizontal axis is for the label that isn't quite as cut and dried: toward the right would be an easy yes, but toward the left is a maybe no (but maybe yes). If you set it up this way, the worst options will *always* be in the bottom left, and the best in the top right. This is why we flipped the urgency axis in the Eisenhower version: it maintains the consistency of meaning we want for the 2×2 quadrants.

Now, let's talk a little about seductive distractions. This is actually the most useful quadrant because it's where so much wasteful conversation happens—from one perspective it's an obvious yes, but from another perspective it's an obvious no. On our version of the Eisenhower Matrix, items in this quadrant are urgent (a "yes" criterion) but *not* important. On the base-case prioritization grid, items in this quadrant are easy but offer little value. In every case, the tasks or options that land in this part of the 2×2 will be appealing for a very compelling reason (e.g., easy or urgent) but are not important enough to merit immediate attention. Jason has found a particularly great example in the world of software development: You'll get a software developer who says "Adding that feature? I can just knock that code out in two hours. Super easy. We should just do it." But if the feature in question isn't important, that team member is actually sucking up time that could be used to accomplish something more valuable. And potentially adding clutter to their code. By "just knocking out" a few seductive distractions, you run the risk of having a net negative impact on your product or outcome.

Items in the Debate & Discuss quadrant truly should be debated and discussed because, quite often, they represent riskier or more unusual choices. The top right items are no-brainers, but the top left items require real investigation and exploration. Think about our anniversary dinner example: We know for a fact that we'll enjoy ourselves at Californios, and that's a good thing—but there's no doubt we're intrigued by Dominique Crenn's restaurant. We're interested but also trepidatious, which means we can dig deeper. What are the risks? Even if the experience is bizarre, we'll still get a great story out of it, so is that enough? Is it more important to us to have a delicious meal or a memorable evening? As you can imagine, in business cases the Debate & Discuss quadrant is where risky investments, relative unknowns, and work outside of the team's known strengths will fall. If you never explore those things, you'll never grow or expand. They're uncomfortable and hold no guarantees but may turn out to be game changers.

If you only spend your time doing sure things that are easy and clearly valuable, you may overlook important—even critical—things just because they're hard or experimental.

FINDING YOUR DECISION CRITERIA

Many years ago, we worked with a client who needed to decide which projects to invest in. They were an online university and, through a series of meetings, we discovered that their top priority was appearing to be a market innovator. Even more important than the potential returns on an idea was the perception that the idea was innovative. They felt those optics would be a market driver for them, so when we used 2×2s with this client, we put "Looks Innovative" on the vertical axis. (Orient Honestly was key to this decision.)

Other groups have placed more value on things like profit (high returns) or speed (it's something that we'll be able to release in sixty days or less). And without those preliminary conversations, we couldn't have known how to set up 2×2s with relevant decision criteria. And to make those conversations as productive as possible, we run an EOF exercise called value finding.

To do this, ask your stakeholders, "What are some characteristics of outcomes that are important to you?" Even with that prompt, they're likely to look at you with blank stares at first, so give them some examples: inexpensive, makes lots of money, saves lots of time, and so on. Or, in the case of a restaurant, how formal, how festive, how excited do we feel. That should get the ball rolling and the people writing. Ask everyone to write down a single characteristic on each sticky note. Then, to evaluate each one based on importance to the team, start by asking them to place their notes in a "1x1," which is our tongue-in-cheek name for a single horizontal line; a definite yes goes above the line, a definite no goes below. Nothing can get placed on the line. Once you have fewer than seven things above the line, you can then stack rank the items above the line and throw away the items below it. Now you have a group of outcomes that everyone agrees are important, and when

More innovative

The 1x1

To simplify the 2x2, do one consideration at a time. The "Yes" criteria goes above the line and "No" criteria goes below.

Then sort half of the items above and half below.

You can do the 1x1 twice with different criteria, eliminating the below-the-line items each time.

Less innovative

you gather for future decision-making meetings, you can label your 2×2 axes accordingly.

HOW TO FACILITATE YOUR TEAM OR FAMILY

As with EOF, it's *extremely* helpful when doing a 2×2 for someone to act as a facilitator. Whether you're doing this at home with your family or at work with a team, everything will run more smoothly if one person is in charge of the process itself. In the previous chapter we mentioned that you can either facilitate or participate, but not both. When the two of us did our anniversary dinner 2×2, we had to bend that rule somewhat, but in most cases it's helpful to have a designated facilitator to ask the questions that we just discussed in value finding. You want someone who can objectively see what would constitute a good decision for the group. Because, after all, that's what a 2×2 is for: it's a sorting grid for the purposes of making a decision.

If you're acting as the 2×2 facilitator yourself, the first thing you need to do is likely value finding. Unless it's already quite clear how the axes of your grid should be labeled, talk with everyone about what they want to understand or accomplish, have them write down their ideas, place them on the 1x1, stack rank, and agree on how to label your axes. Then make your masking-tape plus-sign on the wall. (Blue painters' tape won't damage the paint or wallpaper.)

Next, you need to help everyone generate the ideas that will eventually be sorted onto the grid. Basically, get them to Externalize. In chapter nine, we talked about prompts and filters and those come into play again here. Give the group a guiding prompt that will help them generate a high volume of relevant ideas: specific enough that it offers them guardrails, but not *so* specific that it limits their imaginations. Something like, "I'm going to give you five minutes to come up with ten ideas guided by this prompt: What are the most important projects our team should focus on in the next quarter?" Have them write each idea on a separate sticky note.

As you'll remember from chapter nine, we often recommend a self-edit after this first bout of Externalization. As facilitator, you'd say, "OK, now I want you to look at all ten of your ideas and choose five to move forward with and five to let go of." This filter enables participants to have the freedom to write down any thought, knowing they can be self-critical later. It allows them to give some thought to what they truly want to share and trains everyone on the importance of surfacing only those suggestions that will be truly useful.

If you're working in physical space (as opposed to online collaboration), ask everyone to come up to the grid and stand side by side, shoulder to shoulder, to place their items on the grid. They need to do this without commenting on each other's items. Discussion comes later. For now, just ask them to use their own best judgment in placing their ideas where they belong in the quadrants of the grid. (If you've never used a 2×2 before, you'll be surprised by how quickly people take to it instinctively. Once they see that labeled grid, they know just what to do.)

This step is so valuable for shy people. Being asked to place your own ideas silently on the grid creates a very clear expression of your own thoughts without any risk of being spoken over. It allows for equal expression of equal creativity of equal input, right off the bat. It also can serve as a conversation prompt for your team because now you've stated where you believe your item belongs and the rest of the team will either accept it without question or will want to understand why you think that.

The next step is a quiet read: everyone in the room should take a few minutes to read and consider everything that's been put on the grid and formulate their thoughts. This can be both exhilarating and nerve-wracking for participants. It's reassuring to watch other people read your ideas and give them real consideration, but it can also feel very vulnerable. What's wonderful is that everyone else is having some combination of those experiences as well.

While the quiet read is happening, participants will find themselves with three possible reactions. (It's worth noting that agreeing with an item's placement on the grid doesn't elicit a reaction, and that's part of the tool's power—there's so much that just doesn't need to be discussed.):

1. "This idea isn't where I think it belongs. I wonder why they put it there."
2. "This thing is pretty much the same as that other thing. I wonder if they go together."

3. "This item doesn't make sense to me. I wonder what it means."

That last one is where you start your conversation since your next step is asking questions to create understanding. Let's go back to the anniversary dinner example. Let's say Jason didn't like Californios as much as Janice did. He might say, "You put this here under, 'We Love It,' but I didn't love it. I'm surprised that you loved it. I'm surprised it's even here at all."

And Janice might respond, "Oh wow, really? You didn't love it?"

Jason might reply, "I only barely remember going there, whatever it is. I actually literally don't remember going there at all. Where is it?"

"It's over in the Mission. Dark curtains and overly attentive staff."

"Oh yeah, that's ringing a bell. What kind of food do they serve?"

At this point, the conversation is heading toward the interesting stuff, which is possible because it's dominated by questions rather than attempts at persuasion. As the facilitator, you need to be on the lookout for idea-pitching since—as we've said multiple times—persuasion elicits a Stop Hands response, and questions elicit an Open Hands response. This type of discussion *must* consist of asking questions to understand, and then asking follow-up questions. Only through open, honest questions and discussion can people begin making suggestions about possible changes.

This also applies to ideas that appear to be duplicates. (Reaction 2: This thing is pretty much the same as that other thing. I wonder if they go together.) Encourage people to approach this by saying something like, "You wrote this thing. I wrote this thing. Are we talking about the same thing here?" If it's agreed they're dupes, place one note on top of the other to "merge" them.

At this point everyone has read each other's ideas. We've started asking questions. And now we're engaged in a lot of dialogue about all the items on the 2×2. It's the richness of this conversation where you want to spend most of your time as a leader. This is where all the work really happens.

Over many years of running 2×2 work, we've found that many people have never worked with their colleagues in this way before and have never had this level of open and clear conversation with their colleagues about the decisions that they're making. Many of them tell us they've never felt so aligned with their colleagues as they have after a 2×2 session. And it's the conversation that they have while standing at that wall, moving stuff around on the grid, that is truly critical. That's what binds the team together as a team. It's that conversation that aligns them on the work they're about to undertake together.

Once all the items are placed in spots that everyone agrees make sense, the facilitator can step up to the grid and remove everything below the horizontal axis: nothing in the "don't bother" or "seductive distractions" quadrants even merits further discussion. Throw away those sticky notes, or if that makes the group unbearably uncomfortable you can seal them into an envelope. Get them out of sight so they can be out of mind.

The remaining items above the horizontal axis can be discussed to see if any can be eliminated, and once that last round of winnowing is done, bring out another tool to create focus. Do a stack rank or a dot vote. Give everybody a different color pen and say, "You can put three dots anywhere on any one of these seven remaining ideas. And the question that I want you to be answering with those dots is, 'Which one should we be doing?'"

Once that's done, you will have narrowed the field enough to take action. And you've done so in a way that created alignment and built confidence among all team members.

Now, as a facilitator you may end up with a person or group who insists that all of their ideas belong in the top-right quadrant; every single one is both important and urgent. This is why it's helpful to label the axes with relative terms like "more important" and "less important." That gives the facilitator license to start moving items along the axis gradually, while asking for input, gently forcing people to rank their items by rearranging them and asking for gut reactions. Jason also uses a visual prompt when everything is in the top-right quadrant. Look at the plus-sign of the 2×2 and imagine that it's the crosshairs of a scope. Now imagine that you re-aim those crosshairs to be right in the middle of that big cluster of stickies. And then you imagine zooming in really tight, so you can see a lot of space between each of the stickies. That's what we're going for with this exercise. Once they have that image in mind, he asks them to move the stickies around to match that image of crosshairs in the middle and lots of space between the stickies.

Or if everyone has put all their ideas above the horizontal yes/no line, the facilitator can just move the line to provoke a response. Peel the horizontal tape off the wall and move it up four inches. Then say, "What if that were true? Would that be okay?" Which forces people to instantly reevaluate and reprioritize. As a facilitator, forcing a response through reconfiguration and questioning is a fantastic way to jar people loose from believing that every option is equally meaningful, urgent, and valuable.

In our experience, one of the greatest advantages of using a 2×2 is it gives people a clear view of the breadth of ideas available to them. People tend to think that creativity and innovation are scarce, but they're not. They're abundant. Humans overflow with ideas. All they need is a skilled and empathetic leader to help get those ideas out of their heads and into the world. Get a group of smart people in a room with a whiteboard, show them the 2×2 framework, and in ten minutes you'll have more exciting new prospects than you can handle in a year.

We can get twenty people to come up with two hundred ideas and choose one—in about an hour. That's the power of Leveraging the Brains. It reminds us that we live in a world of abundance, and that the abundance doesn't have to come with a side order of chaos and drama. It's possible to collaborate in ways with such speed and ambition that it feels like $1 + 1 = 42$.

But there's a catch: you need to be able to live with the decisions you make. And the decisions need to withstand challenges. Because they do get challenged, and that's what Part 4 of the book is all about. Creating efficiency through how we make and keep decisions.

Workshop with Janice:
THE "I'M OVERWHELMED" 2×2

Before you start leading groups to collaborate using the 2×2, I'd like you to try to do one yourself. Ideally, the first time you try this, you'll be able to put it on a wall or whiteboard. If that's possible for you, then the first thing to do is pull together your supplies—a Fine Point Sharpie, a pack of 3" square canary yellow sticky notes, and a roll of blue painters' tape (we like the 0.7-inch width).

　　If not, then you can use one of the many online whiteboard tools now available (Google Jamboard and Miro are both good options at the time of writing).

1.　Brain dump all the things that are on your plate. Write down every single thing that is on your mind, keeping you up at night, or giving you heartburn. I assume that most of you will focus this activity "at work," but it's also fine if you want to use it to sort out all of the things you're juggling at home or elsewhere. The focus is just "I'm drowning and need some relief," and step one is to externalize that mountain of items. Now you can see why you're overwhelmed—it's a lot of things, right?

2.　Set up your 2×2 using blue tape. Give yourself lots of room. Make the blue tape about three feet across and three feet high. Label the vertical and horizontal axes the way we have it in the picture.

3.　Now, place each of your sticky notes onto the appropriate spot on the 2×2. Don't put any of them on a line, because we'll make batch decisions about them based on their quadrant. Treat every sticky as its own item (don't cluster them together). If you see that they're all clustering in the top-right quadrant, try to pull them apart a bit.

4.　Take a step back and see what you notice.

5.　Pull off the sticky notes below the horizontal line, stack them up, and set them aside. We like to seal them in an envelope. (Or, even better—tear

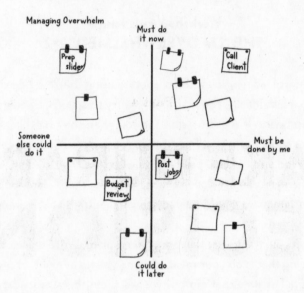

them up and throw them away! You don't need those today!) Doesn't that already feel better?

6. Now, look at the things in the top-left quadrant. Group these by person: Who will you assign them to? Make those assignments now. (Right now, get out your cell phone and send some text messages or make a few phone calls.)

7. What's left is the stuff in the top-right quadrant. Generally speaking, the thing placed at the farthest up, farthest right is the one you should start with. Pull that sticky note off, bring it to your desk, and get to work.

As you're doing this activity, it can be helpful to have a friend or colleague (a spouse? work-spouse?) join you to listen to you talk through it all. They can ask questions, point out opportunities for delegation, and validate that it's just all too much for one person.

Part 4

MAKE DURABLE DECISIONS

Chapter 11

NO BAD DECISIONS

NO BAD DECISIONS

I have great news. It doesn't matter if you made the *best* decision, or even the *right* decision. A lot of the language around decision-making takes the form of a hyperbolic binary, where everything is a win or a loss, excellent or awful. This kind of black-and-white thinking is the source of so much unproductive pressure because it just doesn't work that way. And, starting now, we invite you to opt out of it by reframing how you think about decisions.

Most of the time, there are only two considerations that matter: where you're trying to go and how confident you feel. Becoming a skillful decision-maker involves learning to discern which options will create lasting progress toward the outcome you've chosen as your Point B. Once you eliminate options that won't last, or won't move you toward Point B, then any options left over will necessarily be helpful. And once you know that, your confidence will soar.

About fifteen years ago, Janice was the CEO of a company that decided to invest in an "internal startup," a group within the parent company that would pursue a single business idea with almost complete autonomy. The internal startup asked for investment of $250K, which was a hefty percentage of the parent company's operating capital. It was a risky move. The company's Point B at the time was twofold: have a big impact and make a bunch of money.

There's no question this investment would do the first and could potentially accomplish both of those outcomes.

In the lead-up to the investment decision, after all the facts had been reviewed, some board members were still afraid that the new project might fail. The debate swirled with imaginings and poorly concealed emotions until Janice interrupted to ask, simply, "Is this a decision that we can live with?" And it was. So they took the plunge.

Within ten months the internal startup had sold to Google for a substantial cash return, far beyond the 10x that the company hoped for. That team went on to design Google Analytics and has influenced countless online products. Although this was a remarkably fast and effective outcome, there was a lot of discussion about whether the company had made the "right" decision. One board member said it was "the worst decision we've ever made." People seemed to enjoy armchair quarterbacking, pondering the risks after the fact. But that was just fine, because at the time they'd made the decision to invest, everyone agreed the company could absorb the loss if the internal startup had failed.

By reframing the decision, out of the black or white, good or bad binary, Janice helped her company make a much bolder decision (with far greater impact) than they would have otherwise. **"Is this a decision we can all live with" widens the aperture of possibility, while reducing the chances that someone will back out later.** This is not the middle path or the risk-free path. This is the mindset that enables groups to accelerate together to do important things.

We consider this to be a question of sufficiency. What needs to be agreed upon before we take action? What are the minimum criteria that must be met before we proceed? When we reach that moment of choice, there's always this implied prompt: "Do we all think this is the right thing to do?" We want to replace that with: **"If we went in this direction, is that something we could all live with?"** Because with our alternate prompt, the stakes are different. If somebody says no, that's a really big deal. They're saying they absolutely cannot tolerate the action you're considering as a group. That level of objection makes it worth going back through the previous decision steps, gathering more inputs, reevaluating, weighing more options, and reaching a different conclusion.

And if everyone can "live with" the decision even though they're not thrilled about it, that should be sufficient. Every stakeholder shouldn't believe that they must be overflowing with surety and enthusiasm in order to commit to a path. If they truly believe that progress is the goal, they should be willing to stop testing a decision and get on board.

CAN WE LIVE WITH IT?

Early in her career, Janice worked at Netscape, where Jim Barksdale was the CEO. Jim was the practical, folksy leader from Texas who had led a high-profile turnaround of FedEx, and she admired him greatly. Jim made a practice of addressing Netscape's exploding workforce at a monthly all-hands meeting. One month he got onstage to say, "You know, we have a saying in Texas: If you see a snake, kill it. And don't play with dead snakes." His meaning was simple: once you make a decision, don't second-guess it.

We all know that groups frequently make a decision only to pick it apart and change direction later. **The decisions people make are remarkably fragile. All it takes is one side conversation, and it's back to the drawing board.** And as more people become involved in a group decision or activity, complexity multiplies. (Remember the handshakes exercise from chapter one?)

Agreement becomes even more difficult to reach when the incorrect people are involved. We've all been to meetings where a key decision-maker or stakeholder is not represented and you leave the room without making a call. Or when someone who has no real business chiming in decides to offer endless opinions on a difficult topic. Many decisions fall apart because of who was or wasn't present at the table. We've even seen groups make sound, meticulously researched decisions only to have them torn apart by someone else after the fact.

The reason we've added Making Durable Decisions to our list of motions is because this type of backpedaling and waffling frustrates the pants off us. It's wasteful, corrosive, and antithetical to progress. Much of this chapter stems from our desire to understand the ways in which people will try to shake a decision apart, and our need to create stronger foundations that will withstand attack.

DECISIONS GET TESTED

What do we mean when we talk about a decision being durable? A few months into our son Evan's very physical summer job, his pants had worn spots and tears, so he replaced them with Carhartt's. They're made with rugged fabric, reinforced knees, and riveted joints so that everything holds together. These pants aren't going to wear out easily, even if you're hammering asphalt roofing shingles day after day. It's kind of the same with decisions. Our decisions work hard, and there's a lot of friction wearing away at them. You need your decisions to be tough enough to stand up to doubt, uncertainty, or politics.

We love to tell ourselves that once a decision is reached then the matter is resolved, but decisions are tested all the way through execution. And the bigger and bolder the decision, the more likely that someone, somehow, will challenge it either passively or, sometimes, actively. The entire time you're working to deliver on a decision, that decision will probably be questioned, poked, prodded, and debated. Some decisions can survive this process, others become slowly eroded. If constant questioning leads people to doubt that a "made" decision is the right one, that can slow execution significantly or even obliterate the decision entirely, leaving you with a ton of wasted effort.

While all decisions made by groups of people get tested, there are certain circumstances that make the testing process more vigorous. But before we dive into those, let's examine the stages of decision-making.

Any given decision will typically pass through multiple phases of investigation and debate. There's discussion that happens before you even consider making a decision, there's deliberation and analysis that happens *during* the decision-making event or process, and there's loads of conversation that happens afterwards. Action also follows, though sometimes it happens immediately after the decision and sometimes it unfolds more slowly. If the decision to be made is, "Who should we hire to install our company's alarm system?" then once the vendor is selected, a simple call transforms the decision into action. Decisions at this level are less susceptible to being questioned into oblivion. However, if the decision is, "Whaddaya say we reengineer our entire security infrastructure?" it'll take time, multiple steps, and people will have plenty of opportunities to challenge it.

In earlier sections, we described an idealized decision process that underlies all of our decisions and works something like this:

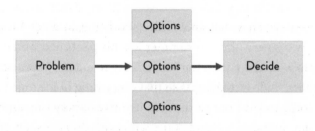

But to Make Durable Decisions, we layer on the complexities, nuances, and wrong turns of real life. You can think of it as a big mess:

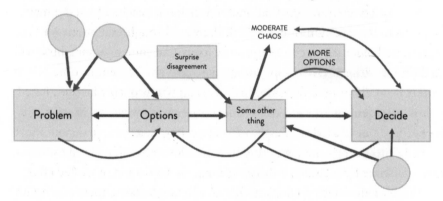

To understand how decisions are constantly challenged from the very beginning, let's look at a single scenario that layers the complexities onto the basic decision framework we're already familiar with. Say Vince and Mary Jo are a pair of empty nesters. After the kids have moved out and they've been on their own for a year, Mary Jo declares, "I want to remodel the bathroom. I've always hated this bathroom. Let's gut it and redo it." There hasn't been any discussion of this previously, but now the two of them need to collaborate.

- **Notice that there's a decision to make:** It's surprising how often this step is missed and how powerful it can be. Simply calling for a decision to be made and framing it up is a big step forward because it engages everyone in a known process that has a beginning, middle, and end. In our example, Mary Jo observes her desire for change and points out supporting evidence like the cracked sink or leaking pipes. Vince may not have seen those same things, so there may be some back-and-forth debate. As they explore the idea, they start *framing the question* at the heart of their decision: "Do we want to renovate our bathroom right now?"

- **Gather inputs:** Gathering inputs, such as costs and potential vendors, will naturally challenge the framing of the question. Mary Jo and Vince may narrow their focus and explore whether making a few repairs would be sufficient. Or they could expand and consider remodeling a whole floor or buying a new house that suits their lifestyle better. This is basically stress-testing the decision in advance and may end up sending them back to the beginning to "notice" that they need to reframe the question. *By refining the question now, they're avoiding bigger challenges later. Making Durable Decisions is frequently an iterative process.*

- **Weighing options:** After several rounds of investigation and exploration, it will begin to feel like they have enough good options on the table, and they stop looking for more inputs. Perhaps Mary Jo and Vince have a sit-down conversation to weigh the pros and cons and decide to invest in a new house. In this period, options are "thrown overboard," priorities are clarified, and we would hope that Mary Jo and Vince would consider both the logical case and their gut feeling. That means discovering which decision criteria are most important to them, and trusting those little voices that tell you what you "want" outside of a logical case.

- **The moment of choice:** If you've done all of the bits and pieces above, and not rushed things, *the actual choice becomes the smallest part of the decision-making process. We think this is the easy part.*

- **Resourcing:** With the decision made, our two empty nesters move
  on to finding a real estate agent, securing financing, getting their
  own house on the market, and pricing out moving companies.
  (Anyone else getting a tension headache just imagining this
  scenario?) As they do this, they will continue to question and test
  their decision when they find out the number of repairs they need
  to make to get their current home up to code, current financing
  rates, and other unforeseen factors. Alternatively, if they've chosen
  to move to a different part of their city, their grown kids may
  have strenuous emotional objections to their parents abandoning
  the family home. In a work context, this would be equivalent to
  excluding a stakeholder in the decision, only to have them swoop in
  later and throw a wrench in the works.

- **Execution:** If all the questions are answered and tests are passed
  in the resourcing phase, Mary Jo and Vince will put in an offer,
  be accepted, and move toward closing. But even at this late stage,
  the decision may need reevaluating. If the inspection on their new
  house reveals massive foundation issues or the seller backs out,
  they may be thrown back to gathering inputs *again*. But so we can
  all breathe easy, let's imagine all goes smoothly and they move into
  their new home knowing they've made a Durable Decision.

Each of these six phases will take differing amounts of time depending
on the decision being made. Some decisions require months in the "weighing
options" phase and then move very quickly, including through a lightning-fast
execution phase. Others will be settled on quickly but take ages to actually
execute; this might be the case for Mary Jo and Vince, since buying a house
takes a frustratingly long time. As we've shown above, at each one of these
six points, the decision can be undermined or delayed by questions leading
to further investigation. And at every phase you may get bumped back to a
previous phase by new information or sub-decisions.

We know this sounds catastrophic, but we promise it's not all bad. Part of
what makes a decision durable is its ability to undergo questioning at every

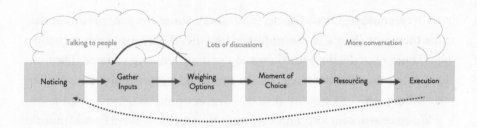

stage, and part of what makes people durable decision-makers is their ability to remain flexible when new facts emerge and they're forced to recalibrate.

DECISIONS CAN BE ERODED, REVISITED, OR REVERSED

In our example, Mary Jo and Vince initially thought the decision they needed to make was around bathroom renovation and they ended up buying a new house, but they didn't fail in any way or make the "wrong" decision. They were thorough in gathering inputs and exploring options and made a choice that fulfilled their true desires.

That's a revisit of the options. They may not have been able to even conceptualize the larger problem until they'd tackled and lived with the smaller one. If that's the case, they still did the best they could; they made a good-enough decision, moved forward, and then lived with the consequences until they uncovered new information. Then they pivoted.

Framing any decision as "right" is counterproductive. The standard of "make the right decision" is too high. It's the wrong metric. Instead, we should focus on making *good-enough decisions*—ones that everyone involved can live with—then move forward, and if something changes, pivot. In the case of Mary Jo and Vince, inaction due to trying to make the "right" decision would have resulted in waiting for years in a home they were unhappy with.

This brings us back to Valuing Outcomes and envisioning Point B. Digging into the ultimate end-result that we want and articulating it clearly enables us to make decisions that support that outcome. If Mary Jo and Vince's ideal outcome/Point B was "We want to be happy in our house," they could have weighed that outcome against the bathroom remodel. Would it have been enough? Or was there much more about the current house that made them unhappy and uncomfortable? If they'd only focused on whether they should remodel the bathroom and not done the deep work of Orienting Honestly to unearth their real needs, they might have ended up revoking their decision.

We once worked with an organization that chose to hire and train up many staff members who weren't very experienced in the jobs that they'd been hired to perform. It was exciting because these were career-changers, so the company made the decision to hire more people into roles that were focused on helping these inexperienced people become better at their jobs. They called these helpers "practice leaders," and they were meant to help the new engineers become better engineers, help the new designers become better designers, help the new product managers become better product managers, and so on. Unfortunately, there were other roles that were also missing from the organization, including key ones like people-manager roles, admin support, and HR. And since those unfilled management roles were actually more urgent to keep the organization functioning, the people hired as practice leaders ended up becoming de facto people managers, admins, and HR folks. The inexperienced new hires still needed the intensive mentoring they'd been getting from those now-relocated practice leaders.

The decision to have practice leaders retrain and support the career-changers was eroded by the second decision, to expand the scope of those roles to include operations. The practice leadership got quashed under the tyranny of operational work, and the organization suffered for it. In this case the undoing was passive: the company saw the practice leaders drift away from the career-changers, and let it happen. Over time, this returned the company to the same position it had been in at the start: employing scores of inexperienced people who needed mentoring and guidance, but lacking the resources to support them properly.

When a decision is undermined systemically over time, it is de facto reversed.

HOW TO MAKE DECISIONS AS DURABLE AS CARHARTT'S

The erosion of decisions isn't a black and white thing—it's shades of gray and death by a thousand cuts. The goal is to make good-enough decisions and move forward with the flexibility to change course if and when we get new insight. We lose time before decisions are made by trying to get the perfect or best decision. We lose even more time after the decision, through inefficiencies caused by erosion and revocation.

Here's how to fix decision-making to make each choice more durable:

Avoid Absolutes: In most cases, there is no "right" decision, so stop thinking you can find one. When we get caught up in making a perfect call that is unassailably correct, we risk spending far too much time gathering inputs and weighing options. We've all heard of analysis paralysis. Make a good-enough decision. And what's good enough? One that moves us in the right direction (toward our Point B) with confidence. One we can all live with.

Get the Facts Right: Some choices are time-sensitive, but short-changing the input-gathering can make a decision vulnerable later. To move quickly, first gather the facts and inputs. Then, get the right people in a room with you. With this setup, you can often make a good-enough call in about an hour using the tools in this book.

Consent, Not Consensus: Striving for consensus is usually wasteful and unnecessary. Making a wise decision requires that everyone is willing to get behind it and support it. That's a much easier standard to reach than everyone agreeing that it's the "right" thing to do. Focus on reaching a decision that everyone can support. Create a standard of comfort that everyone must have with the direction that is being taken, but don't require them all to be completely thrilled at all times.

The Right People, but Not Too Many: To increase the strength of a decision, include in the decision-making process a relatively small number of people who can represent the interests of the right groups.

In chapter five we talked about the three groups who should be represented in every decision. If you don't include these, you really increase the chances that a stakeholder will swoop in later to disrupt the decision. So definitely include:

- People with the authority to say yes
- People who have subject-matter knowledge
- People who have to live with the outcome

And that's it. Nobody else. Including other people in the decision process can detract from your progress. With all good intentions, they can take the discussion in an unproductive direction and use up airtime. Instead, if needed, you can involve these others during the "gather inputs" stage.

Remember also that the more people involved in making a decision, the more likely you are to end up with weak support for whatever decision comes out. We prefer decision groups of three or four. If, say, a group of twelve people needs to make a choice together, there's a good chance that individuals won't feel heard and will worry that their concerns haven't been fully addressed. This weakens their commitment to the decision. Better to have three informed people make the decision confidently, than have twelve half-informed people be wafflers.

Reduce the Scope: If decision scope is large or complex, the perception is that the decision itself carries more risk of failure. The solution to this is to run a process that breaks the big decision down into smaller pieces that are easier to make confidently. The 2×2 is an excellent example of a process that leverages this approach, breaking large decisions into incremental moves. Each move of a sticky note to a different spot on the grid is a micro decision.

Mental Agility and Growth Mindset: If stakeholders come to a decision-making moment with a fixed idea about what must happen, they can block productive discussion. If instead they come with the mental flexibility to consider new information, the insights of others, and a range of options, then you can thoroughly examine the potential outcomes of the decision.

Strong support for a decision comes from belief in the decision-making process, as well as support for the option chosen. We're going to spend nearly all of chapter thirteen addressing that one, so hang tight.

Now, we've just given you several Carhartt's-worthy decision-strengthening tactics. It can be difficult to control for all those variables ahead of time, or all at once. Part of being a humane leader is being humane with yourself, and you are neither psychic nor a member of the Avengers. (We assume.) Keep these tactics in mind as you organize decision-making processes and gatherings, but also use them to diagnose durability and address hiccups *during* those processes and gatherings.

What about decisions that never get made at all? Have you ever felt like your team or group is prone to chasing tangential ideas or getting mired in related projects without ever making a clear choice?

Janice once launched a company with six colleagues—so seven total founders, all with equal standing—and they all spent fifteen minutes every Tuesday for six months arguing about whether to buy a $300 printer for the office. That's a total of forty-five person-hours. They could have bought twenty printers for the money wasted! Eventually, Janice realized the group was incapable of making a yes/no decision, good-enough or otherwise.

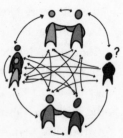

7 people = Too Many Handshakes!!

Remember the handshakes discussion from chapter one? Seven people is too many effing handshakes, so Janice eventually just bought the printer herself.

It's exhausting when discussions about the decisions become black holes into which you pour your time (and patience, and social capital, and your enthusiasm). Plenty of decisions don't get made because people believe they are entitled to keep talking, expressing opinions, and asking questions, even when most folks understand and agree on a direction. (This is a theme you'll see come up frequently in the chapters to come.) When people are afraid that they don't have enough information or worry that moving forward with the "good enough" choice will incur too much risk, they keep pressing for details. When "being wrong" or "making the wrong call" comes with a heavy penalty, groups will avoid making decisions and will engage in all sorts of behaviors to prevent a decision moment.

Eroded and unmade decisions impede progress wherever we lead, including at home and in our communities. In order to get anything done and move forward, groups must find ways to commit. We've found that the best way to ensure this happens is to shift decision-making culture to embrace the standard of good-enough. So now the question becomes, how do you get everyone else to "buy in" to that standard? Well, true to form, we don't believe in buy-in. Instead we look at understanding, belief, advocacy, and decision-making.

Workshop with Janice:
WHY DID THAT DECISION FALL APART?

Think back to a recent decision that you thought was solid and were surprised when sometime later support for it dissolved or it fell apart. See if you can figure out all the ways in which the decision was weakened.

1. Take five minutes and write out how things went wrong. What happened?
2. Outline the steps that were taken to arrive at this decision. You can refer back to this diagram. What steps were glossed over? Who was included in which part? Was there black-and-white thinking? A desire for consensus?

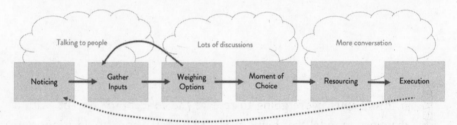

3. Looking back over the recommendations in this chapter, what could have been done to strengthen the decision?

Chapter 12

FORGET BUY-IN AND EMBRACE UBAD

I n this chapter, we're going to replace the concept of "buy-in" with a diagnostic model that helps everyday leaders shore up decisions and helps them guide their folks toward Durable Decisions that everyone can live with. The tools and techniques that we have shared in earlier parts of this book are geared toward driving shared Understanding and Belief (those are the *U* and the *B* in UBAD). If you're using the tools and techniques that we've shared so far, then you're already moving toward Advocacy and Decision-Making (the *A* and the *D*). You've already got the skills; this framework simply provides you with another way to apply them.

We used to work for a company called Pivotal Labs that built software shockingly fast using a very specific methodology. When the company was trying to land a new client, the Pivotal sales team would bring in groups of corporate executives and show them around the workspace to get a feel for how the work got done. In many cases, those executives were floored by what they saw. It was slick, unusual, fast-paced, and very different from what they'd seen elsewhere. Many of them were so blown away, they would close a deal with Pivotal the same day.

Usually it went well, but in one case, not so much. Pivotal relied on setting aside a lot of common habits around doing work. First, instead of Pivotal engineers and developers working out of the client's office, clients came to us. This was done to break them out of their normal ways of working and give them a chance to experience a different way that was much more effective. Four developers and a product manager showed up from this Fortune 100 client's company to start this process. In the first few days, they came to understand that each of them was expected to sit side by side, all day every day, with a partner from Pivotal, co-developing the software in "pairs." They would be dedicating 100 percent of their time to building the software, and they would not be available to check email or attend meetings that didn't pertain directly to the work at hand. The workday started at 9:06, lunch was 12:30–1:30, and at 6:00 everyone left for home. That's how Pivotal Labs worked, and the client employees did not like it. At all.

They almost managed to make it through that first week before they decided they were done. In the middle of the workday, these developers stood up en masse, gathered their stuff, and left the office. They didn't explain, and they never came back.

Pivotal leaders were thunderstruck. What had happened? Did someone say something unforgivable to our clients? But it didn't take us long to make it clear they just didn't want to do what they had literally hired us to do.

Or, more accurately, what their executives had hired us to do, probably without really understanding the implications. The developers and product manager had been tasked with doing something that they were not inclined to do. And the executives hadn't understood how extreme the differences in work culture would be because they hadn't included the people doing the actual work in the decision, and those folks were not interested in experimenting with a completely different way of working.

This anecdote illustrates a problem that's common in modern leadership. The group of executives that were wowed by the Pivotal sales team didn't fully understand what it was they were asking of their own team by signing a contract. And they certainly didn't understand how their team would react to being forced to change the way they worked. The executives at the client company had bought a service based on their strong belief in its effectiveness, but they had very little understanding. But belief without understanding is pretty fragile. So the decision to work with Pivotal got unmade.

When the client execs had come for their walk-through, they saw people working away, writing code, with a clear pipeline to a production environment. They saw people working in pairs, happy and having fun, but still getting the job done. It was a buzzing hive that looked easy to adopt. What they didn't understand were the mindset and behavioral shifts needed for each individual team member to be able to work this way. It's threatening to work with a partner all the time; they watch us make mistakes. No doubt, Pivotal's way of developing software is special—miraculous even—but it's not for everyone.

If the execs had truly understood what they were buying, they would have gone back to their own offices and very carefully considered which employees to put in this situation. If they were compassionate leaders who valued supporting employee growth, they would have chosen people who were already looking for new ways of working. People who were excited about a challenge and eager to work with a team. But they just didn't think to ask more about what they were getting into. And the Pivotal salespeople probably didn't push it. The executives made a decision based on what they believed—that Pivotal's way of working could be instantly superimposed onto their own workforce—but what they believed was not actually rooted in fact. So these decision-makers had strong belief and minimal understanding, which made their decision fragile.

THE MYTH OF BUY-IN

The idea of "buy-in" says that getting key players to believe in a suggested idea or solution ensures its adoption. In practice, however, the tactics we use to get buy-in are more about easing our anxiety than securing genuine and enduring support. We want to rig the game to ensure we won't end up embarrassed for championing a particular idea or project, so we play politics. We shop our ideas around, gather feedback, and listen to various people's opinions. But in the end, buy-in is a myth. And here's why we avoid the term:

- Nobody knows what it is.
- Everyone thinks that they have it (because they're such good persuaders).
- Once we've got it, we forget about keeping it.
- And it disappears based on factors we can't know or see.

The term *buy-in* is so vague. It drives us nuts. Think about it: What really is buy-in? Nobody knows, but everyone thinks they have it. Once they've got it, they forget about keeping it. And best of all, it can disappear without warning based on factors they cannot see.

Buy-in is ephemeral, perhaps even mythological, and yet we end up building mission-critical or life-changing decisions on top of it. Which is foolish, when you think about it. And so, to make Durable Decisions possible without buying into the idea of "buy-in," we created this framework:

UBAD is a four-part approach and diagnostic model that stands for Understanding, Belief, Advocacy, and Decision-Making. Each component is important to creating and maintaining durable support for our decisions.

The UBAD model starts with how we *build* support:

- **Understanding**—Stakeholders need to understand what it is you're proposing. Any decision that's made without understanding is highly vulnerable.
- **Belief**—If you want to accomplish bold things, you're going to need allies. Once a person understands your thinking, you need to help them believe in it. That means hearing objections, exploring concerns, and satisfying curiosity.

The top half of the UBAD model reveals whether we *have* support:

- **Advocacy**—The best feeling is when you hear one of your stakeholders telling someone else about your thing, explaining it correctly, and suggesting they look into it. When someone is putting their social capital on the line to further the idea, you know that they must truly support it.

- **Decision-Making**—The ultimate test is, are people making decisions in support of your idea? This represents the most enduring form of support.

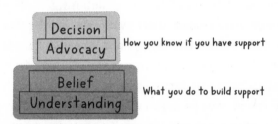

Like buy-in, UBAD is about getting people to support your ideas and proposals. It's about moving your agenda forward. Where it differs is in its specificity. With UBAD, you provide stakeholders what they need to legitimately support your idea (Understanding and Belief), and you have an ability to know whether you have it by testing (Advocacy and Decision-Making).

Now, in order for any decision to hold, the group making that decision *must* have both understanding and belief. Which is why those two steps come first in UBAD. And in this context, "understanding" doesn't just mean reading a bullet point on a slide and allowing it to register in your brain. It means exploring possible misalignments by asking follow-up questions, clarifying definitions of key terms to ensure everyone is on the same page, and ensuring that the facts align with everyone's interpretation of them. Understanding means digging in.

The digging is crucial because, without it, everyone makes assumptions. Janice experienced this when she met with a CEO she'd been advising for several years. This woman had a sophisticated, deep tech startup that was hiring phenomenal people, raising capital, and doing really well. But at a breakfast meeting, Janice could tell she was uneasy. The CEO had lined up a slew of important investor meetings for the rest of her day, so Janice asked, "Are you nervous?"

And she said, "Yes, I am." Then she started crying.

Sensing that her assumption about the investor meetings might've been wrong, Janice asked a few probing, clarifying questions. In short order, she discovered that the CEO felt great about her startup and work life but was struggling to balance the responsibilities of running her company and running her household. Her husband was an active participant in their home, but she still felt like she bore most of the family duties and had some guilt for leaving home to fly to San Francisco for business meetings. Janice helped her manage that stress and surface some solutions, but the salient point is this: the assumed source of discomfort (work) was *not* the true source of discomfort (home and work/life balance). Real understanding always requires follow-up.

This is, in part, because no two people will *ever* have the exact same understanding of an idea/experience/relationship, and this difference in understanding leads to different beliefs. We draw conclusions from information based on our politics, our personal allegiances, our friendships, our cultures, our aspirations, and all sorts of other belief systems. So if we trust ourselves to generate full understanding using only our own perspective, we will inevitably make biased judgment calls.

It's also fully possible for people to understand something but still not believe that it is the right thing to do! That can manifest as pretending, playing politics, lying, or even "going along to get along." If people understand that an idea is popular or favored by someone powerful, they may pretend to have belief in order to protect themselves. But when the time comes to commit resources and act, those folks will back down fast.

Understanding without belief can also manifest as a divergence of interpretations or opinions.

In the context of UBAD, belief means one of two things:

1. Enthusiasm for moving forward
                    OR
2. Shared understanding and a willingness to move forward *despite a lack of enthusiasm*. (This is a principle called "disagree and commit" that we'll explore in-depth in chapter thirteen.)

SIGNALS THAT *U* AND *B* ARE SECURED

Although buy-in and UBAD have many fundamental differences, they share one key feature: they both require exploration and observation. As a leader, you need to put yourself in charge of walking through all four steps, using each as a vetting process for your ideas and endeavors. You need to do the legwork, discussion-leading, and investigation to find out how people are thinking about whatever you're proposing. We recommend ensuring that *U* and *B* are well covered before moving on to *A* or *D*. But just how do you know if decision-makers understand and believe in an idea or project?

Start by honing your observation skills.

Before you do anything else, you need to feel certain that you've secured understanding, and this can be trickier than many leaders realize. Again, you're looking for comprehension that goes beyond the surface level—you don't just want people to grasp the concept; you want them to see the scope, imagine the ripple effects, consider the impact it will have on resources. You want them to think about it from multiple angles and bring their unique perspectives to bear on it. So how do you know if people understand (or are working to understand) your idea? Listen to the questions they ask: Are they smart questions? Do they probe for salient details, or ask for more information about specific elements instead of keeping everything big picture? Notice how they react to your responses to their questions: Do they seem confused? Relieved? Invested? Detached? And observe whether they're deeply engaged in conversation about the idea: Are they curious and expanding their own understanding, or just listening passively?

Once you've observed people's grasp of the concept—in meetings, in casual conversation, in one-on-ones, and elsewhere—you need to begin gauging their levels of belief. How do you know if people believe in your idea? Watch to see if they are advocating for it, resourcing it, or taking action on it independently. Observe if they're saying things about it privately, working together, planning, and prioritizing with you. All of those are evidence of belief. They're more active than signals of understanding, and more collaborative. When people understand something, they may keep it to themselves; when they believe in something, they're more likely to share it with others.

Once you start seeing these signals of *U* and *B*, that's when the *A* and *D* of UBAD can come into play.

The *A* stands for Advocacy, which, in this context, means people going to bat for the idea or project of their own accord. How are people talking about it? What do they say when they think you're not listening? What do they say on Slack or internal chat about it? Are they swaying the opinions of others and marshaling resources? Are they eloquently and accurately telling the story of it? If they are, that means they're putting some social capital on the line to advance the concept, which is a good indicator that you've got advocacy going on.

Way back in chapter one, we introduced you to Wanda Brown, sales genius, and it's time to circle back to her again now. Wanda practiced a style of sales that used "gestures of increasing commitment" to measure advocacy. As she worked with a potential client, she'd ask if they would introduce her to someone in their network—a form of advocacy. She'd ask if they'd be willing to speak to their manager or boss about what she was selling; if they actually did it, another form of advocacy. She was testing the waters to see if the client would advocate on her behalf within their organization. If they weren't willing to do that, that indicated there was not yet strong, durable support. She didn't have the foundation of advocacy she needed to move forward with the sale.

In which case, her course of action was to go back and build more understanding so she could continue cultivating stronger belief. Other leaders have taken a similar approach when testing the waters on new endeavors. We are both trainers and practitioners of an approach to innovation called The Lean Startup, which was developed by Eric Ries. In our experiences with that community, we come across many such stories. In one, a medical device company had an idea for a new piece of equipment that would cost hundreds of thousands of dollars. Before they invested in developing and building it, they wanted to make sure they had the support they needed to actually sell it. The CEO identified the five medical groups in the country that could benefit immediately from this piece of equipment and set up meetings with his contacts within those groups. He gave them his sales pitch, and they all loved the idea. They couldn't say enough good things about it. So he asked each of them, "Would you be willing to send a letter to your chief administrator recommending this piece of equipment?"

Every one of them said "no" after that initial meeting. He thought he had U and B, since they expressed understanding and belief, but because they were unwilling to advocate for the solution, he saw that they didn't believe in the solution strongly enough. So he hadn't quite made it to A.

The CEO went back to the drawing board, created a new value proposition, set up a new round of meetings with those customers, and said, how about now? Still no. He continued to iterate, tweaking various variables—the price, the value, the bullet points outlining the machine's benefits—until all his contacts weren't just excited about the machine themselves, they were willing to advocate for it. They were willing to send a letter to their chief administrators recommending its purchase.

Now for the plot twist. The CEO was thrilled to have reached this level of support but, knowing that the machine would be a massive investment on both his side and the customer side, he decided to do a bit more exploration and negotiation. The medical device he was proposing wasn't something that people wore or had surgically implanted like a pacemaker. This was more like an MRI machine or scanner, something that needed its own space and dedicated techs to run it. The CEO decided to get at least three of his customers—the ones who were already willing to advocate for the idea by sending letters to their chief administrators—to allocate funds and make plans to build brand-new rooms to house these unbuilt machines. Even better if they started planning to hire new staff or train existing employees to operate them.

Three companies proved they were willing to put money toward housing these huge devices. And *that's* when the medical device company started to develop the machine itself.

The CEO had nailed down U, B, and A. He'd also made some serious progress toward D: taking action and committing to a path. The client was assigning resources, creating a timeline, and moving forward, so he could too. If no one had been willing to start assigning people to do the work or invest in the resources needed to proceed, then our CEO would have known that something was amiss, even though he had garnered enough understanding, belief, and advocacy to get those letters sent to the chief administrators. Decisions about allocating money and people power is where the rubber hits the road. If stakeholders slam on the brakes when asked to contribute resources, you likely don't have the levels of understanding, belief, and advocacy you need to see this through. Going back and cultivating more U, B, and A will reveal what's preventing people from committing fully to the decision.

BRYON KROGER: HOW UBAD HELPED TRANSFORM THE AIR FORCE

When Bryon Kroger was just a captain in the United States Air Force, he cofounded Kessel Run, an experimental software lab that transformed the Air Force and defined "DevSecOps" for the entire Department of Defense. You have to understand, Air Force captains are not usually in a position to take generals to school. But for two years, that became Bryon's job—challenging, explaining, teaching, and advocating for software development best practices in an organization that had only ever purchased software from massively expensive outside contractors. He continues to champion a digital transformation within the DoD from his consulting company, Rise8, "to help change agents reinvent government software organizations and deliver a future where fewer bad things happen because of bad software."

Bottom Line Up Front

You have to take responsibility for driving the understanding and belief necessary for others to make good decisions.

After a particularly frustrating week, when our leadership had just made some really bad decisions around HR and resourcing changes that we needed to grow our culture, I was incredibly frustrated. I told Jason, "I just can't get these people to make the right decisions." He walked up to the whiteboard and wrote down UBAD, and he said, "Bryon, you keep thinking it's their bad, but it's actually YOU-bad saying that."

I heard this saying once about how fault and responsibility don't go together—none of these things are your fault, but it's your responsibility to do something about them if you actually want to create change. And so you look at all the challenges in the Department of Defense, literally not a single one of those things was my fault, or my organization's. But we had to take responsibility for them in order to create change.

And that's what UBAD gets at—it's not your fault that these people are making bad decisions, but it's your responsibility. And we weren't taking responsibility in the way that we needed to; we were just complaining. If "they" don't make the decisions you want, what are you going to do about it?

That's when Jason walked me through the steps of UBAD. First you need to drive that understanding that's going to create belief. And belief is what creates advocacy, which in turn drives durable, long-lasting decisions. You need a level of advocacy that drives decisions. Because that's the other thing I was complaining about. Even when I could get people to make decisions, it felt like "leadership by who I spoke to last." I would get General So-and-So to make a decision, then they would go talk to the two-star general and reverse their decision. They were always waffling back and forth.

UBAD was the solution to both of my problems, and that led us to a very different path where we focused on doing the work. We went from, "Hey, the work's going to speak for itself," to really focusing on understanding. I had to become a storyteller and learned to use the terms my stakeholders knew. With UBAD, it's important to speak the language of the people you're trying to reach. Because you'll never get to the "understand" part speaking your own jargon.

And that drives me to the second thing that I've learned. I was always assuming I wanted people to take *my* understanding and get to *my* belief. My method of driving understanding was just to talk *at* people and explain, explain, explain. Somebody told me that the ultimate form of empathy is not even asking somebody to change in the first place, but just meeting them where they are. Now I try to understand the level of proof required for certain people to believe in a product or an idea.

I've had trouble describing this, how we accomplished what we did. Adam Furtado and I were very normal people. Like, painfully normal

> people. The organization we started, Kessel Run, began with six people, and by the time I left, it was a five-hundred-person organization and created huge ripple effects across and even outside of the Air Force.

HOW TO USE UBAD AS AN EVERYDAY LEADER

UBAD is a diagnostic model. Using it helps you determine if your group is ready to take action together. That's why we've suggested circling back to previous levels when you hit a wall. Doing so is the best possible way to diagnose what's missing, misaligned, or misunderstood. Assuming that you're a leader who wants to create decisions that everyone can live with, how do you use UBAD with the groups and teams you lead?

Start by creating opportunities for understanding. When you know who your stakeholders are, gather them, explain your idea, then give them the floor and allow them to poke at the information so they can work through their questions. Give them the additional details they need to start building belief on their own.

To reinforce belief, figure out what the objections are and begin to workshop them together. Your team or family might be stuck for important reasons that merit exploring and doing so together can only help build belief. Remember that an objection is a request for information and, as a leader, it's your responsibility to help others get the information they need to make sound decisions. Don't try to persuade or shift into sales mode. As the person seeking support, you need to have empathy for the viewpoints of others and remain as judgment-free as you possibly can. Listen, encourage active questioning, and share information as a group to see if doing so addresses any objections. Remember, too, that belief flows from deeper understanding, but so does reinforced disbelief: if exploring objections causes someone to dig into their stance, respect that. Leverage the Brains in earnest, and lead with shared outcomes in mind.

To encourage advocacy, you'll want to do many of the same things you'd do to reinforce belief, but go a step further and ask explicitly if group members would be willing to promote the idea to other people. (Like Wanda did in Chapter 1 when she asked the party chair if he wanted her to take over.) Doing this may uncover additional objections that are impeding belief or reveal gaps in understanding. Either way, the most important question to ask when you're testing for advocacy is "why?" If you ask, "Will you promote my idea to others?" and the response is, "No," your next step *must be* to ask, "Will you help me understand why? What would need to change for you to feel differently?" Listen and ask more questions. Make changes to your plans or positioning statements (as our medical device CEO did), then circle back and find out if group members are more willing to advocate for the revised idea.

To propel the group toward a decision, reflect what you're hearing back to everyone. Express your honest observations about or assessments of current sentiment. If there are two camps, say so and talk about how you might become more fully aligned. If everyone is gravitating toward an option or action, point out that you seem to be approaching a decision. When you reach this point in UBAD, people may continue to discuss and ask questions even though they've made their minds up (as we'll explore in chapter thirteen). Be a compassionate leader and tell them what you're seeing and hearing. Doing so may curb unnecessary tail-chasing.

Then reiterate whose decision it is—who will make the final call—and ask, "If we were to go in this direction, could everyone live with that?" Point out the extent to which a decision has already coalesced, but also leave room for any lingering or suppressed concerns. If any such hesitations pop up, say, "Are there other things that need resolving?" If so, address them. If not, place authority where it belongs, support decision-makers in Leveraging the Brains of the smart people around them, and forge ahead together.

UBAD takes more work at the start than buy-in, but saves you work in the end. If you trust buy-in and end up with a flimsy, barely supported decision, you'll have to backtrack much later down the road and potentially start from scratch after investing time, effort, and resources. UBAD asks leaders to do their due diligence at every step and iteratively, which can feel laborious midstream, but is also both prudent and collaborative. This tool allows you to lead with shared outcomes in mind instead of pushing your own agenda, all while Leveraging the Brains of those around you. If you ask us, that's the very definition of leading with less ego and more impact.

Workshop with Janice:
USE UBAD TO DIAGNOSE A DECISION FAILURE

This workshop puts UBAD to work as a diagnostic model. Think about the project we started working on at the beginning of this book. We haven't really touched on it since the Kanban. Is there a high-stakes decision coming up for your project? Or perhaps one was recently made.

Most of what we do in workshops falls into a category I refer to as "semi-structured critical thinking." That's what we're going to do for this workshop. To get started, pull out a notebook or blank paper and set aside fifteen minutes where you won't be interrupted. Even better if you can give it thirty minutes. For simplicity of instruction, I'll assume you're working with an upcoming decision.

1. First, let's explore the dark side. Imagine that a decision has been made. Who might be the detractors? List them. There may be different folks depending on which way the decision goes. Put them all on the list. Think about folks who needed to approve the decision, those who could veto the decision on a technicality, people whose watercooler talk (or politicking) could sway opinion, people who might be threatened by one or another outcome, people who might be afraid.

2. Now, let's explore the light: Who are the current champions of one option or another? Who tends to be an influential voice in these matters?

3. Read down your list and consider, is this person a lynchpin? Circle up to five names. These are the folks that you want to focus on.

4. For each of the five people, you need to know if they Understand the question at hand and the decision options. Rate each one on a scale of 1–7 for their level of understanding. 1 = does not understand, 7 = totally understands. (Be careful, because if they only understand one option but are closed off to other options, there may be conflict later. Best if everyone understands the advantages and disadvantages of all the viable options.)

5. Same again, but this time for Belief. 1 = does not believe in any particular option, 7 = totally sold on an option.

6. Now, ask yourself for each person's scores, how do you know? When they talk, do they frame the question and options accurately and effectively? This is part of advocacy. Have they already started making decisions that are in alignment with the decision? These behaviors are evidence of Understanding and Belief. After considering the evidence, you might need to change a few scores, so do that now.

7. Identify a small handful of spots in this picture where it's important to strengthen someone's Understanding or Belief. How might you do that? Is it best done on a one-on-one conversation? Or perhaps a group setting?

8. Make an explicit plan and then act on it.

Chapter 13

ALIGNMENT VS. AGREEMENT

Several years ago, Jason was selected to serve on a jury in a criminal case at the San Francisco County court. The defendant was charged with selling narcotics and pleaded not guilty. The only witnesses were two police officers who told the jury that the narcotics had been purchased from the defendant by an undercover police officer. They testified to a chain of custody, meaning the police had eyes on the defendant the whole time.

In criminal cases, a unanimous verdict from the jury is required for either conviction or acquittal. Anything else is deemed a hung jury, which leads to disbanding the current jury, reappointing new jurors, and starting the trial all over again. The court will keep doing that until they get a unanimous jury decision, which is costly and time-consuming. This is also one of the reasons that jurors for criminal cases are screened for bias; every juror should be capable of making a decision based on the evidence presented.

Jason and his fellow jurors were told that witness testimony is equivalent to hard evidence and to treat it as such. The jury had elected Jason to be foreman, and when they assembled in the jury room, he led them in discussing everything that had been presented to them during the trial. Then he asked them, "Who votes guilty in this?" Nine people raised their hands, ten including Jason himself. He asked, "Who votes to acquit?" And as the first group put their hands down, the two remaining jurors raised their hands. There was a split of ten to two.

Using every tool in his facilitator's toolbox and respecting all viewpoints, Jason worked with the jurors for a few hours to help them describe why they felt as they did. He spent an hour enabling the two not-guilty jurors to say as much as they could about where they were having trouble agreeing with the majority decision. He led the group in discussing the evidence again and took another vote. Nobody had changed their vote.

For the not-guilty voters, the problem sat with the jury instruction. Their experiences and beliefs made them unable to accept the idea that police officers would not lie on the witness stand. And with only police testimony for evidence, they didn't feel that the case for conviction was strong enough.

Consensus is hard. Good, smart, benevolent people can legitimately hold different interpretations of the same facts. People come to the table with complex belief systems and life experiences, and no amount of skillful facilitation or leadership can change that. *Nor should it.* Varied perspectives are a strength, bringing issues to light that would've been overlooked or ignored by a homogenous group.

In the case of a criminal jury trial, consensus is appropriately required. So the group had to go back into the courtroom and inform the judge that they were a hung jury, unable to make a unanimous decision.

Thankfully, most group decisions are not criminal jury verdicts, so unanimity is off the menu. So many teams and families mistakenly believe that everyone must be in complete agreement before action can be taken! This is simply untrue. Durable Decisions are fully possible without consensus, but they absolutely require alignment.

WHAT'S ALIGNMENT? AND HOW IS IT DIFFERENT FROM AGREEMENT?

When people agree, they hold the same opinion on a certain matter. When people align, they may or may not hold the same opinion, but they are willing to overlook those differences to work together to achieve a shared goal.

Alignment happens when we all understand the direction we're headed in, and we're all willing to support it. Being aligned means saying, "Yes, I get it. Let's move out. Sometimes I get my way, sometimes you get yours. It's all good."

Alignment can also happen even if some participants don't agree that going in a certain direction together is "the *right* thing to do" or "the *best* decision." Words like *right* and *best* only apply when we need to agree, a state in which we believe (often falsely) that everyone involved is 100 percent on board. **Aligning leaves room for dissent, so long as everyone involved agrees to move forward regardless.**

Instead of bludgeoning everyone into agreement, we believe that smart people can disagree. And if we're humble enough, we'll admit that sometimes our own beliefs around "the right thing to do" turn out to be hilariously (embarrassingly, painfully) off base. Only when we create environments that make disagreement (and being super wrong) feel totally safe can we hope to uncover the best possible options for all involved. You make progress faster with a lot less drama.

For most decisions, it is far better to be mostly right and move forward boldly than it is to be 100 percent in agreement and stalled out. In the case of Jason's jury, someone's life was literally on the line, making it one of the rare instances in which consensus is a good idea. But when the decision in question is, "Which hotel should we book for our team off-site," who gives a crap if it's the perfect decision?

What's needed most often is for everyone to be heard and understood, and for someone to just make a f*cking decision. So, while agreement means we all agree that this is the right thing to do, alignment means we understand the direction we're taking and we don't hate it so much that we will stand in the way.

Which is rooted in the philosophy of "disagree and commit."

DISAGREE AND COMMIT

We've already told you the problem with consensus: It's hard. Often too hard to actually reach, even with a group that's like-minded and amiable.

Venture capital (VC) investors know this, so they intentionally avoid consensus. Their approach is diametrically opposed to that of a criminal trial jury. Venture capital investors love to invest in really disruptive ideas and they also like to make giant piles of money. (They're called venture capitalists, not venture socialists. I'll be here all week.) They're looking for big returns, and one way they identify a high potential idea is to look for concepts that inspire extreme views over high conviction and low consensus. Meaning some people believe the company will be totally huge, and other people believe the concept is a hole into which they will pour money.

When they find such an idea, they also find tension within their own ranks. Say one voting partner at a capital firm brought a solar-powered roller skates company to the partner table. That partner thought it was genius! But others believed it was complete lunacy. That disagreement is considered a positive result. The strength of conviction and disagreement is one of their signals that a concept might be worth investing in.

That's where "disagree and commit" comes in. VCs accept that world-changing ideas are often so far ahead of their time that they look preposterous, and to get on board at the right time you need to be willing to trust the vocal minority. They're often willing to vote "yes" on investments they don't fully believe in because they're always looking for the radical new thing that has value unrecognized by the masses.

DAVID KIDDER: TRUST ACCELERATES PROGRESS

David Kidder is one of those kinetic leaders who processes and synthesizes input so quickly, you feel like you're standing still even when you're running as fast as you can to keep up. He is generous, warm, kind, emotional, and vibrant. He has proven over and over that you don't have to be ruthless to "win"—you can be wildly successful by leading relentlessly from a place of love. He's the founder of multiple successful startups, author of a NY Times best-selling book series, and a brilliant, humble, imperfect, resilient human.

Janice: Tell me one thing about how you lead.
I don't even think of it as "I'm going to lead you." I'm more like "I am *with* you and we are going there together." Despite all of my imperfections, which are many, I think people know that I really love them. I care. I may be busy, but they know, I just care: I'm in. And it's not just for the company—I keep relationships forever. I think that's really underneath all of my thoughts on leadership. If you're at my funeral, I hope the people would say, "I know he loved me. He really was there. How I felt when I was with him is that he really was with me and he loved me and we were in it together."

Janice: How do you do that—lead with love? There had to be people who just didn't work out.
I've had employees that I really care about who were just, you know, heretics. What do you do? Of course, I've had to let some of them go, and they needed that from me. I did not want to. It cost me something, it cost the company something, but it was the right decision. It was actually the right decision for their own growth. You've got to be pretty f*cking fearless to love people.

Janice: Tell me about "disagree and commit."
Disagree and commit is a tool that tests and fosters trust. It was first used by Scott McNealy, and notably by Jeff Bezos.

In the last two or three companies where I've been CEO, I've thought of the leadership team as something like a set of puzzle pieces. The pieces had very little overlap, and together they created a complete set of talent and skill needed to deliver on the company's purpose. We can challenge how those roles, those puzzle pieces, are carved up, but "disagree and commit" means that what's in each person's puzzle piece is theirs. Each person's moral obligation is to use their superpower to lead that area of business.

You need to make really good decisions, but you can't run a team by consensus. So we ask, what's the consequence of getting this decision wrong? If a decision is inconsequential or easily reversed, we spend very little time in the debate phase. If it's in your domain of expertise, your puzzle piece, then you need to be able to say, "We've debated this enough. I think we need to disagree and commit."

That's where it becomes a test of trust: Does that person have the moral authority to make that call? Do we trust them? If we don't, then we should talk about why we don't.

Getting to this level of examination is super important because mistrust is the source of corrosive, malignant cultural issues. If we're spending a lot of time second-guessing someone's domain expertise and decision-making, then maybe they're the wrong person. Or maybe they're the iconoclast that creates productive friction.

But if we spend all that time and energy on every decision, it becomes one big fog of lack of trust and lack of accountability and lack of ownership. You have to put people in their superpowers and let them own it. You want consent, not consensus.

"Disagree and commit" is just a decision architecture that signals the deeper issue: Do we really trust each other? And do we trust the person occupying the puzzle piece, which creates a collective whole that can live out the purpose of the company?

UNDERSTAND THE LANDSCAPE OF OPTIONS

And here is where we come back to Wanda Brown, profiled in chapter one. Wanda taught us that, in order to get people to pursue a course of action together, you have to lead them through a set of steps. Virtually all humans will first innately seek to understand the options. Then they want to structure the landscape. Once they understand the structure of the options, then they can match up their needs with the available options. From there, they start throwing options overboard, then they choose. The process is pretty linear.

Over the years, we've seen that Wanda's steps apply to pretty much all people and all decisions. We've also learned that if you try to circumvent this process, things go sideways. You end up going back to the steps you skipped, torturing yourself with "what ifs." When you don't let folks explore options, or when they don't understand how those options relate to each other, they won't fully support the final decision. They may even feel like they were railroaded into that decision. This is why it's possible to go too fast. Creating alignment requires us, as leaders, to help our team members, family members, or stakeholders understand their range of options and what those options represent. We need to support them in matching those options with their needs, eliminating the options that don't fit, and making informed choices. Because when people feel comfortable about and confident in that process, they're way less likely to backpedal or panic. They commit.

Exploring and understanding options is critical to making Durable Decisions. It is more critical than honing in on the one option that you select in the end because confidence springs from a belief that the gamut of alternatives has been explored. Even a cursory understanding of the things we didn't choose and why we didn't choose them underpins our ability to fully embrace the things we *did* choose. It's just the way we're wired.

This goes back to our observation that people stop talking when they feel misunderstood. Short-changing the exploration of options can leave people feeling unheard and misunderstood. Or even like they've been manipulated, especially if you're asking them to align around a decision that they don't entirely agree with.

As we have experienced Wanda's insight over decades, we have come to believe in its universality. It forms the backbone of most decision-making models. For instance, back in chapter eight, we introduced you to a two-meeting model created by Michael Mankins, a leader at Bain & Company. The first meeting in that model is dedicated to exploring facts and options. It allows stakeholders to present cases for how they believe that money should be spent. The second meeting is about decisions and commitments. It's scheduled for about two weeks after the first, which gives everyone ample time to discuss options offline, explore questions and concerns, and decide how they want to proceed.

Consider the overlap with Wanda's model, where you start with the problem that you want to solve, explore a wide range of options, structure that set of options, and once you turn a corner you begin eliminating options.

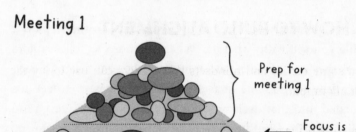

Meeting 1

Prep for
meeting 1

Focus is
here

•"These are the options to debate"
•"These are the salient facts"

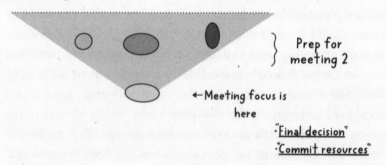

Meeting 2

Prep for
meeting 2

←Meeting focus is
here

•"Final decision"
•"Commit resources"

In Mankins's model, the first meeting is focused on exploring options, too: stakeholders research their facts then present their cases to the group. The group discusses options that match those facts and cases and begins to winnow them down. When the first meeting ends, everyone has a chance to go off and do their own independent research and raise objections and have conversations offline. That interstitial time enables stakeholders to come back and make a choice that they can all align around.

We'd wager that any decision-making model omitting these steps will lead to fragile, untenable decisions. The kind that lack solid and genuine alignment.

HOW TO BUILD ALIGNMENT

We've identified some tactics and mindsets that leaders can use to lay the groundwork for alignment.

Act in Service to the Team

This is about temporarily setting aside any need to persuade and neutralizing your own bias or point of view. (And your ego.) In Jason's jury foreman experience, he never attempted to seize "power" or exert control. After the group gathered outside the courtroom, he noticed no one was speaking or taking charge, so he tried to help everyone reach some decisions. He said, "The bailiff just told us to figure out lunch and choose a foreman. It's getting late, so maybe we should do lunch first. Does that sound good to everyone? Great. So how should we choose a foreman?" And the group unanimously selected Jason. By framing what needed to be done, asking questions that helped everyone Orient Honestly, and making it clear he wanted to Leverage the Brains instead of being a dictator, he earned instant trust. Jason wasn't pushing an agenda or jockeying for power; he was acting in service to the team by de-centering himself and centering shared progress. To be a valuable and collaboration-centered leader, you've got to let go of the notion that you'll always know what to do in every situation no matter what. Practice facilitative leadership instead of directive leadership. (It's also *much* easier for people to Orient Honestly when discussions are persuasion-free.)

Release Pressure

When people feel pressured to fall in line, their defenses go up. Their brains close off as an act of self-protection. To Make Durable Decisions together, you need participants to remain open to possibilities. We've found that the simplest way to release this pressure is to offer an "invitation *not* to buy" (thanks again, Wanda); present them with an easy out, and make sure to do so before they've even expressed which way they're leaning.

This might sound like, "I don't know if it's right for us to pursue this project as a team, but perhaps if I could ask everyone a few questions, we could figure that out together." That first part is critically important because it shows that everyone is on the same side, working toward the same goal of understanding. No one is trying to persuade. We're really trying to figure out together what would be best for us all. That framing for conversation will get people engaged, and engagement cuts a quick path to alignment. You may have a situation where there really isn't a choice. In this case, talk it through anyway. You might surface valuable information that will help you move forward later, and if nothing else, you'll earn trust with your team by helping them externalize their concerns.

Ask Processing Questions

This is another activity that requires leaders to focus on facilitation. Try to help participants reveal how they are mulling and organizing the decision in their own heads. Engaging each other in a direct discussion of mental processing enables everyone to think through what information or proof they require in order to come to a decision. Questions might include, "Can you tell me more about that idea?" or "Would you share how you decided that?"

When we were thinking about buying a new car, we started by asking ourselves, "What do we need to know in order to make an informed purchase?" We agreed that we should make some lists: the characteristics that we would like in a new car, and so on. We talked about moving on from there to internet research, and then test drives. We asked questions about thought processes and the micro decisions that needed to be made. We nodded to affirm each other's suggestions. We echoed what the other had said to ensure we understood each other fully. We processed together, and that helped us remain in alignment. It's not that we always agreed. It's that we always understood.

Processing questions enable self-reflection, which is an essential part of individuals making decisions on their own. To the extent that we are leading people, we are helping them know themselves in a way that moves the whole organization forward.

Enable Micro Decisions

Forcing people to hold the "big picture" from start to finish can induce panic. It will exhaust them mentally and emotionally, while preventing the group from making meaningful progress together. Instead, remember that making many small agreements will lead to alignment.

To go back to our car-buying example, "What car should we buy?" is a big, bold question. And one that we weren't ready to answer without tackling a few micro decisions first. What's our price range? Do we care where the car was manufactured? Do we need a moonroof? Those smaller considerations were ones we felt comfortable addressing right away.

Breaking down a huge decision into smaller decisions lowers the stakes. It enables participants to be honest about their opinions and enables leaders to ferret out areas of innate agreement. This simplifies the work of creating alignment by creating clarity and reducing the scope of disagreement. It also fosters excitement as group members see how smaller agreements build upward toward the bigger picture.

Observe Out Loud When a Decision Is Near

This may sound simplistic or odd, but here's the thing. Frequently, people will keep talking even when alignment has been reached. We don't notice and we don't shut up. We just keep talking for hours (or days, or weeks). So, as a leader, sensitivity to "the done deal" is an essential skill. Keep your finger on the pulse of the discussion, recognize when people are expressing agreement, and ask, "Is it possible that there's a decision here?"

We facilitated a meeting of a large, publicly traded internet firm. It was just before the company's IPO and about eighty leaders were gathering for the annual strategy session where they laid out their objectives for the coming year. Participants were working in groups of ten people, and one group was completely stuck, unable to make any progress toward alignment. Janice asked them to explain what was up, and they spent a solid ten minutes outlining a very complicated set of considerations. There were basically two options on the table, and the group was leaning toward one of them. So she asked, "Can you tell me how many people at this table are comfortable with option one?" Nine out of ten raised their hands. "How about option two?" Just one person signaled. So she said, "Well, it's possible that this second option is really important. Maybe we should hear it out." And she turned to the sole objector and asked him how important it was to stick to option two, and would he be willing to accept the option that everybody else was supporting. He told her, "Oh yeah, I just wanted to make sure we explored all the angles and options. I'd be totally fine with the first option."

They had been talking about this for over an hour. They probably would've kept talking for another hour if Janice hadn't intervened. All they needed was someone to say, "Are we good?" and they could stop talking.

Request Objections

Any objections people raise are really requests for information in disguise. When you, as a leader, encourage them to express their hesitations and questions, you help them articulate what is concerning them. Be as neutral as possible when you do this so they can raise objections without fear. You can try something like, "Who here would be uncomfortable with this direction?" Or ask, "What else do we need to know to make a decision?" which allows folks with objections to articulate them without feeling put on the spot.

To Reduce Drama, Honor Objections

As a leader, it's in your best interest to be objective, which means giving any objections their due. When Janice was at the strategy meeting facilitating the one table of stakeholders, she did this. Only one out of ten people had any concerns, but instead of dismissing those concerns and plowing ahead, she sincerely considered the possibility that he was flagging something valuable and legitimate. She didn't default to "majority rules." She honored what he had brought to the table. Often minority points of view are more accurate. Leaders should assume that every single person in the decision-making process is bringing their best self to bear. Use strategically placed, open-ended, and closed-ended questions to help people articulate their ideas and to curtail wasteful conversation.

Test Alignment

When you're starting to turn a corner toward a decision, don't just lean into it. Make sure that you've got true alignment by asking some key questions; ones that allow people to think through their stances and voice any lingering concerns. Determine the right test to run to determine if you're making a choice that everyone can support. Remember that they don't need to agree with the decision. They don't need to like the decision, or even feel comfortable with it. They need to *be willing to support* the decision.

Some of the test questions we use include, "Could you live with it if we went this way?" "What's at risk if we did this?" "Are there any final points we need to consider?" You don't need to keep poking until someone dredges up an objection, but you also shouldn't gloss over this step. Alignment will withstand testing. That's the whole point.

ALIGNMENT STARTS AT THE BEGINNING

Alignment shouldn't be an afterthought. It's not something you can do as a separate activity; it's a natural outcome of working in an inclusive, humane way. It's a by-product of genuine collaboration and humble leadership.

When you get comfortable using the leadership methods we've shared in this book, your awareness of other people will naturally and steadily increase. That awareness will help you notice when alignment is strong or weak, when agreement is present or absent, when actions are aligned or misaligned. And that awareness allows you to make small adjustments while everyone is working through a project or decision together, rather than sneaking in some monolithic alignment exercise at the tail end.

As a leader, do your best to build alignment from the very beginning: framing the questions, listening and de-centering yourself, and Leveraging the Brains to Make Durable Decisions. When you do, you'll be able to move organically toward the best possible outcomes with ease, grace, and good humor.

Workshop with Janice:
DISAGREE AND COMMIT

No way! This is our last workshop together!

I hope you've been able to make real, tangible progress throughout this series of activities. The one idea I'd like you to take away from the workshop portion of this book is that a workshop is just semi-structured critical thinking. You can craft a workshop anytime, simply by taking a moment to consider how you might prompt some good thinking to move a group from Point A to Point B. Now, let's close out this chapter by looking at decision-making styles.

At the start of the book, you chose a project to focus on for the workshops. Perhaps you've shifted to another project, or maybe you're not "doing" the workshops, just reading and thinking about them. But just for this one, I want you to really remember where you were. If you can, pull out the work you did way back in the chapter one workshop. That was the one where you wrote down a big list of all the challenges you were facing.

1. Scan down the list of problems, and circle all the ones that are resolved. Somehow, some way, they're done with.

2. Of the ones that are circled, put a star next to the ones that involved at least one big decision.

3. Of the Circle + Star items, put a big check mark over the ones where everyone was 100 percent in agreement with the big decision. What do you notice? Do you have any check marks at all? For any check marks, do you think everyone had the same level of enthusiasm for the decision that was made?

4. Now look at the items that are not circled. These are the challenges that are not yet resolved. Which ones involve big decisions? Mark those.

5. From the uncircled items, is there a particularly thorny decision coming up? Write a few sentences about the decision, the options on the table, and who is currently aligned with which option. Or, even better, grab a

partner who is also working on that thing and talk through the options, people, and their alignment.

6. Write (or discuss with a partner): What would be the likely consequences of going for full consensus? Of disagree and commit? Of one person just "making a call"? Perhaps you need to move really fast, so having someone just make the call could speed things up. Or, possibly, there would be dire consequences if you make the wrong decision (as in Jason's jury), so you need full consensus.

7. What is the right level of alignment for this decision?

EPILOGUE

Janice's laptop is getting old, but she doesn't want to replace it because of the sticker on the outside. It says "Regular People," and she's kept it in a prominent spot for several years. She does this to remember that regular people are spectacular. To remind others that super-special people who get to do super-special things aren't the ones making the world move. It's regular people in their regular lives who are making everything happen.

Regular people are the leaders that we're hoping to support with the ideas in this book. They're the leaders that we look up to in our personal and professional lives. Many of the leaders we admire didn't go to Stanford or Harvard or MIT; didn't have perfect GPAs; aren't  the heads of their companies. They think of themselves as regular people who just step up to create order and facilitate forward movement in their companies, families, communities, and lives. There are infinite contexts in which regular people are called on to lead.

Think of an elementary school parent-teacher organization: virtually everyone involved is just a regular person, someone who happens to be the parent or caregiver of a student and is willing to support the system that supports their kids. Think of the twenty-year customer service rep who has never been promoted but mentors every new hire to ensure they feel totally comfortable with the in-house systems. Think of the family member who swoops in to help organize a funeral in order to ease the burden on others. These people are regular people, and they are also amazing leaders.

We believe that leadership goes beyond inventing things, making money, and dreaming up world-altering ideas. Leadership is stepping forward and taking responsibility and doing so knowing that your choices will be highly visible to others. It's helping one or more people accomplish things that matter, part of which is understanding the outcome and framing it so it makes sense. It's organizing or structuring activity to make it as easy as possible for everyone involved.

Ease is increasingly valuable in our complex and fast-moving world. After all, life is hard. *Really* hard. And some of the ways in which we interact with each other make it even harder. Nobody needs that, especially right now. Whether it is political unrest or a pandemic or your first year with a new baby or a cancer diagnosis or studying for the bar exam, the challenges just keep coming. The world is changing so fast, and it's not going to slow down anytime soon. We need ways to be nimble even in a hyperdynamic environment. We need ways to understand and adapt to the current reality and to be effective in the current moment. And we desperately need ways to do all that without creating any more friction because life is hard, and it's also short. There's too much good stuff to do for us to sit in useless meetings or execute meaningless busywork. There's too much great music to listen to. There are too many naps that should be taken. Too many dogs to pet and donuts to eat and amazing outdoor spaces to explore. We need tools and mechanisms to navigate family, life, work, relationships, and the world around us compassionately and efficiently.

As regular people who lead, we can help ourselves and each other get through the hard times together as quickly and smoothly as possible.

Regardless of where you find yourself in the world, there will always be people around you who just want to go farther, move faster, and opt out of the drama. And you, a regular person, are fully equipped to lead them. You just need a deliberate, straightforward way to navigate those challenges yourself, and navigate challenges in community with other people.

Which is what we've given you.

GO FARTHER

With the ideas and strategies you've learned from these pages, you can be more effective. We know you're pretty effective already. But if you're anything like us, you've got some room to improve. The result of being more effective is that you'll waste less time and effort. And when you limit your wasted time and effort, you'll have more energy, which helps you think bigger, focus on high-impact activities, and go farther. You have more resources to make more progress, in all aspects of your life. As a more effective leader, maybe you'll be able to accomplish five things during a single meeting, instead of just one thing. Or maybe you'll have more capacity to support the growth of those around you, while simultaneously achieving your own goals. When you spend less of your time doing the wrong work, you get more bandwidth to do the right work.

Increasing your effectiveness as a leader will take self-reflection. You can't go farther as an individual or with a team if you can't recognize and articulate your destination. **Our approach to leadership asks people to focus on being decent human beings**, then allow themselves to mature as individuals. The mindfulness required to enable that kind of personal growth also helps people grow as leaders, which in turn helps them go farther, dream bigger, and achieve more.

MOVE FASTER

Using the skills and knowledge you've gleaned from this book will make things easier, and when things are easier you can move faster. You can narrow down options, select meaningful outcomes, and accomplish more in less time. More significantly, you know how to avoid doing the wrong work. Think of it this way: You need to retrieve the day's mail, your mailbox is at the end of a long driveway, and a snowstorm has just dumped eighteen inches of snow on the ground. You can certainly slog your way down the driveway in your boots and snow pants to get the mail, but you'll get there faster if you use the snowblower to clear everything off first. The right tools make progress easier and quicker.

As an everyday leader who has read these chapters, we hope you've accepted that you don't need to execute on everything yourself or be right all the time. Being released from that fallacy means you no longer feel isolated and pressured, a dire combination that can cause people to take fewer risks and (you guessed it) slow everything down.

And you don't expect anyone else to do everything or be right all the time, either. All leaders are tasked with making the best use of their people. That means preparing them to find answers no matter what happens, not expecting them to have "the right" answers ready at hand. The first is an adaptive skill; the second is a toxic fantasy. By sharing the load, you facilitate momentum; by Leveraging the Brains, you tap knowledge and skills that accelerate progress without draining people dry. You move faster, organically, and as an elegantly synchronized unit.

OPT OUT OF THE DRAMA

As leaders, we must recognize that everyone has feelings, and they come out in so many ways. People's emotional states and social abilities affect productivity, as individuals and in groups, and it's perilous to pretend this isn't the case.

What will reduce drama is de-centering yourself—when you're busily persuading and insisting you're right, you're moving away from alignment. If you're focused on preserving your power instead of prioritizing outcomes, then you're creating a dynamic in which any disagreement with your stance will produce friction.

Reducing drama means helping everyone put collective progress ahead of their own vanity. It means wanting to be really proud of the work that the team does instead of wanting to be proud of one's own cachet. **Opting out of drama means leading in such a way that no one, including yourself, feels the need to manufacture it.** Collaborating, listening, respecting, aligning, and being flexible all make this possible.

We almost titled this book *Swaggerless* because we wanted it to reach leaders who understand the value of leading without ego. You're one of them. Far too many people believe that leading is violent, being "on-target," "killing it," hacking a path through the world with a giant machete to achieve your reality-altering personal goals. That's Capital-L Leadership. That's the archetype we have held up as a society. It's not, however, an archetype of kindness.

Apply what you've learned. Do it daily if you can. Apply these ideas at home, in your community, with friends, on work projects both large and small. Teach them to others. Change the world by leading in ways that take us all farther, faster, and with far less drama.

ACKNOWLEDGMENTS

This book is twelve years in the making, so there are countless people to thank. If you contributed or supported us, please know we are grateful, even if we don't mention you by name.

First, thank you to Kate Rutter, our partner at LUXr and longtime friend. So many of the ideas in this book are the product of our decades-long collaboration. Your brain is the most delicious. We love you.

Thank you also to our agent, Joy Tutela, for believing in this book, seeing its potential, and pushing us to keep thinking better. You're real good.

Thank you to Sally McGraw, for everything always.

Massive gratitude to Matt Holt, Camille Cline, Katie Dickman, Brigid Pearson, and all the folks at Matt Holt & BenBella books. We feel seen! And to Nora Rosenberger for the beautiful illustrations.

Thank you to every Pivot, past and present, especially those who took facilitator training.

Thank you to everyone who shared their story with us for this book. Though so many of you are anonymous, every story mattered.

Also to our customers and clients, especially Chris B and Karen H, who taught Janice so much. And to Adam Furtado and Bryon Kroger, wizards of the first order. Thank you to the BOLD ladies, Christina Wodtke, Cindy Alvarez, Laura Klein, and Kate Rutter (again!) for being Janice's Old Girls Network for the past decade. Thank you to all of the LUXr-ians, who helped us figure out so many things. Thank you to Wanda Brown, whose epic wisdom changed the way we think about collaboration. Thank you to our career sponsors, Eric Ries, Josh Knowles, and David Kidder, who have brought us so many brilliant opportunities.

Thank you to the many and varied people of the U.S. Armed Forces and the U.S. federal government, for everything you do every day on behalf of the American people. Working with you has changed our lives. So many people never understand the real impact you have in the world.

Also thanks to our cheer squad: Tom, Sharon, Jenny, Jeana, Evan, Shuqiao Song, Aloka Penmetcha, Andi Plantenberg, Kim Dowd, Michele Perras, Paul Bernstein, and Catherine Pulling. We know that we can always count on you.

Thanks to the delivery folks who brought lunch nearly every day in the final months.

INDEX

externalize, organize, focus. *see* EOF
Extreme Programming Explained, Second Edition
    (Beck and Andres), 138–139

F
Facebook, 135
Facilitation, 163, 208, 253
    for alignment, 250
    of meetings, 180–182
    of 2x2, 202–206
fairness, in hiring, 136–137
fatigue, choice, 15
FedEx, 213
Fey, Tina, 131
fidgets, 52
filters, as facilitation tool, 180–182
Five Whys, 56–60, 63-64
flexibility, 90–91, 220, 221
focus
    in EOF, 152, 163–166
    in meetings, 183–184
    narrowing, with 2x2, 193
Ford, Henry, 88
Four Leadership Motions (4LM)
    about, 8–10, 21
    in conjunction, 158
    fractal nature of, 118
    purpose and benefits of, 10, 74
Frame the Problem, 138
Friedman, Milton, 105
Friedman Doctrine, 105
Fulghum, Robert, 46

G
Gantt charts, 89
The Gap, 53–54
gathering inputs, 216, 220
GIVE (Gentle, Interested, Validating, Easy), 67
Goals, in OGSM, 120
goal setting. *see also* Outcome Oriented
    Roadmapping
    in increments, 116
    mechanisms for. *see* goal-setting
        mechanisms
    micro-goals, creating, 117–118, 155
goal-setting mechanisms, 106, 119–123
    DIY Cascading Goaling, 123
    importance of, 119
    OGSM, 119–121
    OKR, 121–122
    V2MOM, 122
Google, 212

"Go Wide, Then Decide," 160-161
grooming outcomes, 117
grounded, staying, 55
group dynamics, 16-18, 20, 150, 186, 213, 222
Grove, Andy, 121
growth mindset, 221

H
handshakes. *see* group dynamics
Harvard Business Review, 106, 175
health, 54
Hill, Linda, 19
honesty, 45–46
"How to Run a Meeting" (Jay), 175
HUD, 140-141
humane leadership, 222
humble leadership, 4, 8, 11, 54, 144, 243, 244, 253
Hurricane Katrina, 18
hyperdynamism, 65–83
    about, 73–74
    coping with, 65
    and dialectical behavior therapy, 66–68
    and ease, 258
    Observe, Describe, Participate (ODP),
        68–72
    OODA Loop, 74–78
    Pivot or Persevere exercise, 78–81
    and purpose, 106
    workshop activity for coping with, 83

I
ideation. *see* "Go Wide Then Decide," sticky
    notes
IDEO, 160
IDI (Intercultural Development Inventory), 53
inclusion, 135
inputs, gathering, 216, 220
Intel, 121
intent, cascading, 107, 112, 113–114
Intercultural Competence Continuum, 53
Intercultural Development Inventory (IDI), 53
Interculturalist LLC, 53
interpersonal respect, 139
"invitation not to buy," 249

J
Jay, Anthony, 175
Jobs, Steve, 1
Jones, Hannah, 107–111
justice, 136

NOTES

Chapter 1

1   Daphna Shohamy, "Lentils or Pasta? Why Small Decisions Feel as Tough as Big Ones in This Time of Crisis," CNN, accessed September 20, 2022, https://www.cnn.com/2020/04 /13/opinions/coronavirus-brains-decisions-shohamy-opinion/index.html.
2   Jill Suttie, "Why Are We So Wired to Connect?," Greater Good, University of California, Berkeley, December 2, 2013, https://greatergood.berkeley.edu/article/item/why_are_we _so_wired_to_connect.

Chapter 2

1   "Barbara Minto: 'MECE: I Invented It, so I Get to Say How to Pronounce It,'" McKinsey & Company, 2019, https://www.mckinsey.com/alumni/news-and-insights/global-news /alumni-news/barbara-minto-mece-i-invented-it-so-i-get-to-say-how-to-pronounce-it
2   Ibid.
3   Erik Asp et al. "Benefit of the Doubt: A New View of the Role of the Prefrontal Cortex in Executive Functioning and Decision Making," *Frontiers in Neuroscience* 7 (2013), https://doi.org/10.3389/fnins.2013.00086.

Chapter 3

1   MindTools Content Team, "5 Whys: Getting to the Root of a Problem Quickly," Mindtools.com, Emerald Works, accessed September 20, 2022, https://www.mindtools .com/pages/article/newTMC_5W.htm.
2   "Genchi Genbutsu," The Economist, October 13, 2009, https://www.economist.com /news/2009/10/13/genchi-genbutsu.

Chapter 4

1   "An Overview of Dialectical Behavior Therapy," Psych Central, Healthline Media, June 19, 2019, https://psychcentral.com/lib/an-overview-of-dialectical-behavior-therapy/.

2   Thomas J. Peters, *Thriving on Chaos: Handbook for a Management Revolution* (New York: Knopf, 1987).

Chapter 5

1   Naina Dhingra et al. "Help Your Employees Find Purpose—or Watch Them Leave | McKinsey," www.mckinsey.com, April 5, 2021, https://www.mckinsey.com/capabilities /people-and-organizational-performance/our-insights/help-your-employees-find -purpose-or-watch-them-leave.
2   Carol S. Dweck, *Mindset: The New Psychology of Success* (New York: Ballantine Books, 2006).

Chapter 6

1   Dhingra, "Help Your Employees Find Purpose—Or Watch Them Leave."
2   HBR Analytic Services and Harvard Business Review, "The Business Case for Purpose," Ey.com, 2015, https://assets.ey.com/content/dam/ey-sites/ey-com/en_gl/topics/digital /ey-the-business-case-for-purpose.pdf.
3   Deloitte, "Thriving in the Future of Work Means Focusing on Your People." HBR.org, Harvard Business Review, April 28, 2021, https://hbr.org/sponsored/2021/04/thriving -in-the-future-of-work-means-focusing-on-your-people.
4   Lieutenant Colonel Lawrence G. Shattuck. "Communicating Intent and Imparting Presence," *Military Review* (March-April 2000), //www.nwcg.gov/sites/default/files /wfldp/docs/Shattuck.pdf.
5   Helmuth Karl Bernhard von Moltke, "Aus den Verordnungen fur die hoheren Truppenfuhrer vom 24. Juni 1869," in Moltkes Militarische Werke, Zweiter Theil, Die Tatigkeit als Chef des Generalstabs im Frieden, Preubischer Generalstab (Berlin, Germany: Ernst Siegfried Mittler und Sohn, 1900), 178.
6   Chad Storlie, "Manage Uncertainty with Commander's Intent," *Harvard Business Review*, November 3, 2010, https://hbr.org/2010/11/dont-play-golf-in-a-football-g.
7   Peter M. Gollwitzer, "Implementation Intentions: Strong Effects of Simple Plans," Psycnet.apa.org, American Psychological Association, 1999, https://psycnet.apa.org/ record/1999-05760-004.
8   Mindtools Content Team, "OGSM Frameworks: Making Your Strategy a Reality," Mindtools.com, Emerald Works, accessed September 20, 2022, https://www.mindtools .com/pages/article/ogsm-frameworks.htm.
9   Sam Prince, "OKRs and OGSM: What's the Difference?," *What Matters* (blog), accessed September 21, 2022, https://www.whatmatters.com/resources/ogsm-vs-okr-whats-the- difference.
10   Soren Kaplan, "Want a High-Performing Team? Try the OGSM Model," Inc.com, Inc., April 4, 2020, https://www.inc.com/soren-kaplan/want-a-high-performing-team-try- ogsm-model.html.
11   Marc Benioff, "Company Alignment: The Salesforce Secret to Success - Salesforce Blog." *The 360 Blog from Salesforce* (blog), May 2, 2020, https://www.salesforce.com/blog/how- to-create-alignment-within-your-company/.

Chapter 7

1 Rebecca Rubin, "Tina Fey on Her 'No A–Holes' Policy and Bringing 'Mean Girls' back to the Big Screen." Variety.com, Variety, May 6, 2021, https://variety.com/2021/film/features/tina-fey-mean-girls-movie-snl-1234967386/.

2 Paul Gompers and Silpa Kovvali, "The Other Diversity Dividend." *Harvard Business Review*, July 2018, https://hbr.org/2018/07/the-other-diversity-dividend.

3 Andrés T. Tapia and Alina Polonskaia, "5 Disciplines of Inclusive Leaders," Korn Ferry, https://infokf.kornferry.com/rs/494-VUC-482/images/Korn-Ferry-5-Disciplines-of-Inclusive-Leaders.pdf.

4 Sundiatu Dixon-Fyle, et al. "Diversity Wins: How Inclusion Matters," McKinsey, https://www.mckinsey.com/featured-insights/diversity-and-inclusion/diversity-wins-how-inclusion-matters.

5 Kate Rooney and Yasmin Khorram, "Tech Companies Say They Value Diversity, but Reports Show Little Change in Last Six Years," CNBC, June 12, 2020, https://www.cnbc.com/2020/06/12/six-years-into-diversity-reports-big-tech-has-made-little-progress.html.

6 Dixon-Fyle, "Diversity Wins: How Inclusion Matters."

7 Judd Kessler and Corinne Low, "Research: How Companies Committed to Diverse Hiring Still Fail," HBR.org, *Harvard Business Review*, February 11, 2021, https://hbr.org/2021/02/research-how-companies-committed-to-diverse-hiring-still-fail.

8 Kent Beck and Cynthia Andres. *Extreme Programming Explained: Embrace Change, Second Edition*. Addison-Wesley, https://www.oreilly.com/library/view/extreme-programming-explained/0321278658/.

9 Delaney Hall and Roman Mars, "429: Stuccoed in Time," February 2, 2021, in *99Percent Invisible*, podcast, https://99percentinvisible.org/episode/stuccoed-in-time/transcript/.

Chapter 8

1 Gollwitzer, "Strong Effects of Simple Plans."

2 Audrey L. H van der Meer and F. R. (Ruud) van der Weel, "Only Three Fingers Write, but the Whole Brain Works†: A High-Density EEG Study Showing Advantages of Drawing over Typing for Learning," *Frontiers in Psychology*, no. 8 (May), https://doi.org/10.3389/fpsyg.2017.00706.

3 Bryan Goodwin, "The Magic of Writing Stuff Down - Educational Leadership." Ascd.org, April 1, 2018, http://www.ascd.org/publications/educational-leadership/apr18/vol75/num07/The-Magic-of-Writing-Stuff-Down.aspx.

4 van der Meer, "Only Three Fingers Write."

5 F. P Lane Gobet, et al. "Chunking Mechanisms in Human Learning," *Trends in Cognitive Sciences* 5, no. 6 (2001): 236–43, https://doi.org/10.1016/s1364-6613(00)01662-4.

6 Anne Manning, "Divergent vs. Convergent Thinking: How to Strike a Balance," Professional Development | Harvard DCE, Harvard Department of Continuing Education, May 11, 2016, https://professional.dce.harvard.edu/blog/divergent-vs-convergent-thinking-how-to-strike-a-balance/.

Chapter 9

1 Peter Economy, "A New Study of 19 Million Meetings Reveals That Meetings Waste More Time than Ever (but There Is a Solution)," Inc.com, Inc., January 11, 2019, https://www.inc.com/peter-economy/a-new-study-of-19000000-meetings-reveals-that-meetings-waste-more-time-than-ever-but-there-is-a-solution.html.

2 Cindy Perman, "Hate Meetings? Why Most Are Complete Failures," www.cnbc.com, September 6, 2012, https://www.cnbc.com/id/48898453.

ABOUT THE AUTHORS

Together, Janice and Jason Fraser have coached teams and delivered their workshops to organizations around the world, including startups, governments, non-profits, mom-and-pop shops, venture firms, and top business schools. Janice built a storied career as a Silicon Valley startup founder, product manager, and confidante for entrepreneurs and enterprise executives alike. Her hobbies include healing generational trauma, challenging the patriarchy, and icing migraines. Jason leads a team at VMware of more than sixty product managers and designers who work with the Department of Defense and other government clients to build mission-critical software. He can say "thank you" in more than twenty languages, holds a fifth-degree black belt in Choy Lay Fut Kung Fu, and has published more than 1,600 chocolate reviews on Twitter and Instagram.

Jason and Janice split their time between San Francisco and Minneapolis, where they live with a derpy dog, a bitter cat, and a very tall college student.